CAIRO PAPERS IN SOCIAL SCIENCE
VOLUME 33   NUMBER 4

The Political Economy of the New Egyptian Republic

Edited by
Nicholas S. Hopkins

Contributors
Deena Abdelmonem   Zeinab Abul-Magd
Yasmine Ahmed   Sandrine Gamblin
Ellis Goldberg   Clement M. Henry
Dina Makram-Ebeid   Hans Christian Korsholm Nielsen
David Sims

THE AMERICAN UNIVERSITY IN CAIRO PRESS
CAIRO   NEW YORK

Cover photo: Nicholas S. Hopkins. Secret Keeper, Mahmoud Mukhtar Museum

This paperback edition first published in 2023 by
The American University in Cairo Press
113 Sharia Kasr el Aini, Cairo, Egypt
420 Lexington Avenue, Suite 1644, New York, NY 10170
www.aucpress.com

First published in an electronic edition in 2015

Copyright © 2015, 2023 by the American University in Cairo Press

All rights reserved. No part of this publication may be reproduced, stored in a retrieval system, or transmitted in any form or by any means, electronic, mechanical, photocopying, recording, or otherwise, without the prior written permission of the publisher.

ISBN 978 1 649 03226 3

Names: Hopkins, Nicholas S., editor. | Abdelmonem, Deena, author.
Title: The political economy of the new Egyptian republic / edited by
    Nicholas S. Hopkins ; contributors, Deena Abdelmonem [and 8 others].
Identifiers: LCCN 2022016015 | ISBN 9781649032263 (paperback) | ISBN
    9781617978500 (epub) | ISBN 9781617976483 (adobe pdf)
Subjects: LCSH: Egypt--Economic conditions--21st century--Congresses. |
    Egypt--Economic policy--Congresses. | LCGFT: Conference papers and
    proceedings.
Classification: LCC HC830 .P65 2022 | DDC 338.962--dc23/eng/20220506

1 2 3 4 5   27 26 25 24 23

Designed by Adam el-Sehemy

Contents

Arabic Abstract   v

Chronology: Timeline until July 3, 2013   vii

1   Introduction: The Political Economy of
the New Egyptian Republic   1
Nicholas S. Hopkins

2   The Egyptian Economy – A Dream Deferred?   19
Ellis Goldberg

3   Tumult, Trauma, and Resilience: Psychological Well-being of
Cairenes One Year Following the January 25, 2011 Uprisings   39
Deena Abdelmonem et al.

4   Labor Struggles and the Quest for Permanent Employment
in Revolutionary Egypt   67
Dina Makram-Ebeid

5   *Islah*, from Gift to Right   87
Yasmine Ahmed

6   Adapting to Change: Tribal Influence on the 2011–2012
Parliamentary Elections in Aswan Governorate   115
Hans Christian Korsholm Nielsen

7 International Tourism in Post-revolution Egypt:
   Value Conflict and Economic Pragmatism   137
   Sandrine Gamblin

8 Militarism, Neoliberalism, and Revolution in Egypt   157
   Zeinab Abul-Magd

9 Affordable Housing Policies in Egypt after the 2011 Revolution:
   More of the Same?   179
   David Sims

10 Islamic Finance in the New Egypt   199
   Clement M. Henry

About the Contributors   233

الإقتصاد السياسى للجمهورية الجديدة فى مصر

ملخص

شهدت فترة ما بعد ثورة يناير ٢٠١١ تغيرات عديدة فى الاقتصاد الاجتماعى للمجتمع المصرى والتى لم يتم دراساتها بالشكل الكافى. وفى محاولة لرصد تلك التغيرات, قامت مجلة بحوث القاهرة فى العلوم الاجتماعية بعقد ندوتها السنوية فى ٢٠١٣ عن الاقتصاد السياسى للجمهورية الجديدة فى مصر دعت اليه أكاديميين من مختلف العلوم الاجتماعية اشتملت على مجالات الأنثروبولوجيا والتاريخ والعلوم السياسية وعلم النفس والتخطيط العمرانى. وقد كشفت الأوراق التى يتم نشرها فى هذا العدد الاستراتيجيات التى تبنتها كافة القوى الفاعلة مثل العمال والفلاحين وموظفى الدولة للتعامل مع هذه المرحلة والتى سوف يكون لها تأثير كبير على مستقبل مصر. حيث يتم القاء الضوء على العلاقة بين المجتمع والثقافة من ناحية والفعل الاقتصادى من ناحية أخرى.

إلى جانب المقدمة. يحتوى هذا العدد على تسعة أوراق تقدم صورة بانورامية عن الاقتصاد السياسى فى مصر الجديدة. يبدأها إليس جولدبرج بنظرة عامة عن الإقتصاد المصرى وتطلعات المصريين فى هذا المجال تليه دينا عبد المنعم وأخرين عن الحالة النفسية للمصريين بعد عام من ثورة يناير. بعد ذلك. تحدثنا دينا مكرم عبيد عن النضالات العمالية ومحاولة الحصول على عقود دائمة. ثم تنتقل ياسمين أحمد للحديث عن الفلاحين ومحاولة استرجاع أراضى الاصلاح التى أخذتها منهم الدولة لإعادتها لملاكها السابقين. أما هانز نيلسن فيلقى الضوء على تأثير القبلية فى إنتخابات برلمان الثورة فى محافظة أسوان. وتتناول ساندرين جامبلان أزمة السياحة فى فترة ما بعد الثورة. بينما تركز زينب أبو المجد على الدور الاقتصادى للمؤسسة العسكرية. ويشرح ديفيد سيمز سياسات الإسكان بعد الثورة. وأخيرا . يقدم كليمنت هنرى تحليلا لفكرة الاقتصاد الاسلامى فى الجمهورية الجديدة.

Chronology: Timeline until July 3, 2013

1981: Hosni Mubarak becomes president after the assassination of Sadat.
Jan. 25–Feb. 11, 2011: Demonstrations in Cairo and elsewhere lead to Mubarak's resignation.
Feb. 11, 2011: The military takes over, dissolves the parliament elected in late 2010, and suspends the constitution.
March 3, 2011: Ahmed Shafik replaced by Essam Sharaf as prime minister.
March 19, 2011: Egyptians approve in a vote the constitutional amendments sponsored by the military.
Nov. 2011–Feb. 15, 2012: Parliamentary elections are held, won by the Muslim Brotherhood and other Islamists.
Dec. 7, 2011: Essam Sharaf replaced by Kamal al-Ganzouri as prime minister.
Feb. 1, 2012: Altercation between football fans in Port Said; over 70 fans from Cairo die.
March 17, 2012: Pope Shenouda III dies.
May 23–24, 2012: First round of presidential elections is held.
June 14, 2012: The Supreme Constitutional Court orders the dissolving of the lower house of parliament.
June 16–17, 2012: Runoff between Muhammad Morsi and Ahmed Shafik. Morsi wins with 51.7% of the vote.
July 27, 2012: Hisham Kandil named prime minister in place of Ganzouri.
Aug. 12, 2012: Abdel Fattah al-Sisi named defense minister in place of Muhammad Hussein Tantawi.
Nov. 22, 2012: Morsi unilaterally declares greater powers for himself.

Dec. 15 and 22, 2012: Referendum on the new constitution, drafted before Nov. 30 and approved on this date.

Dec. 29, 2012: The Egyptian Central Bank declares that foreign reserves have fallen to a critical minimum, to $15B from $36B in 2010; value of the pound slides.

April 6, 2013: *Cairo Papers in Social Science* conference.

June 30, 2013: Millions of Egyptians demonstrate asking Morsi to step down, continue for several days.

July 3, 2013: Military ousts Morsi, suspends constitution, and imposes an interim technocrat government. Adly Mansour named interim president, and Beblawi prime minister. New constitution and new elections promised.

CHAPTER 1

Introduction
The Political Economy of the New Egyptian Republic

Nicholas S. Hopkins

From time to time since its founding, the *Cairo Papers in Social Science* (CPSS) has published an issue which provides an overview of some aspect of the social situation in Egypt, with particular reference to its political and economic aspects. In the first volume of the CPSS, for instance, we presented a collection on *Democracy in Egypt* edited by Professor Ali Eddin Hillal Dessouki (1977), and most recently the CPSS published a collection entitled *Political and Social Protest in Egypt* (Hopkins 2006). In the interval, we have presented collections dealing with elections, human rights, development, the informal sector, the politics of structural adjustment, and the environment. All this of course is in addition to many issues dealing with specific problems, notably focusing on the role and position of women. The full list is given at the end of this volume.

The January 25 Revolution and the subsequent developments clamored for attention, and so we organized our annual conference in 2013 around the topic of the political economy of the new republic. As usual we met for a full-day conference in Cairo on April 6, 2013 and we combined local talent with a few guests from abroad. The presentations led to lively discussions. At the time we chose the topic there was no way of predicting how the new republic was going to evolve, or even if it was going to be a *new* republic. (Frankly the questions are still relevant.) The timing of our conference fell during the one-year presidency of Muhammad Morsi of the Muslim Brothers; most of the papers were not finalized until after the fall of that government, and these political circumstances may have influenced the tone of the arguments. The reader must judge.

Our strategy in this collection has been to put aside all the debate about how the revolution happened—there are many analyses of that—and to focus on what are loosely called changes at the 'grass roots' level, to aim for an idea of how that great lumbering entity called Egyptian society is getting along, socially and economically. The publication cycle of the CPSS is such that we cannot hope to provide up-to-date information on events, but must limit ourselves to more analytical and background pieces. We have also set aside for the time being the interesting topic, which some are now beginning to address, of analyzing how the 2011 revolution compares to earlier Egyptian revolutions, or indeed to revolutions elsewhere.

We decided to call our domain 'political economy' but we could equally well have labeled it the 'social economy.' The critical task is to see how social and cultural patterns interact with economic issues. Our focus is on social relations between individuals. And we always retain as the central insight that the economic is embedded in the social. Thus we recognize the importance of institutions.

This is not political economy in the sense of Samer Soliman's recent analysis (2011) of the finances of government. We chose our title several moons ago in the evolution of postrevolutionary Egypt when it was only clear that the regime would be new and that it would in some sense be republican. We felt it would be presumptuous to give a number to the republic in the French tradition: from 1952 on, how many republics would there have been and who is counting? In any case this nomenclature is not in use in Egypt.

There have been many changes and developments in the social economy of Egypt since January 2011, but not necessarily much detailed information about them. It does not take a genius to assert that tourism has been affected, and with it the whole range of employment linked to tourism. International investment has also declined because of the unrest and uncertainty. Probably there has been less domestic public investment, for instance for the repair of infrastructure. Unemployment and underemployment are high. Poverty is increasing. The informal economy predominates. Wages are low. The debt level is high. The value of the pound relative to the dollar has also declined by around 15 percent: it is to the credit of Egypt's banking managers that it held at that level. Egypt's foreign reserves have been devastated, declining at one point to a third or so of their maximum before recovering some of their value and stabilizing. At the same time one should note that many parts of the administration continue to function and even to plan; as far as we can tell, agriculture has proceeded without a hitch and urban markets are provisioned.

Egypt relies heavily on purchases of fuel, food, and other necessities from abroad, and the lack of replenishment of the foreign currency reserves obviously means that those reserves were drained. After summer 2013 the cash advances from Saudi Arabia, the United Arab Emirates, and Kuwait alleviated that situation somewhat, but that cannot be a permanent solution.

Human societies need to produce and exchange the products of their labor in order to survive and progress. Egyptians do not live by bread alone, but they do live by bread. The critical point to stress is work, where this 'bread' comes from—how do people work to earn their living, and to 'produce'? Do they work singly or cooperatively, and what organizations or institutions do they call on? What role is played by families, teams, partnerships, companies, bureaucracies? What forms of competition enter into the picture? Once they have produced, how does this production circulate among other people, so that it reaches the consumers? How are markets organized?

From this material base one can then observe the development of secondary political and social structures. It is an error of method to make the starting point for analysis the observable political and social structures. We have to go back before that to see how these structures emerged. Simply to focus on 'the political' or 'the economic' or 'the social' does not allow us to construct a viable analysis.

Accordingly we have organized the papers in this collection to start with those which focus on interpersonal relations in a community or set of communities. Gradually we move up the scale until we reach bankers and planners, but still keeping our attention on the fact that they too are involved in dyadic relations built around production, exchange, and consumption.

We might start by enumerating certain enduring problems in Egypt, leaving their elaboration until later. These problems are distinct from the short-run everyday issues. And they persist irrespective of the political crises and governmental shifts.

1. Population: now nearing 100,000,000 (ambiguity of attitude; role of family).
2. Employment: shortage of jobs and lack of fit between education and employment needs.
3. Poverty: generally declining level but much poverty and some real destitution.
4. Self-sufficiency in food: inadequate production for the population, notably in grains, hence reliance on imports.
5. International and national debt; foreign borrowing; IMF and oil states.
6. Budget: state takes over school fees and raises minimum wage; hence the need to increase income.
7. How to raise the money to cover government expenditures: the government as redistribution center.
8. Fluctuation of tourism revenue.
9. Water: will there be enough, going forward? Dam in Ethiopia and other threats.
10. Environmental damage to tourist sites and to agricultural land.
11. Pollution: water, air, noise, garbage accumulation (note China as a negative example), and their health impacts.
12. Hostility between segments of the population (primordial groups, sports teams, classes, partisans of different policies, etc.).

Beginning in January 2011, five broad goals were articulated by Egyptians: bread (economic improvement), freedom (from police harassment mostly), democracy (in the context of voting and choosing their leaders on the basis of a majority), human dignity (also in the face of police harassment[1]), and social justice (which also had a strong component of economic equality). The underlying notion of much of this was that all Egyptians were equal in the face of the law and their neighbors. Some subsidiary notions were also present: gender equality (freedom from sexual harassment, on the street and at home), the possibility for all Egyptians to have a secure place in the economic structures of the country, the existence of state institutions to which all could have

---

[1] See Bayat (2009:178): strict police surveillance in better neighborhoods like Maadi pushed Islamists into the 'opaque' neighborhoods of Ain Shams and Imbaba. See also Ismail (2006) and the reciprocal resentment. She confirms this analysis in Ismail (2013).

Introduction: The Political Economy of the New Egyptian Republic

easy and equal access, the entitlement to the respect of neighbors. They desired to have a constitution which would institutionalize this as much as possible, and that would be in accord with general Egyptian values, meaning primarily the notions expressed through religious texts (such as sharia). Underlying it all was a wish to have a system that would elaborate real solutions that offer stability and create opportunity.

None of this is new. It coincides with what Ellis Goldberg, in his keynote address to the conference, identified when he noted that Egyptians had been promised a robust economy with a place for everyone and good government services, and called this a "dream deferred" for 60 years, two generations. The delivery on the promise was always just around the corner. It would appear that the diverse governments that ruled Egypt between February 2011 and April 2014 (when this was drafted) were not able to make much progress either, and in fact in the short run there has been regression. Only recently (after the 30 June 2013 "revolution") did the Biblawi government promise to improve economic circumstances for the lowest strata by increasing the minimum wage and offering a one-year holiday on school fees. I think we can assume that the school fee holiday was implemented, but we do not know the effect on the government budget or on the schools themselves. Implementing a minimum wage is complicated, and was not quickly carried out, despite the ease of the proclamation. Without going into details one can say that there has been less stability and safety and fewer chances to create opportunity—although perhaps one should note the expansion of 'informal' activities in the housing and marketing (petty trade) areas. The position of Egypt in the world economy has hurt progress, as Egyptian small-scale manufactures have been hit by imports from China and other low-wage countries.

If we wonder what have been the social effects of the rupture in Egyptian society caused by the fall of a long-time president and his regime, some of the answers might turn around the extra degrees of freedom acquired.

One of the most obvious and quickly noticed was the speedy seizure of opportunities to disregard restrictions on building on agricultural land and in other restricted spaces. Newspapers have reported this and provided questionable figures, but the overall trend of the process is clear. People in villages and on the outskirts of cities with land that can be used for housing cash in for the one-time benefit. This has long been a familiar process in Egypt, with some of the best evidence being the fact that street layouts follow the old property boundaries (and streets are often as narrow as possible[2]). David Sims has cited some additional evidence by comparing aerial photographs of the same area at an interval of several years to show how the built footprint has expanded (Sims 2013). The actual construction of buildings may not be so problematic; Sims has also pointed out that the construction methods of these four- and five-story buildings are generally solid. Around Cairo these buildings are very much in evidence, especially on the western and northern edges of the city where they are typically constructed on former farmland (but can also be seen in villages). This construction outside the laws has been made possible by a relaxing of the efforts to prohibit it. Those efforts were anyway not very successful. The attention of the government after the revolution continued to be on large-scale housing projects; there was no evidence of any change, although there was still the rhetoric of providing decent housing for the poor and lower middle class.

A large-scale example of conflict over land in the wake of the revolution concerns the land set aside for a nuclear plant at al-Daba'a between al-'Alamein and Marsa Matruh in the Western Desert. In September 2013 the Egyptian press reported that Bedouin groups, who had broken through the perimeter fence and occupied the land, agreed to relinquish their occupation and return the establishment to the army.[3] This land had been carved out of the Bedouin territory for the nuclear plant in the 1980s and had remained relatively empty since, as the Egyptian government debated the utility of pursuing peaceful nuclear power.

Struggle over the control of farmland has been a continuing theme in rural Egypt. Yasmine Ahmed provides an example of how a dispute over land in Fayoum between a group of peasants and a powerful landlord family was conducted. In this case the chief battlefield was the court system

---

2   I followed debates about this in Musha, Asyut, in 1981. New streets were narrow so that building sites could gain a few extra meters.

3   *Egypt Daily News*, October 1, 2013, "Army Regains Control of Nuclear Plant Construction Site"; *al-Masry al-Youm* (English edition), November 20, 2012, "In Dabaa, the Fight to Halt Nuclear Power Continues." The issue for the Bedouin was not nuclear power per se but access to land which they felt was historically theirs. They also wanted the same terms of land occupancy that were granted to the Sinai Bedouin. The role of the army and General Sisi is noteworthy.

rather than the fields themselves. Veterans of the Yemen war had been awarded land under agrarian reform; then the original owners managed to get it back, and the fight continued. For more than anecdotal evidence we must await the next agricultural census, when land ownership figures over a ten-year period can be compared and regional differences detected.

CAPMAS announced in February 2014 that the population of Egypt was 86 million in the country and an estimated 8 million abroad, for a total of 94 million, and noted that the population had increased by 1 million in the previous six months (*Egyptian Gazette*, February 23, 2014, 1). It appears that the rate of population growth in Egypt has accelerated, and is from 2 percent to 3 percent per year.

CAPMAS pointed to these figures with alarm and noted that population growth is "a major challenge for this generation and the generations to come," adding that population growth is "a key obstacle to the government's efforts for development and improving the standard of living" (*Egyptian Gazette*, February 23, 2014, 1). Nonetheless, Egyptian authorities have a highly ambivalent attitude toward this population growth, and this attitude translates out into very little action to limit it.

The question of the status of women has been hotly debated since January 25. Observers have been watching carefully to see whether there has been any breach in the patriarchal patterns of Egypt (Sullivan 2013), and have not detected any. The different regimes since the January revolution have yielded somewhat different outcomes in terms of the number and quality of women who became members of different committees and assemblies. But feminists have considered all of the appointments or elections as inadequate. And there have been no laws to bolster the role of women.

Apart from their role in public affairs, one of the key issues for women has been their safety in public places, the streets, and public transportation. Deena Abdelmonem and her colleagues provide some figures and some insight into anxiety about safety in the street and protection from robbers and other criminals. Their analysis shows that all the unrest has had its effect on an individual's sense of security. In general there was a feeling that, after the revolution, security deteriorated from an already low level. On the other hand there have never been very good figures on criminal activity, in Egypt or anywhere else, making it hard to document trends in crime, let alone trauma. The apprehension about safety in public areas for women discourages their movement about the city (but they are still quite visible). The study of Abdelmonem and her colleagues was completed before the skirmishing between the Muslim Brothers and their various supporters on the one hand and the government on the other became endemic, but that could only have reinforced these feelings.

The Baseera Center circulated two figures from the undated (but probably 2013) "Study on Ways and Methods to Eliminate Sexual Harassment in Egypt." According to one figure, 49.2 percent of Egyptian women feel they are subject to sexual harassment daily, and according to the other, 87 percent of Egyptian women do not feel safe and secure on public transport, and 82.6 percent do not feel safe and secure in the streets. These figures are more directly a measure of the anxiety of women, however well founded, than of actual events, and they do not compare the situation before and after the January revolution. And harassment of women certainly existed prior to the revolution.

Just as there has been informality in housing, so also in commerce. The lack of salaried jobs and the growth of unemployment have pushed many people into seeking a living as vendors in the streets of Cairo. This already large domain has expanded in recent years. This is generally a fairly precarious living, as compared to the regularity of a salaried job, and clearly works better in some circumstances than others. The patterns of informal vendors tend to be the same the world over: there is a struggle for a favorable spot; there is competition between sidewalk merchants and the storekeepers in front of whose stores they display their wares; vendors are likely to get their wares on credit from a wholesaler with whom they must settle accounts at the end of the day; they have low profit margins; they are vulnerable to police crackdowns and shakedowns, so they are constantly on the lookout (cf. Tadros, Feteeha, and Hibbard 1990). Characteristic of vendors are those frequenting public transport (the metro), where for a few minutes the customers are captive. Vendors of fruit and vegetables are particularly at risk because their goods are perishable, and so they often adjust their price as the day wears on. They are also likely to lie in wait for office workers on their way home.

Dina Makram-Ebeid has stressed the strategies government workers follow in an effort to get and retain a permanent job, and also to get one lined up for relatives. People's goals are to achieve stability, which some prefer to the risk of dealing on the market, where income may fluctuate greatly from one day to another. But Makram-Ebeid also stresses the distinctions the government system makes among workers, with at least three different levels with variations in pay and other privileges. Workers in large private-sector enterprises faced the same situation. After January 2011 there was agitation among workers and would-be workers to try to improve conditions, but improvements have been marginal.

At the very lowest level are the people who rely on charity. In a recent MA thesis at the American University in Cairo, Shanara Frazier sought out the poorest of the poor (the destitute) in a community near Luxor, who relied mostly on an Islamic charity combined with occasional odd jobs, exchanges with neighbors, and in extreme cases simply helped themselves to their neighbors' gardens. Their poverty was mostly linked to their social isolation, as they were often alienated from their relatives or simply too far from them. Her research was carried out during the Muslim Brotherhood government, but her respondents reported no increase in government or private charity during that period (Frazier 2013). Her results confirm what I found in an Upper Egyptian village a generation earlier: a household with an able-bodied male can manage, but without that wage earner it cannot.

Thus we are confronted with a social organization that appears to have a large segment of individualized actors. Some are dealing on the market, either as retailers or buyers and sellers or as middlemen or -women of some sort. Most of these people relate to their family (narrow or extended) first of all, and may have little organized social contact beyond that. Some may belong to large-scale social organizations with a religious focus, but little internal division of labor. The number of factories with large work forces appears to have declined, and the textile factories are the largest remaining. The figure of 4,000 closed factories is often cited in the press. So the largest number of Egyptians working in a formal setting are the 5 million or so who work at various levels of government (including the security forces?). And the informal sector, whether sidewalk vendors or petty craftsmen, is the resort of many.

One vehicle that may bring little businesses out of the shadows of the informal economy may be Islamic banks. Clement Henry has described the people who work in banking, particularly Islamic banking. The issue here is the interface between ideology or even theology and the business world, and this effort has been stimulated by the election of the Morsi government in 2012. Closer economic relations with the GCC both before and after the Morsi era also encourage the development of Islamic finance. Experts have been trying to develop the *sukuk* (Islamic bonds) as a way to facilitate long-term borrowing and investment in development. They appear to be a small community of technocrats familiar with Islamic teaching on the preference for profit over interest, and who have highly overlapping patterns of membership in committees advising organizations on the creation of *sukuk*. This profession, centered in Bahrain, Dubai, and Malaysia, is being standardized across the Muslim world to satisfy the large majorities of Muslims who reject conventional interest-based banking. For now the *sukuk* market has minimal effects on daily life, and only one of Egypt's Islamic banks is pioneering microfinance.

The urban planners whom David Sims describes doubtless share some of the same characteristics, but are all working inside the government. Sims summarizes the urban and regional planning efforts of the government, but with some skepticism with respect to the realism of these plans and their execution. Generally speaking, he argues that the government is too focused on housing for the middle class and above, so pays little attention to providing housing for the poor. The 'poor,' however manage to look after themselves with self-built housing, often laying out their own streets as well. This is the so-called 'informal' housing sector that, according to most estimates, represents well over half of all new housing, and that proportion is growing. Informal housing has been the dominant form of housing for more than a generation (Abt Associates 1982). The paradox is that while government-built housing is usually in the desert because of the availability of land, informal housing is often on agricultural land, which is then taken out of production. As noted, this complicates the drive for food sufficiency. Since 2011, the rate of informal building has probably increased as the bureaucratic structures that somewhat reined it in have atrophied or been distracted. Some very partial evidence that Sims (2013) adduces is that the rate with which ground is covered with buildings has increased in the areas for which he has data, in one area in Giza by 4.5 times, and remittances from abroad jumped to $12 billion in 2012 and inferentially some or much of that must be used for housing (see Abaza 2013). The rate of building and demolition orders in Alexandria also increased by 2.5 times in 2011 and the first half of 2012; these have never led to much action and the assumption would be that that is still true.

Introduction: The Political Economy of the New Egyptian Republic

A critical area for understanding the economic impact of the 2011 revolution and especially the Muslim Brothers government is tourism, at once one of Egypt's largest earners of foreign exchange and biggest window on values and behavior that could run counter to some traditional Egyptian values. This has always been a fraught area in Egypt. Sandrine Gamblin's paper details the conflict between money and values, which appears at the level of both the individual workers and the hotel operators. The key issues are women's attire, especially on the beach, and the consumption of alcohol. But big business is also involved in the form of investments in hotels and tourism companies, and this business closely involved some of the leading figures of the Mubarak regime and the military. The Muslim Brothers government was working out an accommodation with this when it created a second problem by starting to encourage tourism from Iran, to replace the income lost with the drop-off in Western tourism. At this point the opponents of Shi'ism, mostly from the Salafi tendency, rose up and managed to block that effort, which they saw as encouraging the spread of Shi'ism in Egypt. If one of the possible outcomes of tourism is to encourage friendship among diverse peoples, Egyptian tourism was caught between the Scylla of the West and the Charybdis of militant Shi'ism.

Another contentious area, of course, was elections. Elections for parliament were scheduled for late 2011 and early 2012 in Egypt to establish a solid base for political action in the new period. Hans Christian Korsholm Nielsen's account shows how those elections displayed continuity with the past while introducing new elements. His research drew on his previous research in the governorate of Aswan. Probably no two successive elections in Egypt have been held under exactly the same rules, and these were obviously no exception. The 2011–2012 elections can probably claim to have been the most open elections ("free and fair") in Egyptian history in that there was almost no pressure from the government to achieve a given result. That the elections in Aswan, as elsewhere in Egypt, produced an overwhelming victory for the two main Muslim parties, the Freedom and Justice Party of the Muslim Brothers and the Noor Party of the Salafi tendency, can be taken as a true indication of people's sentiments at that time. Nielsen's account of the campaign issues illustrates that. So that was the new. The carryover from past elections can been seen in the tactics, in the occasional role of primordial groups such as tribes and neighborhoods in the process, and in the tendency to see a member of parliament as a broker to funnel rewards to his constituency. Nielsen's account also shows the people of Aswan committed to electoral democracy and quite familiar with the tactics and issues involved. That the outcome of the elections was overturned by the courts several months later is another story.

One of the critical questions for any government is the source of the money to cover its costs. Funding has to come from somewhere. Let us say that the standard answer is through taxes and fees, and that assumes a minimum willingness on the part of the citizens to pay those taxes. There are of course many kinds of taxes, of which income taxes and sales taxes (or value-added taxes) are the most common. Property or land taxes and customs dues are also very common ways of raising money. Except for value-added taxes and customs, the other forms of taxation in Egypt are highly progressive. The efficiency of collection is another question. There have been several efforts to increase revenue from taxes, most notoriously the effort under Mubarak to tax owners of valuable real estate, but these efforts have often bogged down and instead publicity given to tax reduction. In May 2013 the Egyptian (acting) 'parliament' (Shura Council) approved a new income tax law that would raise taxes on the wealthy and reduce them for the poor (signed by Morsi on May 21, 2013). A proposal to increase the sales tax was not discussed, nor was subsidy reform tackled.[4] The tax on farm land held in units of more than three feddans that existed around 1980 (Hopkins 1987) was then abolished, and agriculture is not subject to direct taxes.

Obviously the point is that the gap between income and expenditure, if the latter is greater, represents a deficit. And the bigger the deficit the greater the interest due on that deficit. If Egypt is committed not to fall (further) into debt, then it has a problem. It must generate the income from somewhere. In recent years Egypt has solved this problem in part by cash assistance from friendly countries, most recently at this writing Saudi Arabia, the United Arab Emirates, and Kuwait. As with any country receiving large amounts of money from outside (income from oil or from aid, 'rent') rather than from the work and productivity of its people, this situation can negatively affect the relationship between the

---

4   See Aya Batrawy, "New Egypt Tax Law: Cuts for Poor, Business Hikes," Associated Press, May 21, 2013, downloaded from Yahoo News, October 13, 2013.

government (the rulers) and the people. When people support a government through taxes they have a right to demand accountability; a government supported otherwise can easily ignore public opinion. At the same time it matters how the funds to support the government are raised in a country, and that has implications for the political economy (redistribution and reciprocity; the market). (On the other hand, if the money from outside is generously redistributed, people may be grateful.)

An idea that is firmly entrenched, or at least often cited, in Egypt is that the role of government is to "solve the problems of the people." In practice this means either spending money or forgoing taxes and fees. The interim government after June 30, 2013 has engaged in both these activities. Have they given any thought to what will happen when the bill comes due? Governments redistribute their income to their citizens, but they do have to have income. One is beginning to hear local leaders say that Egypt is "too big to fail," but they have not spelled out the implications of this sentiment.

Another area of concern is the 'youth.' In Egypt, 'youth' is often considered a category,[5] and the elders refer to it collectively: "Let the youth solve the problems." But observations suggests that the patriarchs have no intention of ceding too much power to the youth (Sullivan 2013). Their deference is a misleading and fake show. No sooner does the dust settle a little bit than the gerontocrats are back, and the youth are ushered back to their symbolic role. They may be allowed the floor in certain general assemblies, but rarely if ever accede to leadership positions in established institutions. In fact the young defer to the elderly.

Some interesting reflections on the role and place of youth are provided by the organization of sports, particularly sports where individuals compete against each other such as swimming, wrestling, or track and field. Paralleling the international organization of such sports, there is an Egyptian federation for each sport. This organization is run by bureaucrats, who may or may not be former athletes. But the competitors are youth, and they are ambitious. They frequently run afoul of the bureaucrats over issues of training and money. The youth must cede to the bureaucrats, quit, or rebel by moving abroad. The impression one has is that talent is often stifled.

---

5 In the big sporting clubs supervised by the government, the elected governing boards have 'set-aside' seats for members under 35 years of age.

From the point of view of the political economy, the major economic role of the youth as a category derives from the various marriage expenses (and the efforts to raise money to marry and support a family). For details see Singerman and Ibrahim (2003:81), who estimate that "Egyptians spend more than 13 billion Egyptian pounds annually on the costs of getting married" (and that was then) and present this as a major way in which wealth is transferred between generations. Some of the frustration of Egyptian youth with the economy at various times has been linked to what they see as the difficulty, if not the impossibility in the short run, of getting married.[6]

Like many other large Third World countries (Pakistan, Indonesia, Thailand; see Siddiqa-Agha 2007), Egypt's military is heavily involved in both military production and the civilian economy. Zeinab Abul-Magd examines the situation in Egypt and lays out the details. This is as yet a poorly known area (and comparison with other countries in a similar situation would be beneficial). Abul-Magd suggests the overall picture, but the internal operations are still a black box. How centralized are the activities, and how much control is exerted outside the military domain by 'retired' officers? How is the flow of benefits organized ?

An interesting case not analyzed by Abul-Magd concerns the extension of military control over the Ministry of Environment, symbolized by the long tenure of an army general, Maged George, as minister under Mubarak. This presence facilitated the extension of army investment into coastal tourism (beach hotels and the like); because the coastal areas are a sensitive military zone, military influence and authorization were necessary to build hotels. And frequently retired or active officers ended up as investors/owners of these new hotels. Sad to say, despite the involvement of the Ministry of Environment, little attention was given to protecting the marine and shoreline environment, so that, for instance, many coral reefs near the shore were destroyed in the process of building infrastructure (Sowers 2013).[7]

---

6 One could also refer to the propensity to seek out high-end consumer goods, at least for those in the wealthier strata. Or it could be linked to the dream of migration to a more lucrative and flexible situation outside Egypt. All this remains to be researched.

7 After summer 2013 the Minister for Environment has been more independent.

Some have observed that the situation in Egypt was not a revolution in the literal sense that the social order was not turned upside down, with the have-nots taking over from the haves. Notably the property alignments were not affected, either in the city or in the countryside, and a whole new generation of leaders did not appear in place of the old ones. (There was no rabble occupying ministerial offices with their feet on the desks.) Nor was the institutional structure reconstituted. In fact there was a great deal of continuity in terms of both property and leadership. The Muslim Brothers might have represented such a shift, but even had they been successful, the change might have been minimal—one group of businessmen for another, with only the ideology as a differentiator. Different animals, same trough.

Looking back, it is worth wondering in what sense the 1952 coup produced a revolution. There was a fairly significant land reform, eventually, and it basically amounted to promoting the middle rather than empowering the destitute. The landless remained and some of them were eventually absorbed in urban employment. There was the growth of industry and an industrial proletariat that has been described and analyzed by many observers, including Ellis Goldberg. There had been an industrial working class, of course, but it grew and acquired a somewhat different social role. But eventually its independent power was reined in under Abdel Nasser and his successors before it could go too far.[8] The efforts to make sure that the workers and peasants were represented in parliament were soon circumvented by the loose definitions given to these two categories, and by the powerlessness of the parliament anyway.

So after a while the revolution became symbolic rather than effective. The managers of the political and economic system could claim a revolutionary heritage while still maintaining a bourgeois lifestyle. It is true that for a while the bourgeois lifestyle was pretty thin because of the lack of imported luxury goods in the market.

So that was then. In terms of the political economy of Egypt, one can also speculate what a revolution that turned everything upside down would look like now. This is a thought experiment. Egypt is certainly a very different country now than it was in the 1950s—the population is five or six times greater, literacy is widespread, there is a

---

8 The union never acquired the durable independent existence that it did in Tunisia, where it continues to play a major role in national politics.

much more differentiated economy, and so on. Also the 1950s revolution did two things that cannot be easily replicated: it created an industrial proletariat and it redistributed land. In the present situation the focus has been on a competition for power at the top. There seems to be no body of resources whose expropriation and redistribution could feed a revolution. If that is the case, then what kind of a revolution can we expect? There is not likely to be a cornucopia of new resources that would suddenly provide a better income and a higher standard of living for Egyptians. Given the rapidly increasing population, even generous aid from oil-rich countries is not likely to make a difference (and we have to assume that they are offering this aid in their own interest, not Egypt's). That being the case, can any government offer anything more than blood, sweat, and tears in the context of a long struggle to raise the quality of life for the people and generate a radically new and different society? The pie is not going to miraculously expand.

But from an individual point of view, will there be new opportunities? Will education provide a viable set of paths to accomplishment and financial success? Will there be technological breakthroughs? Already we hear stories of entrepreneurial success, and we can hope for more. But we also know that new business opportunities are often circumscribed by bureaucratic concerns, including the need for payoffs. (Perhaps the real revolution would consist of totally easing the process of starting up a business—down with what the Indians used to call a "permit raj." Throw in the abolition of police controls. And reduce the cost of marriage . . . .)

The 1952 revolution largely replaced the ruling elite, most significantly by destroying their agrarian base. Of course, arguably the next generation of this elite rose again, and some estates remained, albeit reduced. But we also have to see that Egyptian society no longer is built on an agrarian base as it was in the 1950s (Ammar 1940; Abaza 2013). Even in the rural areas the basis of social stratification is no longer the amount of land held, but a mixture of factors including wealth, education, and political position.

The bottom line on the evolution of the situation since January 2011 is that there may be a 'new' republic but that no social revolution occurred. Our authors repeat this in most of the papers. There has been change in personnel but with the same social categories represented. The most obvious change has been the slow deterioration of the economic circumstances in most domains. Egypt needs a new start. And that new start must cope with the problems listed at the beginning of this introduction. Fresh ideas may be hard to come by, but a fresh enthusiasm and determination are necessary, along with imagination. Egypt has never been short of talented people, but there must be a greater sense of organization and discipline. People must set aside their individual interest to work for the common good. There must be a balance between central direction and self-directed energy. There appears to be a consensus on this point.

References

Abaza, Mona. 2013. *The Cotton Plantation Remembered: An Egyptian Family Story*. Cairo: American University in Cairo Press.

Abt Associates. 1982. *Informal Housing in Egypt*. Cambridge, MA: Abt Associates. Submitted to the US Agency for International Development.

Ammar, Abbas M. 1940. "Conditions of Life in Rural Sharqiya: A Brief Account of a Socio-economic Study of 238 Households of the Province," *Sociological Review*, 32: 171–215.

Bayat, Asef. 2009. *Life as Politics: How Ordinary People Change the Middle East*. Cairo: American University in Cairo Press.

Dessouki, Ali E. Hillal, ed. 1977. *Democracy in Egypt. Cairo Papers in Social Science* 1(2).

Frazier, Shanara. 2013. "Understanding the Extremely Impoverished: An Exploration into the Lives of the Poor in Upper Egypt." Unpublished MA thesis: Department of Sociology-Anthropology, American University in Cairo.

Hopkins, Nicholas. 1987. *Agrarian Transformation in Egypt*. Boulder, CO: Westview Press.

Hopkins, Nicholas, ed. 2006. *Political and Social Protest in Egypt. Cairo Papers in Social Science* 29(2/3).

Ismail, Salwa. 2006. *Political Life in Cairo's New Quarters*. Minneapolis: University of Minnesota Press.

———. 2013. "Urban Subalterns in the Arab Revolutions: Cairo and Damascus in Comparative Perspective," *CSSH*, 55(4): 865–894.

Shehata, Samer. 2009. *Shop Floor Culture and Politics in Egypt*. Albany: State University of New York Press.
Siddiqa-Agha, Ayesha. 2007. *Military Inc.: Inside Pakistan's Military Economy*. London: Pluto.
Sims, David. 2010. *Understanding Cairo: The Logic of a City out of Control*. Cairo: American University in Cairo Press.
———. 2013. "Understanding Cairo's Informal Development." In Beth Stryker, Omar Negati, and Magda Mostafa, eds. "Learning from Cairo", electronic publication. Originally as a conference paper in May 2013, Cairo.
Singerman, Diana, and Barbara Ibrahim. 2003. "The Costs of Marriage in Egypt: A Hidden Dimension in the New Arab Demography." In Nicholas S. Hopkins, ed. *The New Arab Family, Cairo Papers in Social Science* 24(1/2): 80–116.
Soliman, Samer. 2011. *The Autumn of Dictatorship: Fiscal Crisis and Political Change in Egypt under Mubarak*. Stanford, CA: Stanford University Press.
Sowers, Jeannie. 2013. *Environmental Politics in Egypt: Activists, Experts, and the State*. New York: Routledge.
Sullivan, Earl (Tim). 2013. "Youth Power and the Revolution." In Dan Tschirgi, Walid Kazziha, and Sean McMahon, eds. *Egypt's Tahrir Revolution*, 67–87. Boulder, CO: Lynne Rienner.
Tadros, Helmi R., Mohamed Feteeha, and Allen Hibbard. 1990. *Squatter Markets in Cairo. Cairo Papers in Social Science* 13(1).

CHAPTER 2

The Egyptian Economy— A Dream Deferred?

Ellis Goldberg

Introduction

Writers had been predicting the collapse of the Mubarak government almost since it began, but when it occurred it was unlike anything anyone expected.[1] Whether the events of 2011–2013 can usefully be called a revolution remains contentious, but in this essay I am going to use precisely that term.

There are many ways in which recent events in Egypt do not resemble the classic instances of social revolution immortalized by Barrington Moore and Theda Skocpol; not least among these are the absence of any particular moment in the outbreak of revolt when the central government lost the ability to violently repress mass protest and the absence of any uprising in the countryside (Moore 1966; Skocpol 1979).[2] Whatever its failings may have been in regard to the Egyptian people, the government was neither bankrupt nor experiencing an inability to pay the salaries of its policy, and despite policies that have deprived significant numbers of people in the countryside of access to land or unequal access to goods and services provided by the state there has been no rural revolt.

In the absence of a single point at which the state broke down, we can at least provisionally consider a different approach which you may most immediately connect with the work of Joel Beinin and the late

---

1 See "Actually the Experts Did Predict the Revolution," on nisralnasr, http://nisralnasr.blogspot.com/2011/06/you-say-you-want-comparative-revolution.html.
2 It is revealing that Moore's book is subtitled "Lord and Peasant in the Making of the Modern World," although certainly that set of power relations is not relevant to Egypt in 2011 or indeed to the largely urban setting of the uprising. Skocpol's concern with the sudden onset of fiscal crisis also seems beside the point here.

Samer Soliman: the idea of an ongoing set of problems that finally reached a crisis in 2011. One problem with this approach is that it is wholly ad hoc because, as with stock market bubbles and the outbreak of war, we can have a sense that a crisis is approaching but cannot predict the moment at which dramatically unexpected events will occur.[3]

What is peculiar about the events of late 2010 and early 2011, especially in Tunisia and Egypt, is that while there was certainly economic distress in both countries, looking at most of the quantitative indicators, things were going relatively well. Not, obviously, as well as they were going in the countries of East Asia or even parts of Latin America, but in many ways relatively well indeed. Economic growth and the macroeconomic balance of the government appeared to most observers to be at least at the world's average in Egypt and somewhat above average in Tunisia. The distribution of income was less even than 30 years earlier but it remained, in comparison to Brazil or even the United States, relatively egalitarian.[4] Money income figures are notoriously problematic but many other indicators also indicate significant changes: school attendance is up and illiteracy appears to be down. Girls are attending school in equal numbers with boys; infant mortality is down; life expectancy is up (Noland and Pack 2011:60–69). Measured unemployment was high but it appeared to be lower than several years earlier, and while there had been spikes in the global price of many commodities (especially wheat), most Egyptians were somewhat sheltered from them due to subsidies for bread.[5] Labor economists such as Ragui Assaad believed that the youth bulge was finally working its way through the labor market and expected that Egypt might in the near future enjoy a payoff from a decline in the dependency ratio.

My reason for repeating this account is not to show that life was wonderful in the last days of the Mubarak era, but to recall that the economic situation did not, to most observers, suggest the imminence

---

3 There were attempts to do this using so-called 'catastrophe' theory about 20 years ago; for a variety of technical and other reasons these attempts led nowhere.

4 The World Bank "Gini Index," measuring how much the distribution of income or consumption expenditures differ from equality, gives Egypt an index of 30.8 in 2008; Brazil's is 55.1; China's is 42.1, and India's 33.9. The Gini index for the United States as a whole is 46.9.

5 The degree to which this is so depends in part on how much of their food or other basic requirements could be met through subsidized goods.

of massive protests. Accounts of the uprisings of 2011 spend more time on explaining why the monarchies survived than on explaining why several of the republics fell, as if the collapse of government was somehow self-evident while the continuation of regimes was problematic. The most common culprit is said to be the failure of the security forces. The problem here is that, in contradistinction to the theory, the security forces collapsed after the demonstrations were well under way rather than occurring sufficiently early to allow the massive demonstrations to occur. What we would like, analytically speaking, especially from the economy, is a prompt and exogenous occurrence that detonated a revolution and preferably made the state unable to deploy coercion. That does not seem to be the case. There are other possibilities: a much longer and slower process that finally reached a tipping point or an explanation that does not rely so heavily on economic factors at all.

In 1951 the African American poet Langston Hughes wrote the poem "A Dream Deferred" (Hughes 1951). The poem is an elegy for a political order that promised universal equality and political rights but failed to deliver them. His particular point of reference was the failure of the U.S., especially in the wake of a war fought to defeat the power of racism and anti-Semitism, to make good on its promise for black equality. Not for another 15 years would significant legislative steps to redeem that promise be taken, but any observer of the U.S. from 1945 until 1963 would have been aware of the profound discontent among African Americans and of the profound ways in which the country was beginning to change. And yet the changes that occurred in the wake of the civil rights movement and because of it were far deeper and more profound than anyone might have expected when the poem was written.

Egyptians have been promised for at least 60 years that they would live in a country with a robust economy in which industry played an increasingly important role that provided education, health care, and a decent standard of living for all citizens. From the dawn of the republic in 1952, Egyptians were implicitly promised—if only in the slogan "from the needle to the rocket"—that their standard of living would not merely improve over time but would approach that of the European countries. That dream has been, for most Egyptians, deferred for six decades and continues to be deferred indefinitely. Following Langston

Hughes's brief exploration of the implications, we might say that students of durable authoritarianism thought the dream would simply dry up in the sun or else sag like a heavy load; puzzled students of economics thought it might sag or, given some luck, might crust and sugar over and turn into a syrupy sweet. And more recently analysts such as Beinin and Soliman have argued that, in the end, it simply exploded.[6]

What we know about dreams deferred from other settings, notably the last years of the Soviet Union, is that their ends are often politically nasty, brutish, but not short; that they are rarely sweet except for a privileged few; and that whatever poor information was available under the old regime decreases in quality and quantity. The Soviet dream, indefinitely deferred, was communism. The Egyptian dream has been either more realistic or less speculatively inclined: a mixed economy in which the government provided investment in areas crucial for growth but where, for whatever reasons, profits were low and a modest safety net for the poorest had to be put in place.

Roughly speaking, we have a perfectly plausible picture of the last 80 years of the Egyptian economy and a set of highly stylized facts.[7] An open, market economy in the first half of the twentieth century based on specialization in the export of one primary good (cotton) was transformed after 1952 into a mixed economy in which government pursued a variety of strategies (investments, redistribution, regulation) to engage in import-substituting industrialization (ISI). For both endogenous and exogenous reasons the ISI policies no longer seemed to work, and the cost to government budgets led the state to a lengthy and not always very successful pursuit of privatization. While industry was, after 1952, very largely in the hands of the state, many physical assets—especially land—remained in private hands although there were no factor markets and not even very many free markets for domestically produced goods.

The open market economy was governed by a political system in which a powerful constitutional monarch was supported, albeit with occasional tension, by foreign troops, and whose rule was lightly constrained by an elected parliament. This liberal experiment was, unfortunately, never repeated with sufficient changes in the variables to know under what

---

6 Joel Beinin, "Egypt at the Tipping Point," *The Middle East Channel*, January 31, 2011; and 2011b.

7 The following paragraphs are drawn mainly from Hansen (1991:64–108).

circumstances it might have succeeded. Obviously one crucial concern is whether the events of the past two years will provide an opportunity for another trial of limited liberalism or authoritarian statism.

The creation of a state sector of the economy in the late 1950s was accomplished partly through sequestration and nationalization of existing firms and partly through government investment. The underlying strategic logic was to pursue the then-popular policy of import-substitution industrialization as well as to move in the direction of self-sufficiency for a regime threatened by boycotts, sanctions, and the possibility of war. There are many reasons to believe that government employment policies, coupled with overly capital-intensive investments, created significant limitations of economic growth, although they also increased equity.

More important, under Anwar al-Sadat's presidency attempts were made to contain inflationary pressures by increasing subsidies of basic goods. Subsidized goods, it was believed, would relieve the pressure for increases in money wages. Over time the subsidies, many of which were poorly if at all targeted, became an increasingly large burden on government expenditures. There is a basic conundrum of Egyptian economic, political, and social history embedded in these years and these policies that continues to affect the present. Egyptian economic growth has been, by the standards expected by policy makers and probably desired by Egyptians, weak at best. Perhaps paradoxically, however, Egyptians have experienced after 1952, relative to many other countries, relatively less unequal distribution of income and, perhaps more important for many, access to a variety of commodities—both goods and services—that have made their lives materially better off.

If we want to understand the relationship between the economy and the revolution without focusing on a single actor or event, where should we begin? We have no longitudinal studies of attitudes or interests or latent groups that would help us to understand what may be the most important differences between 2011 and, for example, events in 1952–1954 or in 1919: transformations in attitudes toward governance and the kind of political economy Egyptians, even if only vaguely, want. As an example of what might be useful I want to focus on several different areas of Egypt's political economy to gain some traction on recent events and what the future may be like.

Government Employment

Since the 1960s, the government has offered employment to graduates as a way to induce Egyptians to pursue education and thereby increase the stock of human capital. Government employment, along with employment in the public sector, has been an important tool for the government to influence the twin goals of equity and capital investment. As educational attainment has increased in Egypt and more Egyptians complete not only primary but also secondary and tertiary levels of education, the cost of providing government positions has become an increasing burden on the state budget.

One question about increasing levels of education or human capital is that we are not sure exactly how it is best deployed or, frankly, even exactly how it contributes to growth, although it definitely does. While most people would believe more education is a good thing in its own right, there is some question about its role in the economy. One argument is that higher levels of education are especially useful as technical innovation is introduced or pursued because it allows that innovation to be more productively used. To the degree that educated people do not work in areas where new technology is deployed, there may not be much of an economic return to society from the education (this of course does not mean education is not still a desirable good, simply that it won't have an economic return).

And yet state employment plays a complicated role in Egyptian life. Determining the appropriate size and social goals of that employment, as well as ensuring that state employees carry out their work effectively, will be a challenge for any post-revolutionary government. It is worth recalling just what the challenges include. Government employment may often be influenced wholly or in part by patronage, corruption, or political exchange. Nevertheless government employment is (to a far greater degree than private employment) bound by rules in regard to dismissal, raises, and advancement.

Employment in government agencies and the public sector where dismissal is quite difficult played a significant role in enhancing equity, although it also played a significant role in the growing government deficits in the 1980s.

First, we know from the work of Richard Adams and others that government employment plays an important role in the countryside insofar as equity is concerned (Adams 2002:359). The two major sources of income equalization among the rural population are remittances and access to some form of government employment. Government employment is not universally available and it certainly does not eliminate significant disparities of income in the countryside, but it appears to be one of the few tools available that directly, if in Adams's words bluntly (that is, without much direction or discrimination), affects income inequality. These positions presumably range from those involving significant education (irrigation engineering or agronomy) to those involving very little (guards or laborers).

Second, we know from the work of Ragui Assaad that government employment plays an important role in the employment of women (Assaad and El-Hamdi 2009). Assaad has written extensively on the unexpected de-feminization of Egyptian employment.[8] Economies such as Egypt's often experience extensive feminization of employment, especially in industries that are labor-intensive or geared to export or both. This has been true, since the early twentieth century, for places as diverse as New England, Japan, South Korea, and Egypt in the 1960s and 1970s.

Egypt, over the last several decades, has witnessed the de-feminization of the workforce except in government employment. There is disagreement about the reasons for this trend, although Assaad leads us to believe that it arises from the collision between social expectations about women's roles at home, the length of the working day, and the exigencies of travel.

Assaad's argument, I note in passing, is not only distinct from but in contradiction with an argument by Lisa Blaydes and Drew Linzer about the role of women, employment, and fundamentalism (Blaydes and Linzer 2008). Blaydes and Linzer argue that some subset of Egyptian women have a predisposition to fundamentalism as a signaling mechanism to potential mates. Blaydes and Linzer hypothesize that a poorer woman is more likely to be fundamentalist because, in the absence of job opportunities, this is the best way to let a husband know she will be a good wife. Somewhat surprisingly, Blaydes and Linzer never refer to Assaad's body of empirical work that suggests women

---

8 See, for example, Assaad (2009) and, in light of what follows, his discussion of decreased employment opportunities for educated women in government.

leave employment on marriage rather than refrain from entering it before. Nor do they refer to the long-standing and well-known demographic studies by Philippe Fargues and others showing that marriage in Egypt has been characterized both by delay and what appears to be, over a lifetime, the near certainty of marriage.[9]

There are also some important implications for post-revolutionary government policy. If Blaydes and Linzer are correct, then increasing equity along gender lines would seem to imply a focus on changing public attitudes about marriage, marriageability, and the behavior through which lower-class women can signal their status as appropriate partners. If Assaad is correct, the reconstitution of the public transportation network that still existed in the 1960s and 1970s before the introduction of private transport through automobiles, mini-buses, and the like may be more efficacious not only for men but for women's equity as well (although there may be other constraints that Assaad did not investigate, such as child care). The creation, for example, of the kind of network of dedicated bus lanes or light rail that has become popular in Latin America in place of heavy capital investment in subways will not be a panacea. It might have unintended and important effects on the Egyptian economy and society in terms of overall employment, women's employment, and perhaps even the demand for buses, which can be more easily produced locally than light rail cars.

Looking forward, therefore, Egyptian governments will have to work with the legacy of the last 30 years, and the choices they make about public investment, employment, and retention policies alone will have significant effects on a broad variety of issues. The problem seems to be less one of government employment as such than of what particular policies are chosen.

Privatization and Macroeconomic Stabilization

Since the middle of the 1970s Egyptian governments have struggled with budget imbalances. Key causes were employment guarantees and the growing size of subsidies. They have also sought to increase investment, especially in industry, as a way of providing employment for a

---

9 See, for example, Fargues (2011). Obviously Blaydes and Linzer could not have read an article published in 2011 when they wrote before 2008; however, this is not a new finding by Fargues. See, for example, Fargues (1988:982).

growing population. Almost the entire Mubarak era was a lengthy series of attempts to decrease annual deficits as well as the accumulating debt. Usually these attempts registered some initial success and then were swamped by newly increased deficits and debts. In the 1990s the Egyptian government undertook policies known as economic reform and structural adjustment (ERSAP) but also frequently referred to as "neo-liberalism." It was one attempt to reduce the size of subsidies by reducing the number of items provided at subsidized prices, as well as to change the balance of public and private enterprise. Partly this was done through the privatization of public firms and partly through allowing private capital to invest in areas of growth (Korayem 1997; Soliman 2011a:56–61, 84–90).

Here again we have wonderful anecdotes, many of which suggest that although Egyptian privatization was better managed than the chaotic free-for-all that characterized the process in the former Soviet Union, it nevertheless did not achieve many of the larger goals its adherents claimed it would bring. Unlike the Soviet Union or Eastern Europe, Egypt had a significant private sector, a legal system accustomed to the role of private property, and the personnel and technology to engage in something like fundamental accounting procedures. It is also clear that in many cases the actual structure of ownership and the flow of resources was sufficiently opaque that little of this mattered. This also suggests that much of the damage that privatization can inflict on societies with large state-owned sectors was, unlike Eastern Europe or the Soviet Union, already behind Egypt when the revolution occurred.

Egyptian governments have been engaged in privatization for more than 30 years and the results have been, at best, mixed. Two primary issues hampered privatization: the existence of an extremely wide-ranging coalition opposed to it, and widespread corruption, looting, and distortion of the process itself as well-placed individuals gained significant private advantages through protected access to public resources. As the late Marsha Posusney pointed out, the trade unions vehemently opposed privatization but so did many of the directors of public firms, government officials in the ministries to which the firms were subordinate, and even members of the private sector who feared the impact on their own protected niches developed in the shadow of the public sector (Posusney 1992). We know, again from anecdotes, that some firms were looted before they were privatized. We also know that some firms really were insolvent and that still others benefited from privatization (Weiss and Wurzel 1998). What we lack is any overall balance sheet and much of a sense of whether there were any systematic differences. Samer Shehata and others suggest that less heavily capitalized and more labor-intensive firms may have been better candidates for privatization.[10] What we also know is that privatization allowed the creation of new, private sources of enrichment through privileged access to the government.

Among the most important cases of privatization was the steel industry, which also became the object of foreign investment under the direction of Ahmed Ezz. "The most fundamental and game changing development that occurred in the [steel] industry within the MENA region, and especially during the nineties, was the entry of the private sector. Prior to the nineties, the steel industry was dominated by governmental institutions, as massive amount of capital and the strategic nature of steel as a commodity made it difficult for private investors to enter this sector" (Global Investment House 2009:16). Economic reform allowed Ezz to take over the Alexandria Company for Iron and Steel to create Ezz Steel, which, along with Saudi Arabia's SABIC Hadeed Company, Qatar Steel, and Libyan Iron and Steel, was among the region's giants. One problem for the Egyptian steel companies, whose prices are sometimes above world prices, was competition especially from Turkey—which may have engaged in dumping in the second half of the first decade of the twenty-first century (25).[11]

The textile industry does not exhibit such high concentration, primarily because the costs of entry and exit are much lower and because it does not appear to exhibit important economies of scale. As far back as

---

[10] Shehata notes that the less well-capitalized factory with older machines was one of the few profitable public sector mills in Egypt. He also notes that the older machines require the worker pay greater attention to the work process. Although Shehata studied worker resistance it is apparent that resistance by the workers is equivalent to lower productivity and profitability for the firm and lack of attention or commitment by workers is one potent form of resistance (Shehata 2009:12–13, 78–80).

[11] The Egyptian steel industry consists of 27 producers with an annual capacity of 5.5 million tons of long products and 2.2 million of flat products. Of the combined 7.7 million tons, the Ezz companies had 5.3 million tons while Beshay, another private producer, had another million and Kandil Steel had a million.

the 1930s productivity in the Egyptian textile industry (catering mainly to low-income buyers) was below Japanese competitors. The textile industry is often cited as a likely source for export-led growth, but it was unable to meet its quota for foreign markets when it still benefited from the now extinguished Multi-Fiber Agreement.[12] How it will do in the future is at best uncertain. Although the textile industry is not usually associated with rents, tariffs on imported textiles can be as high as 54 percent, a figure that suggests the need for relatively high protection in a country with low wages.

Egypt's textile industry has long been based on the premise that the raw material was locally available and that it was an extremely viable export industry as well as an important item of import substitution. While both of these points are true (and, as Robert Tignor's study of the Bradford Dyers' plant shows [Tignor 1989], have been plausible since the 1940s), it is not clear that Egyptian firms and the government have been able to develop (or have even tried to develop) a set of strategies to encourage Egyptian textile products as a whole to fit into global or regional markets or even to develop a clear consensus about their connection to the local market (Tignor 1989). As incomes in the private sector have not only approached but in some cases exceeded those in the public sector, and as parts of the textile/clothing industry may be one of the areas where increased employment of women is likely, this is a problem. Without descending into a kind of left-wing Madison Avenue hyperbole it might also be the case that developing a stronger Egyptian presence in global markets for processed agricultural products would be possible. To accomplish any of these tasks, however, the quality of Egyptian goods would have to be higher than it is now, and this, in part, would probably require a larger share of the returns to quality or reputation flowing to actual producers (workers and farmers) than is now the case.

The Military

We simply have no idea of the true size of the military economy. One oft-cited figure, that the armed forces control as much as 40 percent of the economy, appears to have derived from a statement of Robert

---

12 See Magder (2005:11–14).

Springborg and is evidently based on his 1989 book.[13] Much has been made of the military's economic interests, especially in industrial production and tourism, where it competes with the private sector and state-owned firms. Unfortunately we lack any systematic information on the overall size or specific areas of military investment. We know it produces many of the goods it needs itself and maintains significant excess production capacity in many areas, but in most areas it is far from being a monopolist or even oligopolist. It is, in other words, an actor like others, although more effective due to the presence of free labor in the form of conscripts, and perhaps also more efficient. American academics have long had an infatuation with the military, from the days of the debate about whether it was part of the new middle class to the belief that military industries would outperform their civilian counterparts. Less clear has been the way in which the military itself has played a role in deforming the economy in the search for sinecures.

What seems clear is the interest of the military in land over the last 50 years. If Springborg has tended to overstate the role of the military in the national economy, he has been a lonely pioneer in studying their interest in landed property since his biography of Sayyid Marʻi (Springborg 1976; see also Springborg 1982). In the 1950s, tourism was a decaying sector in Egypt and the gold rush into hotels was not

---

13 On February 17, 2011, David Kirkpatrick reported in the *New York Times* that "some Western analysts have guessed that the military's empire makes up as much as a third of Egypt's economy," although it also cited former trade minister Rachid Mohamed Rachid, who put the figure at 10 percent. Springborg appears to have been cited in a news report filed by Andrew S. Ross on February 13, 2011 (www.sfgate.com), placing the military's share of the economy at between five and 40 percent while acknowledging that this is guesswork. What seems to be at work is a confusion between the scope of the military's activities across many industries and the size of its economic activities, as well as the absence of distinction between 'the economy' as a flow of resources and as a stock. By way of comparison, General Electric's total (international) revenue in 2012 was about $147 billion or 1 percent of the US GDP of $14.7 trillion; GE's net income was about $13.5 billion (or 0.1 percent of US GDP). The base budget of the US Defense Department was about $664 billion, or about 4 percent of US GDP. Absent any argument about the relevant context it is difficult to know what the claims about the size of the Egyptian military economy are supposed to mean. In 1997 Lieutenant Stephen Gotowicki of the US Army published "The Role of the Egyptian Military in Domestic Society," which proposed that Egyptian military expenditures (not production) had shrunk to less than 10 percent of the government budget by 1994.

yet even a glimmer in anyone's imagination, but the Armed Forces were already alert to the possibilities of trading land, although at the time their dominant concern was agricultural development.

In those days the armed forces were already contending over land, although their pursuit of gain was probably far more detrimental to the national economy than their more recent efforts. In 1952, Magdi Hassanein sent army engineers to investigate the area of the Western Desert that would later become Tahrir province. From 1954 until 1973, the army and civilian experts vied for control of land reclamation in Tahrir and elsewhere. Three-quarters of Egypt's investment in agriculture during the 1960s went to land reclamation in the Western Desert, of which less than two-thirds was cultivated, at high cost and with meager (and probably not positive) returns. The creation of state farms on reclaimed land allowed the military to create sinecures for retired and active-duty officers (Hansen 1991:120–121). The tragedy here is not so much that the armed forces control a portion of the state budget far removed from their primary task, as that whole sections of state expenditures were captured and deployed to disfigure the economy in order to provide positions whose holders had no particular substantive interest or knowledge in land reclamation, farming, or environmental issues (see Sowers 2013:35–37, 48–51).

In the last 30 years the armed forces have discovered what are arguably more effective but also more socially useful ways to deploy their interest in landed property and the creation of sinecures by leasing land to hotels, as well as creating a variety of industrial ventures. Among those most frequently mentioned by Springborg and others are bottled water, butane gas cylinders, and automobiles and tanks.

When we look more closely at Springborg's own account from 1989, however, all that becomes clear is how murky everything is. Thus, it is often said that the armed forces control the automobile industry in Egypt because of the links between the military and GM for the assembly of Jeeps from kits. And yet what Springborg tells us about that enterprise, at least in the 1980s, was that the joint venture between the Nasr Automotive Company and GM was funded in such a complex way that "even the most dedicated of the state's accountants would ... have extreme difficulty in tracing the government's original investment ... a very significant share of such funds have ultimately been siphoned off by private interests" (Springborg 1989:84). The existence today of several other assembly plants by foreign car firms to assemble kits probably reduces whatever role the armed forces play in automobile production. The armed forces do assemble Abrams tanks and some other military equipment, tasks which in the US would be assigned to private enterprise, and although these do increase its share of GDP it is hard to imagine that they crowd out other actors (except perhaps through the channel of limited state resources).

Again, I do not bring these forward as a way of arguing that the military-industrial complex is a progressive or negligible force in the Egyptian economy. But I do have several questions: Has the military component of the economy (of which we have some fairly good descriptions in the 1990s, which indicate it was still based primarily on military production) grown at the same or even a faster rate than the rest of the economy? Is the real problem with the role of the military in the economy its gross size or the degree to which (in both the military and non-military components) economic decisions are distorted in the interest of providing sinecures to officers or draining off profits to undisclosed private channels? It could of course be both, but I am inclined to see the latter as more of a problem.

The armed forces have long fascinated American policy makers and academics. Jason Brownlee has written extensively of the policy connections, especially in the period since the 1970s, but the roots go deeper: the army was seen and may still be seen or may present itself to be seen in Washington as a pure Weberian instrument for modernization (Brownlee 2012). I think this is more than simply the reliance on stability. In the 1950s and into the early 1960s there were incessant debates about the role of the military and the so-called New Middle Class, of which the Egyptian army was the outstanding representative.[14] I can still remember colleagues in the 1980s lauding what they presumed were the efficiencies of military discipline brought into the industrial production process in an expanding network of army-run factories.

By Way of a Conclusion

The paradox of the past 50 years thus looks like a more or less steady increase in the command Egyptians have over commodities without a correspondingly great increase in economic growth. In fact this

---

14 There was once a vigorous debate about the role of the army as a force for modernization. See for example Halpern (1963); Abdel Malek (1968); and Huntington (1968).

seems to be exactly the same debate in slightly different terms that structured many discussions of Egypt in the 1980s: growth without development, as it was then put. It is often asserted that rents account for this, especially rents derived from tourism, the Suez Canal, remittances, and (for a while at least) oil. We should be cautious about placing too much emphasis on rents, however, because Egypt has made significant and growing investments in the areas that provide the greatest 'rents.' Whether remittances, for example, are really a rent or simply a payment for human capital created in Egypt and exported would be an interesting question and one difficult to solve. It is worth recalling, however, that payment for human capital was exactly how the exodus of Egyptian workers abroad was perceived in the 1970s. So, too, while the Pyramids are unique, much of Egyptian tourism competes for European and American clients in a world market: the beaches at Varadero in socialist Cuba and at Phuket in capitalist Thailand look remarkably like the sandy shores along a deep blue sea in the southern Sinai.

If, however, Egyptians are better educated, live longer (perhaps with some new debilitating diseases, as diabetes and hepatitis C have replaced schistosomiasis), and have greater access to the world (reportedly there are 92 million cell phones in Egypt and millions of people use the internet), then perhaps attitudes have changed. This is an idea along lines proposed by Robert Springborg and Clement Henry more than a decade ago, that Egyptian demands are driven by their knowledge of incomes and expenditures abroad but no longer limited to perceptions of wages (Henry and Springborg 2001). Now Egyptians might want political participation as well as incomes similar to what they know obtains in industrial economies.

Thus, the population's well-being has converged in some areas (notably mortality and education) toward Europe even as money incomes have only diverged. The paradox therefore is that Egyptians in general have access to more goods and services than was the case 50 years ago although incomes have diverged to an ever greater degree. Some authors, such as Galal Amin, see this as the hallmark of a society about to collapse; others, perhaps including Timothy Mitchell, see this as the fatal result of inclusion in a global economy (Amin 2000:174; Mitchell 2002:215–218).

The economic and political dreams promised by the Nasser regime and the revolutionary upheaval of 2011 both now appear to have been deferred. When Langston Hughes wrote, it appeared as if the American dream was again about to be foreclosed for his African American audience. No more so than in 1955 when fourteen-year-old Emmett Till was lynched in Mississippi while visiting relatives for the supposed offense of flirting with a white grocery store clerk. Had anyone suggested that a decade later a dramatic movement to transform the legal and social norms of the American South would be well underway it would have seemed absurd. We might well be cautious in believing that we fully know the outcome of the events that began in 2011.

The broad trend of the last half century in Egypt (and perhaps also Tunisia and Syria) resembles to me nothing quite so much as the period Jan DeVries calls the "Industrious Revolution" (DeVries 1994). DeVries' argument is controversial, but his discussion of changing consumption patterns and increased commodity consumption in the absence of productivity increases is certainly worth thinking about as an antidote to Amin's and Mitchell's jeremiads. One implication of his work is that, given new consumer preferences and education, it is possible that some new technologies would be rapidly adopted and deployed to positive economic effect.

This was also a period in which very different and contradictory ideas about the nature of political community were being quite literally fought out in much of Western Europe and the US. To comprehend further these kinds of events, however, we may need a different concept of political community than the one we have now. Our current concept, at least in American and European academia, is an image from late in that period of the industrious revolution: a union of individuals. This vision of the social compact envisioning political community as the outgrowth of a nation of Robinson Crusoes agreeing, even if only in thought experiment, on the outlines of justice may serve us well for some areas of political theory. It does poorly, however, as a guide to what happens as people actually attempt to remake political community in the midst of revolutions or restorations. The revolutionary turmoil of the last several years in Egypt suggests that the dream deferred was not only one of economic growth but of political participation. That dream, as much as any economic one, has exploded not merely because it was deferred, but because the changes induced in Egyptian society over the past five decades have made people less patient about its indefinite delay.

The explosion, for the moment, seems to have divided Egypt into two basic camps. Going forward, the problem is not so much whether the camps are religious and secular or authoritarian and democratic as that they seem to inhabit very different worlds morally. What I mean by that is that, broadly speaking, there is not much sense within each group that the other is made up of responsible moral agents. And here we have a paradox as well: despite all the attempts by economic theory to escape from these issues through the discussion of third-party enforcement, game theory, discount rates, and institutions, in the end it seems to matter what kind of community people believe they are part of and what kinds of obligations they believe are incumbent upon them both to participate in those communities and to recognize the possible participation of others. This brings us back to Hughes in a somewhat different vein. When Hughes wrote, the US was already in the throes of a profound transformation (which, for those of us who lived through it, had its revolutionary although not apocalyptic qualities) about the nature of citizenship, political community, and obligations. The "Great Migration," the experience of the Second World War, and the existence of a new set of political actors in the North set the stage for the civil rights movement. These obligations (and rights) are more deeply felt than whatever drafters put into constitutional documents, and until a broader consensus is achieved about the nature of the Egyptian political community, it is hard to imagine much economic progress.

References

Abdel Malek, Anouar. 1968. *Egypt: Military Society*. New York: Random House.

Adams, Richard H. 2002. "Nonfarm Income, Inequality, and Land in Rural Egypt," *Economic Development and Cultural Change*, 50(2) January: 339–363.

Amin, Galal. 2000. *Whatever Happened to the Egyptians?* Cairo: The American University in Cairo Press.

Assaad, Ragui. 2009. "Labor Supply, Employment, and Unemployment in the Egyptian Economy, 1988–2006." In Ragui Assaad, ed. *The*

Egyptian Labor Market Revisited, pp. 1-52. Cairo: The American University in Cairo Press.

Assaad, Ragui, and Fatma El-Hamdi. 2009. "Women in the Egyptian Labor Market: An Analysis of Developments, 1988–2006." In Ragui Assaad, ed. *The Egyptian Labor Market Revisited*, pp. 219-257. Cairo: The American University in Cairo Press.

Blaydes, Lisa, and Drew A. Linzer. 2008. "The Political Economy of Women's Support for Fundamentalist Islam," *World Politics*, 60(4) July: 576–609.

Brownlee, Jason. 2012. *Democracy Prevention*. Cambridge: Cambridge University Press.

DeVries, Jan. 1994. "The Industrial Revolution and the Industrious Revolution," *The Journal of Political Economy*, 54(2) June: 249–270.

Global Investment House. 2009. "Egypt Steel Sector Reinforcing Demand." Kuwait, July, 16.

Fargues, Philippe. 1988. "La baisse de la fécondité arab," *Population*, 43:6 (Nov.-Dec. 1988): 975–1004.

———. 2011. "Croissance et mutations démographiques au XXeme siècle." In Vincent Battesti and François Ireton, eds. *L'Égypte au présent*, 62–65. Paris: Sindbad.

Halpern, Manfred. 1963. *Politics of Social Change in the Middle East and North Africa*. Princeton: Princeton University Press.

Hansen, Bent. 1991. *Egypt and Turkey*. Washington, DC: The International Bank for Reconstruction and Development.

Henry, Clement M., and Robert Springborg. 2001. *Globalization and the Politics of Development in the Middle East*. Cambridge: Cambridge University Press.

Hughes, Langston. 1951. *Montage of a Dream Deferred*. New York: Henry Holt and Company.

Huntington, Samuel. 1968. *Political Order in Changing Societies*. New Haven: Yale University Press.

Korayem, Karima. 1997. "Egypt's Economic Reform and Structural Adjustment (ERSAP)." Working Paper 19. Cairo: The Egyptian Center for Economic Studies.

Magder, Dan. 2005. "Egypt after the Multi-Fiber Arrangement." Working Paper 05-8, Institute for International Economics, Washington, DC.

References

Mitchell, Timothy. 2002. *Rule of Experts: Egypt, Techno-Politics, Modernity*. Berkeley: University of California Press.

Moore, Barrington. 1966. *Social Origins of Dictatorship and Democracy: Lord and Peasant in the Making of the Modern World*. Boston: Beacon Press.

Noland, Marcus, and Howard Pack. 2011. *The Arab Economies in a Changing World*. 2nd ed. Washington, DC: Peterson Institute for International Economics.

Posusney, Marsha Pripstein. 1992. "Labor as an Obstacle to Privatization: The Case of Egypt." In Ilya Harik and Denis Sullivan, eds. *Privatization and Liberalization in the Middle East*, 81–105. Bloomington: Indiana University.

Shehata, Samer S. 2009. *Shop Floor Culture and Politics in Egypt*. Albany: State University of New York Press.

Skocpol, Theda. 1979. *States and Social Revolutions*. Cambridge: Cambridge University Press.

Soliman, Samer. 2011a. *The Autumn of Dictatorship: Fiscal Crisis and Political Change in Egypt under Mubarak*. Translated by Peter Daniel. Stanford, CA: Stanford University Press.

———. 2011b. "The End of the Rentier/Caretaker State." In Peter Daniel, trans. *The Autumn of Dictatorship: Fiscal Crisis and Political Change in Egypt under Mubarak*, 138–162. Stanford, CA: Stanford University Press.

Sowers, Jeannie L. 2013. *Environmental Politics in Egypt: Activists, Experts, and the State*. London: Routledge.

Springborg, Robert. 1976. "Patrimonialism and Policy Making in Egypt: Nasser and Sadat and the Tenure Process for Reclaimed Lands," *Middle East Studies*, 15(1) January: 45–69.

———. 1982. *Family, Power, and Politics in Egypt: Sayed Bey Marei—His Clan, Clients, and Cohort*. Philadelphia: University of Pennsylvania Press.

———. 1989. *Mubarak's Egypt: Fragmentation of the Political Order*. Boulder: Westview Press.

Tignor, Robert L. 1989. *Egyptian Textiles and British Capital, 1930–1956*. Cairo: The American University in Cairo Press.

Weiss, Dieter, and Ulrich Wurzel. 1998. "Politics and Microeconomics of Reform." In *The Economics and Politics of Transition to an Open Market Economy: Egypt*, 105–138. Paris: Development Centre of the OECD.

CHAPTER 3

Tumult, Trauma, and Resilience
Psychological Well-Being of Cairenes One Year Following the January 25, 2011 Uprisings[1]

Deena Abdelmonem,[2] Salma N. Mohamed,[2] Tiya Abdel-Malek,[2] Seham Kafafi,[2] Salma Khalifa,[2] Rana Khalil,[2] Basma Abdelaziz,[3] Mona M. Amer[2]

On January 25, 2011, Egyptians began a series of uprisings that led to the end of President Hosni Mubarak's 30-year regime, and the military took over governance of Egypt. These uprisings took place in Cairo's Tahrir Square as well as other gathering grounds in cities throughout the nation. In the midst of the eighteen-day uprisings between January 25 and February 11, 2011, demoralized police officers retreated from their posts on the streets. Police stations were stormed and set on fire, and prison inmates were released. The sudden absence of a functioning police force led communities to fend for themselves in groups known as 'popular committees' in order to protect their neighborhoods from thugs and criminals (Bremer 2011).

Before the events of January 25 2011, Egypt enjoyed a relatively low crime rate maintained by Mubarak's police state through the use

---

1 Acknowledgment: This research was supported by a grant from the Community-Based Learning Program at the Gerhart Center for Philanthropy and Civic Engagement, The American University in Cairo. The authors would like to dedicate special thanks to the Gerhart Center for the generous support and financial contributions they donated to this study.
2 Psychology Unit, The American University in Cairo, Egypt
3 General Secretariat for Mental Health, Egypt Ministry of Health

of excessive force to uphold order.[4] In the years before the uprisings, Egypt was known to have a lower crime rate than many European countries.[5] Petty crimes such as pickpocketing were always common, but more violent crimes were virtually absent, largely due to the harsh methods employed by the Egyptian police force to crack down on criminal behavior. Even people such as opposition bloggers, conventional criminals, and members of Islamist groups experienced torture in jails carried out by the Egyptian police,[6] and the state's implementation of emergency law further contributed to the police's power over citizens.

Subsequent to the events of early 2011, Egypt faced an unprecedented spike in crime. Reports show that the rate of armed robberies increased by almost 83 percent in May 2011 compared to the rate before January 25 of that year, and the murder rate was up 75 percent as well.[7] In 2011, 2,774 murders were reported in Egypt,[8] compared to 992 murders in 2009 (UNODC 2010). Additionally, Egypt witnessed a reported 2,229 kidnappings in 2011,[9] compared to just 47 in 2008 (UNODC 2009). Some of these incidents occurred more frequently in poorer neighborhoods and remote areas in Egypt, causing citizens to fear leaving their homes.[10]

Many citizens took matters into their own hands to remedy the country's increasingly unsafe conditions, such as installing more locks on their doors, preventing their children from staying out too late, engaging in vigilantism, and acquiring gun licenses.[11] The increased proliferation

---

4   H. Hendawi, "Crime Wave Grips Egypt, Absence of Police Blamed," Associated Press, April 4, 2011, http://www.msnbc.msn.com/id/42427900/ns/world_news-mideast_n_africa/t/crime-wave-grips-egypt-absence-police-blamed/

5   J. Fleishman and A. Hassan, "Rise in Crime Intensifies Unease in Once-Safe Egypt," *Los Angeles Times*, February 20, 2012, http://articles.latimes.com/2012/feb/20/world/la-fg-egypt-unease-20120221

6   L. Harding, "US Reported 'Routine' Police Brutality in Egypt, Wikileaks Cables Show," *The Guardian*, January 28, 2011, http://www.guardian.co.uk/world/2011/jan/28/egypt-police-brutality-torture-wikileaks

7   H. Hendawi, "Egypt's Latest Crisis Puts Pressure on Leadership," *Daily News Egypt*, July 12, 2011, http://www.dailynewsegypt.com/2011/07/12/egypts-latest-crisis-puts-pressure-on-leadership/

8   Fleishman and Hassan, "Rise in Crime."

9   Fleishman and Hassan, "Rise in Crime."

10 Hendawi, "Crime Wave Grips Egypt."

11 E. Arrott, "Egyptians' Fear of Crime Soars," *Voice of America*, October 5, 2011, http://www.voanews.com/content/egyptians-fear-of-crime-soars-131265079/173250.html

of guns on the streets was another security concern. Guns for civilians can be acquired with a license or illegally through the black market, and many Egyptians were choosing to arm themselves. The licensing process requires training for proper gun use but many weapons were unlicensed and unregistered, causing fear among the population over inexperienced gun owners. Some estimates revealed that the number of licensed guns in Egypt had doubled since the uprisings, and black-market availability had increased tenfold (El Sayed 2011).

In addition to these new conditions, the events that unfolded in Egypt over the 18 months following the uprisings also caused concern among citizens. Ongoing protests that occurred in response to various political decisions taken by the ruling military junta contributed to feelings of danger and instability. Violent clashes in Imbaba in May 2011, Maspero in October 2011, Muhammad Mahmud Street in November 2011, Port Said in February 2012, and Abbasiya Square in May 2012 further contributed to citizens' feelings of anxiety, especially as they followed media coverage of these events or witnessed clashes first-hand.

The Psychological Effects of Violence, Chronic Conflict, and Political Unrest

Mass conflict and violence can take a toll on populations in the forms of increased stress and anxiety. Stress is defined by psychologists as the hindered ability to meet life's demands due to real or perceived challenges that exist beyond the range of available coping resources (Gunnar and Quevedo 2007). If the stress response negatively affects a person's daily functioning, such as occupational or social obligations, it indicates that the person may have a stress disorder (Olfson et al. 1997). One feature of stress disorders is their debilitating nature, which involves a loss of energy that can manifest as depression, as well as poorer quality of life (Liverant, Suvak, Pineles, and Resick 2012). Similarly, stressors can trigger anxiety, which is defined as fear and apprehension of future events. Anxiety affects a person's cognition and behavior in the form of preoccupations and avoidance of certain events, respectively (Barlow 1988).

Stressors appear in varying degrees, but when a person encounters an extreme stressor that threatens their physical integrity, they may experience trauma (Flannery 1999). Additionally, trauma can arise if a person is threatened with violence or has learned that violence was inflicted on others (Breslau 2009). If the person continuously relives the traumatic event, avoids items or settings that remind them of the event, and shows a heightened sensitivity for stimuli, the person may be experiencing post-traumatic stress disorder, or PTSD (Flannery 1999). PTSD combines aspects of stress and anxiety, and its pathology is causational in that it must follow a traumatic event (Breslau 2009). However, most people who experience traumatic events do not develop PTSD, but may succumb to a comorbid disorder such as depression or drug abuse in order to cope with the trauma (Breslau 2009). While men are more likely to experience traumatic events, women are more frequently diagnosed with PTSD. The reason for this gender difference in PTSD prevalence remains unclear (Breslau 2009).

While trauma response is widely universal, different cultures express the results of trauma in diverse ways. Current discourse on trauma reactions and PTSD is mainly a product of a Western cultural paradigm, rendering attempts to include other populations under this standard problematic. This is because people in other parts of the world have varying social and cultural contexts that create different backdrops against which to express reactions to trauma (Afana 2012). For example, Arab populations are more likely to describe their trauma symptoms using local, non-technical terms rather than medical or specialized language. In doing so, they often incorporate all aspects of their lives including the social, political, cultural, and economic in order to formulate an understanding as well as an expression of trauma symptoms (Afana 2012). When measuring the psychological state of non-Western populations following traumatic events, researchers have concentrated on revealing PTSD symptoms while ignoring other potential conditions such as psychosis (De Jong 2005). Additionally, non-Western populations have been found to express PTSD symptoms (as outlined by Western populations) throughout their daily lives and not necessarily as a result of a trauma or crisis (De Jong 2005). It is therefore important to formulate research designs related to trauma within non-Western populations in a way that is tailored to the specific population's cultural habits.

Traumatic stressors can occur on an individual level (e.g., resulting from sexual assault or rape) or at a community-wide level such as natural disasters or political violence. Severe community-wide stressors, or disasters, can be natural (such as earthquakes) or manmade (such as chronic violence or war), and each type of disaster has its own adverse effects on communities. However, mass violence has been shown to cause more widespread psychological damage than natural disasters. Furthermore, some members of society may be more at risk for disaster-related stress than others. Negative psychological effects of disasters tend to be higher among youth, women, people of lower socioeconomic status, and citizens of developing countries (Norris et al. 2002). Understanding the patterns through which trauma-related stress emerges can help predict the outcomes of turbulent events on populations.

Effects of Mass Violence on Middle Eastern Populations

Political turmoil is no stranger to the Middle East, and thus mental health researchers have studied the prevalence of trauma and related psychological disorders in response to political upheaval and internal conflicts. For example, in the Iraqi city of al-Nasiriyah following the 2003 US military invasion, the rate of depressive disorders was found to be 10.2 percent, anxiety disorders 8.4 percent, and a combination of both disorders 25 percent (Hussein and Sa'adoon 2006). Palestinians have also been victims of chronic political turmoil as they live under Israeli military occupation. In the Gaza Strip, PTSD symptoms were prevalent among 29 percent of the overall population and 36 percent of those who personally experienced a traumatic event (Afana et al. 2002). In South Lebanon, which has experienced numerous conflicts with the Israeli army, including a military occupation of the region, PTSD of the population was measured at 29.3 percent (Farhood and Dimassi 2006).

Gender differences among these populations that experience traumatic events are consistent with global trends in that women tend to reveal more signs of post-traumatic stress than men. In Iraq, 15 percent of women in primary healthcare settings displayed higher levels of anxiety disorders compared to 3.7 percent of men (Hussein and Sa'adoon 2006). In the Gaza Strip, PTSD symptoms were significantly higher among women (34.4 percent) than men (21.7 percent; Afana et al. 2002). In southern Lebanon, PTSD among women was 36.6 percent, and 20.9 percent among men (Farhood and Dimassi 2006).

These results show that populations that are exposed to violence and instability may experience stress on a large scale. Therefore, community-wide interventions may be beneficial in dealing with the onset of these disorders as they coincide with turbulent events.

Aims of the Study

Egypt experienced a significant increase in crime, violence, and political turmoil after the uprisings began in early 2011. Due to the likelihood of community-wide traumatic stress based on risk factors, mental health professionals at Egypt's Ministry of Health recognized the necessity to gauge and address psychological needs in the form of public services. Thus, this project was originally developed as a needs assessment for an emerging intervention program that aimed to target Egyptians living in Greater Cairo who may have been affected by the events of the uprisings. The aims of this assessment were to: 1) determine if there was a need for this new program, based on levels of stress and trauma the community was facing in response to heightened political violence; 2) document how the population was coping with these new political stressors and what new behaviors they adopted to come to terms with these changes; and 3) evaluate attitudes toward seeking mental health services for stress and trauma related to the current events. In accordance with the target populations identified by the program at the ministry, we developed a needs assessment that comprised a survey distributed to predominantly middle-class Cairenes and two exploratory focus groups with women in economically disadvantaged areas in Cairo. The program development components of the needs assessment, such as respondents' preferences for counselors and psychological intervention formats and their suggestions for outreach and advertising methods, are not reported in this chapter.

Part 1: Street Survey on Psychological Effects of the Uprisings on Middle-Class Cairenes

Measures

An Arabic-language survey was designed for this study. Aside from demographic questions, which were presented at the end so as not to intimidate participants, the questions asked respondents about their feelings regarding living in Egypt since Mubarak's ouster, the traumatic events they had been experiencing, levels of trauma, and ways in which they had been coping with those stressors. Respondents were also invited to provide their opinions on mental healthcare practices and their willingness to seek services for problems. The survey also asked respondents about their level of activity during the protests that took place both during and after the initial uprisings.

The original survey was drafted in English, translated into Arabic, then back-translated into English once more by the researchers and other collaborators in order to ensure accuracy in the way the questions were presented to the Arabic-speaking population. The survey was piloted on eight people who were selected based on socioeconomic characteristics they shared with the target population. These eight participants provided comments that were used to modify and improve the final version of the survey.

Feelings about life in Egypt after the uprisings. The first segment of the survey explored respondents' general feelings about life in Egypt nearly a year and a half following the uprisings. This section consisted of a list of twelve possible feelings, such as "worried," "confused," "less safe," "optimistic," "more free," and so on, from which respondents were asked to select those that they were experiencing. Respondents were also given the opportunity to mention additional feelings they were experiencing that were not included in the list. To construct this list of feelings, the researchers gathered observations from newspaper articles, conversations with others, and anecdotes from friends, family, and colleagues.

Stressors and trauma. In order to understand the nature of the stressful events that people experienced during and after the revolution, the survey provided a list of 15 stressful and potentially traumatic experiences related to the revolution's events and post-revolution instability. The items on this list were chosen based on news reports, researchers' personal observations, and suggestions given during the piloting process, as well as information extracted from previous literature on populations that faced political trauma. When answering the survey, respondents were asked to mark all of the stressors they had experienced. These included statements such as "I stayed up all night watching violent events unfold on television," "I was detained and/or tortured," and "My financial situation declined."

To assess the respondents' potential for post-traumatic stress disorder, the self-report PTSD Symptom Scale (PSS; Foa, Riggs, Dancu, and Rothbaum 1993) was used. This instrument was selected due to its validity for use in research worldwide, including in the Middle East (e.g., Mirzamani et al. 2007). It consists of a list of 17 symptoms that people often face after experiencing particularly stressful or traumatic events. The items are grouped into three different subscales: four items addressing re-experiencing events, seven items related to avoidance, and six items pertinent to arousal. Examples of statements include "Feeling emotionally upset when you are reminded of the traumatic event" (re-experiencing), "Trying to avoid activities or people that remind me of the traumatic event" (avoidance), and "Being jumpy or easily startled" (arousal).

Participants were asked to respond to the items based on how they were reacting to the stressful and traumatic events associated with the uprisings that they had selected in the previous set of questions. They marked how frequently they experience these statements, from 0 (Not at all) to 3 (Very much; three or more times a week). The total sum of each participant's responses (with the highest possible score being 51 points) indicated the severity of the traumatic stress they were experiencing. This measure can also be used to predict the potential and likelihood of a PTSD diagnosis. To meet the diagnosis, a respondent must select at least one re-experiencing, three avoidance, and two arousal symptoms. For this study, we calculated the responses of participants who had completed at least 15 out of the 17 items on the PTSD Symptom Scale. Cronbach's alpha for the sample was .84.

Coping strategies. The next section assessed respondents' coping mechanisms using the Brief COPE scale (Carver 1997). This instrument was selected due to its validity for use in research worldwide, including Arab countries such as Egypt (Elsheshtawy and Elez 2011), Syria (Abdul Khayat 2007), and Palestine (Abdeen, Qasrawi, Nabil, and Shaheen 2008; Pat-Horencyzk et al. 2009). The scale measures 14 domains of coping strategies, including behavioral tendencies, emotional support, humor, self-blame, positive reframing, religion, and denial. Participants were asked to reflect on their coping methods in relation to the stressful post-uprising events by rating how often they used each coping mechanism, from 1 (= not doing this at all) to 4 (= doing this often). Each coping domain is measured by two items. To make the measure more culturally appropriate, a third item was added to the religion coping domain. Examples of items from this measure include statements such as "I've been getting emotional support from family and friends," "I've been criticizing myself," and "I've been trying to find comfort in my religion or spiritual beliefs." Average scores on each domain are then calculated. Cronbach's alpha for the sample was .82.

Respondents were also asked to indicate which new safety precautions (if any) they had begun taking to avoid danger as a result of increased security concerns. A checklist of possible precautions was provided to the participants, the items of which were chosen based on personal anecdotes from peers, information derived from newspaper reports, or input from participants who were involved in the survey piloting process. These items include examples such as "Earlier curfew," "Carrying self-defense (e.g., pepper-spray, stun gun, gun, knives)," and "Avoiding walking in the streets at night."

Attitudes toward mental health supports. Respondents were asked if they were receptive to the idea of seeking professional help for post-revolution psychological distress, as well as their opinion regarding the importance of such programs. If they were disinclined to solicit these services, they were asked to give reasons based on a list devised by the researchers that included items such as "I do not trust these services," "It may be too expensive," "I do not need help," and "It is too shameful."

Sociodemographic characteristics and political activism. The final section of the survey consisted of two subsections: a demographics subsection and a political activity subsection. The demographic questions asked participants to provide information about their location of residence, age, gender, marital status, educational level, and occupation. The other subsection asked participants to describe their political activity during the protests from January 25, 2011 until February 11, 2011 and throughout the year that followed in terms of the number of times they participated in organized protests. Participants who indicated that they had participated in the protests that took place after February 11 were asked to specify how often they did so by marking one of the following options: "Never," "1–2 times," "3–4 times," "5–10 times," "10–20 times," or "more than 20 times."

Procedures

This needs assessment was approved by the Institutional Review Board at the American University in Cairo and the research office at the Egyptian Ministry of Health's General Secretariat of Mental Health. The survey targeted lower- to upper-middle-class Egyptians in Cairo and Giza, and was distributed between April and May 2012, about a year and a half after the initial uprisings began. Areas for survey distribution were chosen based on the electoral voting districts of the November 2011 parliamentary elections. This provided a total of 14 areas: nine in Cairo and five in Giza. Throughout the course of the study, however, some areas (such as Abbasiya Square) were eliminated due to logistical and safety concerns. The final data sample consisted of 313 valid surveys from Haram (19.5 percent), Helwan (18.5 percent), Sayyida Zaynab (17.9 percent), Downtown and Tahrir Square (13.7 percent), Shubra (9.9 percent), Imbaba (7.3 percent), Nasr City (7.3 percent), and Maadi (5.8 percent). In order to optimize data collection, the research team recruited a group of university students as volunteers to assist in distributing the survey and trained them on the ethics and administration methods of the survey. This allowed volunteers to distribute surveys near their own areas of residence, which gave them the advantage of familiarity with the areas.

Participants for the survey were recruited using non-probability, purposive sampling. In each district, a main thoroughfare was selected for data collection based on how likely it was to provide a diverse sample in terms of the participants' socioeconomic level, gender, or age. Participants who were targeted included shop owners, employees, customers, and pedestrians. In each area, prospective participants were approached by the researchers and asked if they would like to participate in the study, and informed consent was reviewed. In most cases, participants were able to complete the surveys themselves. If they could not read or write, the surveys were dictated to them in the form of a structured interview. A total of 93.3 percent of the surveys were self-completed, while only 5.1 percent were read aloud. The remaining 1.6 percent of the surveys were both read aloud and self-completed. The process yielded 313 valid surveys out of 336 participants. Due to the length of the survey (seven pages total) and the inconvenience of answering it on the street, 23 surveys were insufficiently completed and therefore discarded.

Results

The information gathered throughout the data collection process was then analyzed using several types of statistical analyses, including descriptive statistics for the demographic variables and the survey checklists. It also incorporated bivariate statistics such as independent samples t-test, ANOVA testing, Pearson's correlation, and Spearman correlation to explore differences in trauma and coping based on demographic and political activity variables.

Results

Participants. The age range of the participants was between 18 and 74 years with a mean of 30.18 years (SD = 11.5). The majority (71.5 percent) of the respondents who specified their gender were males, and 28.5 percent specified that they were females. Sixteen percent of the total participants did not indicate their gender. Marital status of participants consisted of single (50.8 percent of those who specified their status), engaged (9.1 percent), married (37.5 percent), divorced (1.1 percent), and widowed (1.5 percent). There were missing data for 15.7 percent of participants.

With regard to highest level of education, among those who answered this question, most had a college degree at the bachelor level (57.8 percent), technical or trade diploma (14.8 percent), or a high-school diploma (13.3 percent). About 5.5 percent did not have an education past the preparatory level, and 4.0 percent had a postgraduate master's- or doctoral-level degree. A total of 18.2 percent did not indicate their education level. Participants were also asked to indicate their occupation, which yielded 203 responses and about 30 varieties of jobs. Most of the responses were student (22 percent), store employee (14.2 percent), engineer (6.8 percent), sales (5.4 percent), and manager (5.4 percent). About 7 percent of the responses were not specific enough to be classified into a category.

A substantial portion of the total sample indicated they lived in the working/middle-class neighborhoods of Helwan (11.5 percent), Haram or Faisal (11.5 percent), and Sayyida Zaynab (7.7 percent). Other areas of residence included Imbaba, Shubra, Nasr City, Maadi, Downtown, and others. Nine respondents indicated that they resided outside of Greater Cairo. About 28.8 percent of the participants did not indicate where they live.

In response to the set of questions that asked participants about their political activity, 29.4 percent said that they protested during the 18 days of revolution, 48.2 percent did not, and 22.4 percent did not mark any answers. A total of 51.8 percent did not protest during the months after February 11, while 24.9 percent did, and 23.3 percent of the total surveys did not indicate an answer.

Feelings about life in Egypt after the uprisings. For the first segment of the survey in which respondents were asked about their general feelings toward life in Egypt after the revolution, table 3.1 lists the percentage of participants who reported each feeling, in descending order. Negative feelings such as worry and insecurity were more frequently chosen than positive feelings such as bravery or excitement.

Table 3.1: Feelings about life in Egypt after the uprisings

Feeling	Percentage
Worried	40.9
Less safe	30.0
Confused	29.7
Optimistic	27.8
Pessimistic	22.0
Frustrated	21.4
Angry	20.8
Brave	18.2
Hopeless	14.7
More free	12.1
Excited	12.1
More safe	3.2

If participants felt something that was not provided in the list, they were asked to check "other" and state any other feelings they might be facing. A total of 33 participants provided additional responses. These responses were divided into four general themes: optimism, anxiety, feelings of negativity, and political responses. Examples of participant comments were: "I'm scared of what might happen tomorrow," "I'm scared for my children," "I feel very optimistic that we are finally reaching democracy," "Political parties are doing nothing but claiming their share of the pie," and "Nothing has changed, and the members of the old [Mubarak] regime have simply created a new party."

Stressful and traumatic events experienced. In response to the provided list of potentially stressful and traumatic events experienced, a majority (61 percent) reported staying up during the night watching the news of violent events on television. Additionally, 47 percent of the sample indicated that they had witnessed violence in the streets, and economic stressors (such as deterioration of one's financial situation) were also common (27.8 percent). Table 3.2 lists the percentage of the sample that reported the different types of traumatic stressors.

Table 3.2: Stressful and traumatic events experienced

Types of traumas faced	% of respondents
Staying up at night watching news of violent events	61.0
Seeing violence in the streets	47.0
Deterioration of the respondents' financial situation	27.8
Having a car stolen from them or from someone they know	22.0
Knowing someone who was injured in violent events	19.8
Being stuck in traffic for more than 2 hours due to protests	19.5
Witnessing an injury or death	18.8
Personally getting robbed	13.4
Deteriorated relationships as a result of differing political opinions	12.8
Losing their job	10.5
Knowing someone who was kidnapped	8.9
Getting attacked in the street	8.0
Getting injured in protests	8.0
Getting tortured	2.6
Knowing someone who was detained or being detained themselves	1.6
Other	18.6

Forty of the participants mentioned that they had experienced traumas that were not covered in the list provided in the survey. These responses were clustered into eight categories: negative feelings and anxiety (12 respondents), direct trauma such as witnessing murder or torture (8 respondents), complaints about current situation (4 respondents), positive feelings (3 respondents), problems with work and personal life (3 respondents), obstacles in getting home due to strikes (2 respondents), and miscellaneous responses (8 respondents).

The survey also asked participants who sustained injuries during or after the events of January 25, 2011 to provide a description of their injuries. In total, this yielded 15 answers that included inhaling tear gas (five people), being struck by bullets or stones (five people), beatings (two people), lacerations (two people), and broken limbs (one person).

Levels of post-traumatic stress and its relation to demographics and political activism. Results from the PSS scale showed that 59.7 percent of those who completed this portion of the survey were likely to meet the diagnosis of PTSD. However, 34.2 percent of the sample did not complete at least 15 from the 17 items of the scale and therefore were eliminated from these statistics. Despite this, the results yielded in this section are a powerful indicator within this sample of the notably elevated level of trauma experienced by Egyptians in the aftermath of the revolution.

Regarding demographic differences in trauma, females reported significantly higher trauma levels compared to males ($t = 2.23$, $p < .05$). There were no significant differences in trauma levels based on age or marital status. There was also no significant correlation between the frequency of participation in protests following February 11, 2011 and total scores on the trauma severity scale.

Coping strategies and their relation to demographics and political activism. In order to identify how participants were reacting to post-uprising stressors, the Brief COPE domains were computed for the 222 participants who completed at least 70 percent of the items on the instrument (see table 3.3). The most utilized coping mechanisms were acceptance of the post-uprising situation, planning for the future, and turning to religion. To the community's credit, the coping mechanisms used the least were substance abuse and denial.

Table 3.3: Coping strategies

Coping domain	Mean	Standard deviation
Acceptance	2.89	0.86
Planning	2.84	0.91
Religion	2.81	0.85
Active coping	2.78	0.91
Positive reframing	2.58	0.94
Self-distraction	2.42	0.88
Using instrumental support (advice and help from others)	2.39	0.86
Self-blaming	2.39	0.99
Using emotional support	2.35	0.89
Venting	2.17	0.92
Humor	2.06	0.99
Behavioral disengagement (giving up)	1.89	0.89
Denial	1.74	0.99
Substance use	1.32	0.75

With regard to demographic differences, males scored significantly higher than females on the active coping subscale ($t = 4.13, p < .001$). Males also scored higher on the substance use subscale ($t = 2.25, p < .05$). Older people were more likely to use the coping mechanisms of religion ($r = .24, p < .01$), and less likely to use drugs ($t = -.19, p < .01$). Similarly, compared to those who were single, married respondents were also more likely to use religion ($t = 3.75, p < .001$) and less likely to use drugs ($t = 2.64, p < .005$). There were no significant differences in coping styles between those who participated in protests after February 11 and those who did not.

Coping with the use of safety precautions. A total of 66.5 percent of the respondents reported that they did indeed start taking extra safety precautions against the new dangers they were being exposed to as a result of the security vacuum and increased violence. The precautions that were most reported were avoiding walking in the streets at night (37.7

percent), carrying around less money (36.4 percent), self-imposing a curfew (31.6 percent), and securing the household (e.g., with additional locks; 31.3 percent). Other new precautions were related to transportation and travel, such as avoiding unsafe areas such as Tahrir Square (26.8 percent), staying close to home (21.4 percent), avoiding public transportation (17.9 percent), and traveling in groups (14.7 percent). A total of 16 percent reported carrying self-defense items such as pepper spray, stun guns, or knives.

Those who resorted to methods other than the ones provided were asked to specify what those precautions were. This yielded 36 alternative responses. An example was: "I do not leave my house at all unless it is for an emergency. My house and its rooms are my nation." Responses such as this one indicated that some people were particularly fearful for their safety during and after the uprisings. Other respondents turned to religion with more positive responses, such as "There are no precautions I need to take other than believing in God and not worrying about anything no matter how bad the situation gets."

Views on mental health services. A total of 60.1 percent of the participants agreed that services offering help for people facing violence, injury, or stress after the uprisings were important. However, only 26.5 percent of participants agreed that they would be personally interested in receiving psychological help from such a program. The reasons respondents gave for not wanting to do so are listed in table 3.4.

Table 3.4: Reasons why people were unwilling to seek psychological help

Reason	% of those who answered this section (n = 202–204)	% of overall sample (n = 313)
Don't need professional help	56.9	36.7
Don't trust services by the Ministry of Health	23.2	15.0
Negative reputation of psychiatric hospitals	15.3	9.9
Might be too expensive	14.9	9.6
Don't trust these services	14.7	9.6

Reason	% of those who answered this section (n = 202–204)	% of overall sample (n = 313)
Embarrassing or shameful	12.9	8.3
Time-consuming	11.9	7.7
Psychological treatment is not effective	7.8	5.1
Transportation issues	7.0	4.5
Other reasons	21.2	13.7

Participants who were not willing to receive these services were asked to provide additional reasons that were not listed in the survey, yielding a total of 36 additional answers. These included the arguments that the country's energy and resources should instead be channeled into making things safe again or continuing the revolution, and that relying on faith and religious practices was sufficient to help them with their problems.

Part 2: Focus Groups with Lower-Income Cairene Women on the Psychological Effects of the Uprisings

According to several reports, the highest incidences of crime have taken place in poorer and isolated areas since the revolution began in January 2011.[12] One of the limitations of the street survey was that its main demographic was Cairo's and Giza's middle class, and thus it did not capture the experiences of the vulnerable populations in the city's informal settlements. Additionally, the survey respondents were overrepresented by men, including some men of lower-income backgrounds, possibly because they work in middle-class areas during the day while lower-income women tend not to leave their areas of residence. Therefore, two focus groups with women were conducted in economically disadvantaged areas in order to gain preliminary insight as to how people's lives changed after the revolution. Due to the low literacy rate in these lower-income areas, and a desire to gain richer insight into the respondents' experiences, we chose to conduct focus groups rather than written surveys.

---

12 Hendawi, "Crime Wave Grips Egypt."

Methods and Participants

Focus groups were conducted in Ain al-Sira and Mit Oqba. The Ain al-Sira focus group was held at a non-governmental organization's office on location, and the one in Mit Oqba was held in a participant's home. These sessions took place in April 2012. Each focus group was conducted by three researchers with one primary facilitator and two note-takers, and composed of four to six women, with one man (the owner of the apartment at which the focus group took place) present in the Mit Oqba group. Their ages ranged from late teens to early sixties, and most of the women were mothers and wives or widows who did not work. The sole man present was in his late forties and worked as a tax accountant. Since most participants in both groups were not literate, the moderators read and explained the consent form aloud. The focus groups were conducted in Arabic.

The focus group questions were related to the participants' current conditions living in these areas, political leanings with regard to 'the revolution,' and how they had been coping with new stressful events after the uprisings. The sensitive subject matter of the questions, namely those related to the current dangers these community members faced, sparked intense and expressive conversations regarding the negative effects of the revolution on these communities and their families.

Results

Impact of the uprisings on respondents' lives. Within both communities, there was a general consensus of negative feelings toward the outcomes of the revolution due to the security vacuum that resulted from it and the shift from a previously safe society to a more dangerous, unstable one. The women in Mit Oqba said they felt "great sadness" when they watched Egypt undergo a revolution the previous year because they anticipated that some of the outcomes, such as a less secure environment and economic inflation, would not work in their favor. Due to their lack of support for the revolution's cause as well as safety reasons or schedule conflicts, none of the participants went to the protests in Tahrir. While most participants did not agree with the demands of Tahrir, they sympathized with those who were hurt or killed.

Although the women of Ain al-Sira recognized that Mubarak was a "corrupt" leader, they were still nostalgic for the safety they enjoyed under his reign. The women of Mit Oqba shared similar sentiments toward Egypt's State Security apparatus. Despite acknowledging the harsh methods these institutions used to maintain order, they felt safer when these institutions were in place. They believed that the revolution did not yield desirable results, and in general, they did not welcome the revolutionary movement.

While these communities were comparatively underprivileged before the revolution, they believed their situation had become considerably worse because of the vulnerability of their areas to violent crime and economic decay. At the time of the focus groups, they believed that government officials were not working to meet people's demands or to minimize crime on the streets, but were working toward positions of power.

Life and politics in Egypt after the uprisings. Focus group respondents could see a stark contrast between the lives they led before and after the revolution. Many reminisced about leaving the home late at night (past midnight) to go out or run errands prior to the revolution. Now, they feared leaving home after sunset due to the increase in crime and harassment. Most of the mothers were afraid to send their children to school or to the store because they feared something would happen to them. They readily shared stories of incidents of crime that had happened to family members or acquaintances. In the case of Mit Oqba, community members were aware of the increase of drug use and trade in their neighborhood. Both groups expressed anxiety for the future, and some individuals had nightmares about getting hurt or killed.

Most of the participants from both areas voted in the parliamentary elections in November 2011, and for most it was the first time they voted in any form of elections. However, they were dissatisfied with the way the newly elected officials were handling affairs, especially the Muslim Brotherhood's Freedom and Justice Party (FJP), which won a plurality of seats. They were also frustrated with the strikes that had increased since the revolution, and believed people should spend their time working and not striking, as it brings the country to a standstill. One example they cited was the garbage collectors' strike, which resulted in an increase in garbage in their areas and, they feared, more pathogens and eyesores. They also expressed dissatisfaction about the unstable employment opportunities and the rising prices of goods.

According to the focus group participants, the increase in crime brought to light an incompetent police force that was slow to respond to calls and capture criminals. The women of Ain al-Sira spoke of this extensively, and described incidents when they called the police for a problem and the police showed a up few days later or not at all. With this lack of support from the police and the parliamentarians they elected, they concluded that life was not as good as it had been just one year before.

Sense of community before and after the uprisings. The dynamic of the focus groups was a testament to the strong sense of community these women shared. They were open to each other's opinions and had friendly discussions when they agreed or disagreed. Due to the small size and crowded environment of these communities, it was previously common for members to know each other well on a personal level. For example, participants recalled community members keeping their apartment doors open, allowing their neighbors to enter as they wished. They also helped their neighbors by lending them ingredients and food supplies. The women of Ain al-Sira recalled that this sense of community was very strong during the 18 days of the revolution before Mubarak stepped down. During that time, Christians and Muslims of Ain al-Sira worked together to defend their neighborhood from thugs. Community members organized popular committees as a replacement for the retreated police force.

However, both focus groups recalled that their communities found themselves slightly less cohesive after the revolution. Residents became more wary of their neighbors and of society in general; they approached community members, whether acquaintances or strangers, with caution. Many noticed that people were no longer polite with one another and instead resorted to rudeness or force when they interacted. Community members stopped leaving their doors open and began closing and securing them. Additionally, neighbors no longer shared foodstuffs with one another because increased prices meant they could not afford to do so. There was more competition among community members for both resources (such as food and gas tanks) and jobs, both of which had become very limited in quantity. People became more concerned with their personal welfare than the welfare of the community, contrary to what was reportedly the case prior to the revolution.

Coping strategies. Participants had different ways of dealing with these new stressors. Most were unable to afford psychotherapy or other such "luxuries." The women of Ain al-Sira said that they made jokes about current events and tried to laugh about it. Even throughout the session, they showed good spirits and shared laughs with the moderators. The women of Mit Oqba said they listened to more Qur'an and continuously prayed to God to make things better for them. They liked to be aware of the political situation in the country and follow political news very closely. At the end of each focus group, most of the women said that discussing their problems with the moderators made them feel slightly better.

Discussion

Cairo has witnessed many new stressors since January 2011 and has had to grapple with significant changes in the months that followed. The political instability of the country generated a predictable feeling of confusion and anxiety among the population. Participants in our survey and focus groups reported that their lives generally took a turn for the worse following the initial uprisings. Although most participants were not directly injured by street violence from protests or crackdowns, they were affected by the uprisings' aftereffects, such as the economic decline, increase in political disputes, escalation in crime rate, and especially the violence shown on television. One of the most frequently mentioned reactions was feeling less safe due to increasing crime rates and street violence. Participants from the economically disadvantaged communities indicated that many were nostalgic for the stability of the "Mubarak days." This stability had been shaken, especially with many respondents reporting a deteriorated financial situation.

High rates of post-traumatic stress were found in the sample, with about 60 percent reporting symptoms that are consistent with a diagnosis of PTSD. Severity of traumatic stress was higher among women compared to men, which is consistent with previous research (Afana et al. 2002; Breslau 2009; Farhood and Dimassi 2006; Hussein and Sa'adoon 2006). Moreover, women in the lower-income areas expressed high levels of stress due to their vulnerability to violent crimes and pre-existing financial stressors that worsened after the uprisings.

Despite these new stressors and anxieties, many participants remained politically engaged and well informed about the country's current events.

The participants in the focus groups were up to date on political events and voted in the parliamentary elections. About a quarter of our survey sample participated in the protests after February 11, 2011, indicating that they were striving to make a change in the political scene in Egypt. However, there were no differences in trauma levels and coping strategies between those who were involved in subsequent protests and those who were not.

As many struggled to handle newly encountered stressors in Egypt, participants demonstrated resilience by using active coping methods to counteract the changes in their environment. Measures such as planning, religion, and humor were utilized by the sample in order to cope. Rather than accept this new life in an unstable Egypt, many participants took matters into their own hands in order to reduce their risk of becoming victims of violence. Participants reported walking less in the streets at night, carrying less money with them when outside the home, implementing curfews, and protecting their abodes. These strategies demonstrate participants' use of active coping.

Another means of coping with stress and trauma could be for participants to turn to mental healthcare professionals to help with their problems. However, despite reports of stressors and post-traumatic stress, most respondents were not willing to seek psychological help. Many did not feel they needed psychological help and expressed distrust in these services and negative aspects associated with mental health settings. Thus, in order for community-wide interventions to take place, mental healthcare professionals should address psychological problems in parallel with tackling the stigmas related to this field in Egypt.

These potential services should target specific groups in order to accommodate the community's needs. Previous research suggests that lower-income areas are most susceptible to crime,[13] and also supports our own survey findings that women show higher trauma levels than men (Breslau 2009). Based on these risk factors, community-wide interventions should pay special attention to reaching women and residents of informal settlements.

Challenges and Limitations

Throughout the course of this research, we encountered several challenges regarding data collection. Logistical constraints prevented us from

---

13   Hendawi, "Crime Wave Grips Egypt."

accessing survey participants in more areas and, in particular, organizing more focus group sessions. These constraints were related to safety concerns, high levels of protests in certain areas, and inflexible hours to meet with people. In the areas we were able to access, we faced challenges in orienting participants to the format of the survey. Many participants were not accustomed to the practice of taking surveys and expressed suspicions of authority and data collectors. Despite the data collectors' supervision, many participants misunderstood questions on the survey, especially the rating scales in which the task was to select one from several possible options on a spectrum for each of the items in the instruments. This resulted in missing data.

Other possible reasons for missing data include the length of the survey, the impracticality of distributing it to people on the streets, and respondents' fear of giving personal information. These problems occurred despite a smooth piloting process with similar participants.

In addition, the fact that the sample size was relatively small provides another area for improvement in future studies. While the number of participants was relatively small, it showed diversity in terms of age, gender, occupation, and income level. Another problematic aspect of this study is the fact that it did not utilize a probability sampling method to recruit participants. Although the sample was diverse, it may not be entirely representative of the Cairo population. For further expansion on this study, more focus groups with a diverse sample (such as including more men) would have to take place in order to draw substantial conclusions.

Implications for Future Research and Psychological Services

The significance of this study in post-Mubarak Egypt is shown by the diverse sample of participants, the range of topics included in the survey, and its focus on the little-studied question of Cairenes' mental health state following a series of historic uprisings. It provides ground for further research that can have potential implications for developing community-wide prevention programs in Egypt and gaining a better understanding of how different groups cope with historic transitions. Future researchers can use this data to periodically track the progress of Cairenes' psychological state as events in Egypt develop over time.

While this study mainly targeted adults, children living in politically turbulent countries in the Middle East region have been seen to have considerable trauma responses in the form of behavioral and academic issues (Dimitry 2011). Therefore, it would be important to conduct future studies on the effects of the ongoing traumas on children in Egypt, where about 33 percent of the population are under the age of 14 years (Central Intelligence Agency 2013).

This study was also focused on the Greater Cairo population, even though other areas throughout Egypt, such as Alexandria and Suez, also witnessed political turbulence and violent crackdowns. Future studies could conduct similar research on other urban areas in Egypt, as well as rural areas in the south and throughout Sinai.

Our results suggest a growing need for mental health services in Greater Cairo, as about two-thirds of the sample met criteria for PTSD symptoms. Along with resolving the current economic and political instability, policy makers should also work to establish services that can help alleviate the community-wide trauma that emerged subsequent to the uprisings. These services should target areas that are close to popular protest grounds (e.g., downtown Cairo, where Tahrir Square is located), as well as lower-income areas where violent crime is more prevalent. Services should also aim to treat high-risk populations such as women and children.

In conclusion, as events continue to unfold in Egypt, Cairo residents may find themselves having to navigate among new challenges in order to proceed with their lives. The majority of respondents in our research were struggling to cope with previously un-encountered stressors that developed out of the uprisings. Community-wide interventions may be beneficial in treating these problems related to trauma and can help Egyptians better understand the course of revolutions and their tumultuous nature. It may take years for the revolution in Egypt to succeed in achieving its goals, but despite thunderous protests, the majority of Cairo suffers—and actively copes—in silence.

References

Abdeen, Z., R. Qasrawi, S. Nabil, and M. Shaheen. 2008. "Psychological Reactions to Israeli Occupation: Findings from the National Study of School-Based Screening in Palestine," *International Journal of Behavioral Development*, 32(4): 290–297.

References

Abdul Khayat, R. 2007. "Perceived Stress, Coping Styles, and Periodontitis: A Cross-Cultural Analysis." Unpublished doctoral dissertation: University of Michigan.

Afana, A. 2012. "Problems in Applying Diagnostic Concepts of PTSD and Trauma in the Middle East," *The Arab Journal of Psychiatry*, 23: 28–34.

Afana, A., O. S. Dalgard, E. Bjertness, B. Grunfeld, and E. Hauff. 2002. "The Prevalence and Associated Socio-Demographic Variables of Post-Traumatic Stress Disorder among Patients Attending Primary Health Care Centres in the Gaza Strip," *Journal of Refugee Studies*, 15(3): 283–295.

Barlow, D. H. 1988. *Anxiety and Its Disorders: The Nature and Treatment of Anxiety and Panic*. New York: Guilford.

Bremer, J. A. 2011. "Leadership and Collective Action in Egypt's Popular Committees: Emergence of Authentic Civic Activism in the Absence of the State," *The International Journal of Not-for-Profit Law*, 13(4): 70–92. http://www.icnl.org/research/journal/vol13iss4/art_2.htm

Breslau, N. 2009. "The Epidemiology of Trauma, PTSD, and Other Posttrauma Disorders," *Trauma, Violence, and Abuse*, 10(3): 198–210. http://tva.sagepub.com/content/10/3/198

Carver, C. S. 1997. "You Want to Measure Coping but Your Protocol's Too Long: Consider the Brief COPE," *International Journal of Behavioral Medicine*, 4(1): 92–100.

Central Intelligence Agency. 2013. *The World Factbook Page on Egypt, Section: People*. https://www.cia.gov/library/publications/the-world-factbook/geos/eg.html

De Jong, J. 2005. "Commentary: Deconstructing Critiques on the Internationalization of PTSD," *Culture, Medicine and Psychiatry*, 29: 361–370.

Dimitry, L. 2011. "A Systematic Review on the Mental Health of Children and Adolescents in Areas of Armed Conflict in the Middle East," *Child: Care, Health and Development*, 38(2): 153–161.

Elsheshtawy, E., and W. A. Elez. 2011. "Coping with Stress and Quality of Life among Patients with Schizophrenia in Egypt and Saudi Arabia: Effect of Socio-Demographic Factors," *Middle East Current Psychiatry*, 18(2): 72–77.

Farhood, L., and H. Dimassi. 2006. *Symptom Prevalence of PTSD, Anxiety, Depression, Effect of Exposure and Mediating Factors on a Population from Southern Lebanon.* New York: American University of Beirut. http://www.dtic.mil/dtic/tr/fulltext/u2/a454234.pdf

Flannery, R. B. 1999. "Psychological Trauma and Posttraumatic Stress Disorder: A Review," *International Journal of Emergency Mental Health*, 2: 135–140.

Foa, E. B., D. S. Riggs, C. V. Dancu, and B. O. Rothbaum. 1993. "Reliability and Validity of a Brief Instrument for Assessing Post-Traumatic Stress," *Journal of Traumatic Stress*, 6(4): 459–473.

Gunnar, M., and K. Quevedo. 2007. "The Neurobiology of Stress and Development," *Annual Review of Psychology*, 58: 145–173.

Hussein, A. H., and A. A. Sa'adoon. 2006. "Prevalence of Anxiety and Depressive Disorders among Primary Health Care Attendees in Al-Nasiriyah, Iraq," *Journal of Muslim Mental Health*, 1(2): 171–176.

Liverant, G. I., M. K. Suvak, S. L. Pineles, and P. A. Resick. 2012. "Changes in Posttraumatic Stress Disorder and Depressive Symptoms during Cognitive Processing Therapy: Evidence for Concurrent Change," *Journal of Consulting and Clinical Psychology*, 80(6): 957–967.

Mirzamani, S. M., M. R. Mohammadi, J. Mahmoudi-Gharaei, and M. S. Mirzamani. 2007. "Validity of the PTSD Symptoms Scale Self-Report (PSS-SR) in Iran," *Iran Journal of Psychiatry*, 2: 120–123.

Norris, F., M. Friedman, P. Watson, C. Byrne, E. Diaz, and K. Kaniasty. 2002. "60,000 Disaster Victims Speak: Part I. An Empirical Review of the Empirical Literature, 1981–2001," *Psychiatry: Interpersonal and Biological Processes*, 65: 207–239.

Olfson, M., B. Fireman, M. M. Weissman, A. C. Leon, D. V. Sheehan, R. G. Kathol, et al. 1997. "Mental Disorders and Disability among Patients in a Primary Care Group Practice," *American Journal of Psychiatry*, 154, 1734–1740.

Pat-Horencyzk, R., R. Qasrawi, R. Lesack, M. Haj-Yehia, O. Peled, M. Shaheen, et. al. 2009. "Posttraumatic Symptoms, Functional Impairment, and Coping among Adolescents on Both Sides of the Israeli–Palestinian Conflict: A Cross-Cultural Approach," *Applied Psychology*, 58(4): 688–709.

El Sayed, N. 2011. "Load Up," *Egypt Today*, 32(11) October. http://egypttoday.com/news/display/article/artId:323/Load-Up/secId:1/catId:2

References

UNODC (United Nations Office on Drugs and Crime). 2009. "Kidnapping at the National Level: Number of Police-Recorded Offences." www.unodc.org/documents/data-and-analysis/Crime-statistics/Kidnapping.xls

———. "Homicide Statistics—Latest Available Year." http://www.unodc.org/documents/data-and-analysis/statistics/Homicide/Homicide_level.xlsx

CHAPTER 4

Labor Struggles and the Quest for Permanent Employment in Revolutionary Egypt

Dina Makram-Ebeid

Daily-waged workers led a truly inspiring struggle from the onset of the January 25 revolution.[1] If you followed the news coverage of labor protests since January 2011, you would not have missed their regular protests. You would have heard them call for *tathbit* ('fixing'), *ta'yin* ('appointment'), or simply access to *wazifa* ('office'—often denoting white-collar employment but also blue-collar employment in the public sector). The stable employment they aspired to extends from permanent contracts in the public sector to secured contracts in the private sector with social and medical welfare provisions.[2] Despite their lack of access to work contracts and the basic rights these guarantee, daily workers drew on very militant tactics. From blocking railways and highways to occupying government institutions and from locking up managers to shutting ministry gates, daily workers put their bodies in direct action in order to be heard. This chapter addresses two questions: first, why, unlike other workers in Egypt, did daily workers utilize such radical tactics; second, what does their struggle tell us about the control mechanisms of labor and the limits imposed on

---

[1] Let me forewarn the reader that this chapter does not address whether we should consider the events since January 2011 an uprising, revolt, revolution, or even "refolution," to quote Bayat (2013). These events are still unfolding and it is best to adopt the language my informants use to refer to them. I will therefore use 'revolution' to describe the events since 2011.

[2] There is a stark difference between the demands of private- and public-sector workers for stable work. But their demands for stable work are articulated in the same language of *tathbit* ('fixing') and *ta'yin* ('appointment').

workers' movements in demanding transformative change? The contrast between their precarious position—occupying the lower ranks of the labor hierarchy and acting mostly as a reserve army of labor—and their militant tactics explains why the struggle of daily workers is central to Egyptian labor movements.

The mobilization of daily workers at the Ministry of Culture—namely, workers at the Public Authority for Cultural Centers *(Hay'at Qusur al-Thaqafa)*—and at the Ministry of Agriculture by the forestation workers *('ummal al-tashgir bi wizarat al-zira'a)* grew stronger over several months. In April 2013, following a prolonged battle with the minister, the agriculture workers stormed the Ministry of Finance when their requests for meetings were repeatedly denied. Cultural Centers workers also had enough and shut down the gates of the Public Authority of Cultural Centers until their demands were met. These two cases shed light on the desperation of daily workers who aspire for stability but fail to achieve it. A similar battle was waged by daily-waged workers with whom I conducted fieldwork prior to the revolution, between 2008 and 2010, and later between August 2013 and April 2014. My ethnographic research was at the Egyptian Iron and Steel Company (EISCO). EISCO is Egypt's oldest fully-integrated public-sector steel company, where the complex hierarchy of work in the public sector is unmistakable.[3]

So, Who Is the Worker?

Researchers have sought to define who the worker is since the heyday of early capitalism. In the public imagination, however, workers remain a well-defined group of dispossessed people whose living and working conditions are relatively similar. The media, labor activists, and the general public often consider them a homogenous group, at most divided between public and private sector. While the public–private divide is crucial to people's experience of work, the deregulation of capital and of labor-protection regimes over recent decades render intra-sector

---

[3] This chapter focuses on workers' struggles for permanent employment in the public sector. The reference to the public sector denotes the governmental sector, which is governed by Law No. 47 of 1978, companies fully owned by the state, and joint-stock companies between the state and private entities, under Law No. 203 of 1991, where the state owns the absolute majority of shares.

distinctions among workers equally important. It turns out that, on the ground, this public imaginary is more complex.

Academic research on workers is often influenced by Marxist theory. It considers the working class a uniform group that lacks capital and the ability to escape their social position. As with public discourse, the distinction in academia between private- and public-sector workers, as affluent stable workers and precarious informal ones, is predominant. More nuanced research brought gender, kinship, and generational politics to the forefront of the analysis of work (De Neve 2005; Kondo 1990; Ong 1987; Holmström 1976). Skills, seniority, and unionization have also been central to mapping workplace distinctions (Mollona 2009a; Burawoy 1979a, 1979b; Braverman 1974).[4] Studies of class in industrial sociology that highlight the potential futures of various workers began to take into consideration often overlooked social backgrounds, such as religion and ethnicity (Sanchez 2011; Parry 2005).

These different trajectories of work cast doubts on the 'homogenous experience' of the working class and suggest that dispossessions need to be contextualized and that class formation is "an open-ended, on-going process," a process where "classes are constantly remodelled by changing economic, political and cultural forces" (Lockman 1994a:xxvi). Class is thus a dynamic social relation developed in interaction with the locality. Crucially, who is a worker is contingent upon how multiple identities intersect and overlap (Lockman 1994a). Seeing labor in this way enables an "expanded idea of class" (Kalb 1997:6) as mostly relational. Struggles over job stability thus make class antagonism within, and not just with, working communities vital to how people become marginalized, excluded, and forgotten. It also explains how bourgeoisification occurs over the long term, enabling some to escape their perpetual exploitation, albeit at the expense of others.

The move toward late capitalism and the transition to post-Fordist flexible production inscribed the distinctions between workers in company structures.[5] When employment legislation later reinforced these

---

4   The distinction between skilled and unskilled workers is an old and prominent one in the literature. It has attracted the attention of seminal writers as early as Frederick Taylor in 1911.

5   Land ownership, revenues from moonlighting, or marrying into well-off families had often made some workers better off than others. But the advance of capitalism rendered distinction among workers quite methodical.

hegemonic distinctions they became systematic. This became part of an ongoing global strategy to make employment relations flexible and subject to market rules. Since the late 1980s, daily-waged, 'contract,' or seasonal workers, who have no formal contracts, have been given more attention in labor studies accounts.[6] As Mollona (2009b) suggests, our role now as "anthropologists of 'the global factory'" is to "look at the spatial and temporal interconnections between the visible, stable, respectable labor at its core and the precarious, invisible and degrading labor at the margins" (Mollona 2009b:xxi).

Academics Engage with Egyptian Labor Movements

Although public plants played a predominant role in Egyptian postcolonial history, there is little academic work on the social world of those who spent their lives behind those factory walls. A rich body of literature covers the history of labor in Egypt in the late nineteenth and early twentieth centuries, including memoirs written by labor activists (Abbas 1968; Beinin 2001; Beinin and Lockman 1987; Chalcraft 2001; Goldberg 1986, 1996; Lockman 1994b; Uthman 1972). These texts address the struggles of labor against capitalism and the state, although they underplay the discrepancies within the working class. The controversies over neoliberal reforms since the early 1990s are framed in the literature within the triad of the coherent and too-well-delineated groups of workers, the unions, and the state (Goldberg 1992; Handoussa and Potter 1991; Posusney 1997). This leads Goldberg to conclude that "we are almost wholly ignorant of how these transformations are occurring in individual lives" (Goldberg 1996:186).

The clampdown on academic research and the policing of workers means the lives of Egyptian workers remain unintelligible. Under the regimes of Nasser, Sadat, and Mubarak, state security intelligence monitored the working days of labor, especially in public factories and government institutions. Accessing workplaces thus put workers and researchers at risk, which made the latter resort to archival research or the official documentation of strikes by journalists, labor rights centers, and activist workers (Posusney 1997). It was only with the relative relaxation

---

6 Daily workers sustained industrial work prior to the introduction of flexible capitalism. For an informative account see Toth's work with *tarahil* (seasonal) workers since the 1960s (Toth 1999).

of state controls in the late Mubarak era that some scholars were able to conduct limited research inside workplaces. Two of these remarkable studies are Toth's (2002) research with workers following their layoffs from Kafr al-Dawwar's plant in northern Egypt and Shehata's (2009) research in two textile plants in Alexandria. Since Mubarak's ouster, more opportunities to engage with workers and document their mobilizations have emerged, though the mounting repression since June 30, 2013 has renewed the crackdown on academic research.

The informal sector, easier to access without alerting the radar of the authorities, enabled some ethnographic research on working lives in Egypt. Toth's (1999) study of rural migrant workers in the construction sector and Elyachar's (2005) among workshop masters in al-Hirafiyin in Cairo explained respectively the invisible contribution of seasonal rural workers to the state's economic stability in the 1960s and its use of social values to expand markets since the 1990s.

The labor hierarchy between permanent, temporary, and daily workers, however, remains largely understudied, even when that hierarchy is no longer just a custom but one inscribed by law. The adoption of a new labor law, Law No. 12 of 2003, recognized, for the first time in Egyptian postcolonial legal history, the existence of temporary, fixed-term employment contracts on public-sector payrolls. The law also included special provisions for daily workers to work in this sector. The politics of work, now conditioned by law, remains unaccounted for.

Making the Public Private: Public-Sector Hierarchies

Today the public sector includes workers under three employment types working side by side: permanent labor (*'ummal mu'ayanin* or *muthabatin*), with indefinite employment contracts for life; temporary labor with fixed-term employment contracts of six months to one year *('imala mu'aqata)*; and daily labor *('imala yawmiya)* that is paid by the day, with no formal contract, social insurance, or benefits.

Despite the low pay in many industries and government institutions, permanent contracts in the public sector continue to attract many in Egypt. These contracts offer lifetime stability and a capacity to plan for the future unmatched elsewhere. Crucially, they also offer perks and benefits that alter the quality of life of workers and their households. They include a pension fund, union representation, subsidized housing, free health care, transportation to and from workplaces, recreational and sports clubs, subsidized holidays, interest-free loans, a cooperative that sells consumer goods on installments, and a monthly food allowance. Of course the existence and quality of these perks and benefits vary from one place to another, and the risks of liquidation, privatization, and general layoffs have made workers bear the aggressive attacks of late capitalism over the last three decades. Yet for many, this is by far preferable to working in the private sector.

Temporary labor with fixed-term employment contracts was officially introduced in the public sector after a 16-year hiring freeze (from 1991 to 2007), which was meant to slim down the labor force on government payrolls. The legalization of temporary work under the new Labor Law No. 12 of 2003 confirmed this trend. But a ministerial decree annexed to the new law instructed that temporary contracts were to be made permanent for those who worked three consecutive years in the same workplace. This fueled an enormous demand for temporary jobs. Lucrative permanent jobs that had disappeared since the early 1990s were now a possibility.

Those who did not get temporary contracts joined the public sector as daily-waged workers in the hope of climbing up the labor hierarchy, from daily to temporary and eventually to permanent positions. Secure employment that would guarantee that one wouldn't be abruptly laid off was difficult to find with unemployment rates estimated at 30 percent (al-Naggar 2010). Because unemployment rates were highest among university graduates, educational qualifications also no longer guaranteed a good life.[7] A new labor politics around work contracts was initiated.

Daily-Waged Work, Daily-Waged Waiting

Daily-waged work was introduced at EISCO in 2007 in tandem with fixed-term temporary contracts to accommodate the overwhelming demand for jobs. It became an unofficial entry route for those who lacked a strong *wasta* ('connection') to find temporary work. They were encouraged to join as daily workers and thereby to obtain temporary

---

7 Although the official unemployment rate calculated by the Central Agency for Public Mobilization and Statistics (CAPMAS) was 9.9 percent in 2003, al-Naggar (2010) reveals that the real numbers were disguised through accounting techniques that hid the more accurate figure of 30 percent. He estimates unemployment of university graduates to constitute 93 percent of total unemployment.

contracts within "a few months"—which in practice ranged from two months to two years. During this waiting period, many were repeatedly promised contracts, sometimes by the end of the following month, but such promises were often broken. In some places, this politics of hope (and despair) was standardized in work agreements. The work agreements of daily workers at the Ministry of Culture, for instance, explicitly mentioned that they would work by the day until a job competition was announced. As the waiting period grew longer, however, many doubted whether they would ever get a formal contract. The inability to predict how contracts were allocated made it a frustrating affair, which added to the exasperation of being at the bottom of the labor hierarchy and doing the most degrading and hazardous jobs. Not being able to plan a future became the quintessential condition of the daily laborer.

Daily-waged laborers are not on plants' and government agencies' official accounting books. They are recruited under special funds—*sanadiq khasa*—that exist in various governorates and are not part of the state's budget accounting.[8] A labor contractor who deducts his own fee from their wages often recruits them. Sometimes institutions annexed to the host company/agency, such as EISCO's social and sporting club, makes deductions from their wages.[9] This outsourcing of work in public plants highlights the interdependence between organized, stable, and respectable work and dodgy, unaccounted-for, and degrading jobs. The dependence on the *sanadiq khasa*, whose financial status is disputed and is considered a major source of corruption, demonstrates how the state's 'progress' is inherently built on legalized crime.

Crucially, the daily wage in the public sector is far below the market in daily wages. At the Ministry of Culture, a university graduate earns LE15 ($2.15) a day; at the Ministry of Agriculture, no daily pay is provided but workers are paid *badalat* ('per diems') of LE65 ($9.30) a month. Daily wages at EISCO between 2008 and 2010 varied between a standard LE14/day ($2.00/day) and LE22 ($3.60/day) for the more skilled such as welders. These wages are strikingly different from the

---

8 The value of the special funds *(sanadiq khasa)* is estimated at LE37 billion ($5.3 billion). "The Minister of Finance Admits: There Are Attempts to Conceal the Special Funds Finances," *al-Shorouk*, May 1, 2012, http://www.shorouknews.com/news/view.aspx?cdate=01052012&id=80466c88-7cd5-4659-a478-4c662afcb5b1

9 Between 2008 and 2010 the sporting club of EISCO played the role of labor contractor. It subtracted LE1 ($0.14) from the daily wage of every worker.

daily rates in the private sector, which in 2008–2010 ranged between LE35 ($5.00) a day for agriculture workers and LE50–75 ($7.10–$10.70) a day for construction workers.

By 2009 around 800 young men worked as daily waged workers and 2,246 were on the payrolls of EISCO as temps.[10] The majority of the new recruits were indeed men—only three females were recruited as temporary workers—which speaks to the sexism ingrained in these new work policies. The new recruits were overwhelmingly sons, relatives, and *baladiyat* ('people who originate from the same home village or town') of permanent workers. By mid 2010 all were given permanent contracts. This was exceptional. Mubarak's regime, like those that preceded it, considered EISCO a strategic plant and a symbol of Egypt's postcolonial strength. This offered workers relative protection. Workers' militant occupations of the plant in 1989 also made the regime mindful of a historical repeat. Over time, EISCO became favored by the ruling regime and its party and was considered a potential source of electoral support in parliamentary elections in 2010.[11]

But most public-sector workers were not treated similarly—definitely not the forestation workers in the agriculture ministry, who were hired in the mid 1990s as 'trainees' to join the official ranks of the ministry when stable jobs became available. Their struggle therefore centered on the unjust employment discrepancies between them and other stable workers in the Ministry of Agriculture. Daily workers at the Ministry of Culture, though recruited much later, were also subject to the same waiting game that forestation workers experienced. Tamer, for instance, worked in a private company that was liquidated following the uprising in early 2011. He then joined the Ministry of Culture as a daily worker. His uncle took on his case and encouraged him to join as a daily worker until an official job competition was announced. By early 2014, however, neither Tamer nor the rest of the Ministry of Culture workers had been given permanent contracts. Neither had the 23,000 forestation workers.

---

10 The total labor force at EISCO at the end of 2009 was 13,225.

11 The chief executive officer (CEO) of EISCO, for example, was required by state security intelligence to be a member of Mubarak's National Democratic Party and, once in office, to hold the position of the head of the party's branch in al-Tibbin district. The minister of industry visited the plant during my first fieldwork in 2010 and out of the blue ordered an extra 15 days' bonus pay to all. The gossip in the plant considered that this was because of upcoming parliamentary elections in late 2010.

The rage and fury of daily workers is understandable given the politics of hope and despair. But something particular to their past also fuels their militant resistance. Amgad, a daily worker at EISCO who worked there for two years before getting a permanent contract, explained that no one would try their luck at EISCO unless they had a connection that might get them in. The rest, he believed, did not think it was worth tempting their luck. Ali, for one, did not think it was worth the wait. Ali worked in a painting workshop in Helwan. He did not have any connections at EISCO, but worked nonetheless on a daily basis for six months. He grew tired of the broken promises and the nepotistic calculations involved in securing a contract, lost hope, and quit. Instead he worked at the paint shop as a daily worker. Another old permanent worker at EISCO echoed Amgad when he said, "Those who come here are the lucky ones who know somebody who brought them here and promised to help them. The rest of the kids are all outside. Look at the Sixth of October [City—an area known for proliferation of private-sector enterprises]. That is the real youth cemetery."

The daily laborers at EISCO, the Ministry of Culture, and the Ministry of Agriculture were paid less than daily workers across Egypt. But they were also much 'better off.' Their backgrounds and qualifications were no different from those of the newly recruited temporary workers or permanent workers' sons. Most daily workers at EISCO, for instance, had an industrial middle qualification, which is the minimum requirement for employment at a temporary job at EISCO. A few also had university degrees. The same applied to the Ministry of Culture and the Ministry of Agriculture workers. They too were often sons and daughters of permanent workers, or their relatives, which is the undisclosed criterion for recruitment. And yet, they failed to get a permanent job.

Not only did the youngsters not get the job that they deserved, given their education, but permanent workers considered giving jobs to their children an unquestionable right, which is justified by their labor over the years. They regarded their job contracts as a potential property they could bequeath to their children (Makram-Ebeid 2013).[12] Daily

---

12 This is not particular to Egypt. Many permanent workers in India regard their jobs as "a quasi-property right" (Parry n.d.) and consider the employment of their children part of that right. Although passing on jobs to children has been a tradition in Egypt, especially in public plants since their inception, the precariousness of life today and the lack of job opportunities, especially for educated graduates, have turned this 'custom' into a 'right.'

workers were thus discriminated against by the same custom-based recruitment practices that the state had previously legitimized. This was, however, a particular kind of discrimination based on the commoditization of intimate, relational, and emotional factors within the structures of bureaucracy. The embeddedness of the social and the economic multiplied the hurt, insult, and exasperation of the workers.

Hamdy, for example, a son of a permanent worker at EISCO, had a university degree in commerce. He was married with two children, and came to EISCO after working in the university administration for LE300 ($43) a month, but quit that job when he realized that hanging out at the local coffee shop with neighbors was more promising, given the opportunities for moonlighting and for the expansion of relations. The father gave Hamdy's family a monthly allowance to live on, including when he was working on a daily basis at EISCO. He also lived on the upper floor of the house the father had built. Hamdy's sister had become a successful doctor and had married a pharmacist, and her father had opened a private clinic for her in the same building. Hamdy was frustrated that he had to depend on his father at his age. His inability to keep up with the social mobility of his family also added to his sense of inferiority and broken masculinity.

Securing a contract was important to Hamdy's sense of independence from his father. But it was equally a question of establishing his 'value' *(qima)* within his family and his community. The awaited, yet so far unmet, *istiqrar* ('stability') to which Hamdy and other daily workers aspired should thus be understood in the light of their position relative to permanent workers they had often been tied to. They too had 'played by the rules of the game' and were failed by it (Graeber 2013). Their anger and frustration are totally appropriate.

Whose *Istiqrar* ('Stability') Is It Anyway?

As I saw daily workers do the most tiresome and unrewarding work on the shop floors of EISCO I began to wonder how they accepted such low pay. Why did they not work for higher daily wages in the private sector? The standard answer I got at EISCO, and later the ministries of culture and agriculture, was that they were working "in the hope of a contract" *(shaghalin 'ala amal al-'aqd)*—that is, a permanent contract. The permanent contract, I was told, was *istiqrar* ('stability') and *mustaqbal* ('future'). In Egypt, between the Free Officers coup of 1952 and the January 25 Revolution of 2011, 'stability' embodied access to both tenured employment and the means to reproduce the conditions of 'a good life' in the context of the family, including through marriage. Being *mustaqir*, stable and settled, you could invest in long-term relationships in the community and pursue not short-term gains but longer-term ones.[13] *Istiqrar* was a social value that gave workers respect in their communities and meaning to their work.

Management capitalized on workers' valuation of relationality and reproduction, embodied in their aspiration for *istiqrar*, by reappropriating the meaning of work in their lives. As the revolution of January 2011 unfolded, *istiqrar* was repeatedly evoked, often by counterrevolutionary forces who referenced Mubarak's *istiqrar*. Mubarak adopted a discourse of *istiqrar* as a governing technique. Over the years, he reminded the Egyptian people that *istiqrar* was his legacy both domestically and internationally, using it as a pretext for repressive policies and to limit the democratic field. His use of *istiqrar* implied an ability to maintain production and prosperity, control 'terrorist' activities, and suppress war and maintain 'peace' in the region. In February 2011, in a last-ditch effort to hold onto power, Mubarak threatened the Egyptian people that they had a choice between his *istiqrar* or "chaos."

Stability as a governing logic was reproduced after the January 2011 Revolution. Throughout the next three years, *istiqrar* was invoked to defend state interests. *Istiqrar* was publicly represented as being "jeopardized by the revolution." Those in power, from the Supreme Council of the Armed Forces (SCAF) to Muhammad Morsi's regime, attacked workers for threatening *istiqrar*. Strikes were criticized as factional *(fi'awiya)* and selfish. *Istiqrar* became part of a political discourse that saw the crisis in the corruption of a few rather than the injustice of an entire system. Those legitimately afraid of layoffs, or those who suffered from the deteriorating security situation and wanted an end to protests, supported these claims. I suggest that the power and ubiquity of *istiqrar* as a mode of governmentality (Foucault 1991) cannot be fully

---

13 *Istiqrar* is defined by the *Dictionary of Modern Written Arabic* (Wehr and Cowan 1979) as, among other things, 'stability,' 'settledness,' 'remaining,' 'constancy,' 'continuance,' 'permanency,' 'stabilization,' 'strengthening,' 'consolidation.' The different meanings of *istiqrar* all capture the focus on the long term.

appreciated at the level of political discourse only. Rather, as a practice of government, it is entangled with people's values, aspirations, and the intimate politics of everyday life.

Istiqrar is also a value shared by EISCO's labor force and the workers I interviewed at both ministries. The discourse of work as stability is common among permanent workers, who have benefited from the durability of their contracts in living a good life. In essence, stability expands relationships and is another way to express the importance of relationality as a value vital to Egyptian popular communities (Elyachar 2005). But *istiqrar* is often reclaimed by capitalists and the state as a means of controlling people. There is an increased convergence between the capacities of the Egyptian popular classes and the aims of neoliberal rule, which draws on these capacities (Elyachar 2005). Exchanges made between workshop masters and customers based on money, referred to as business relationships *(bi-l-bizniss)*, thus often replace relationships based on *gad'ana*, which capitalize on and reproduce the value of neighborly relations (Elyachar 2005).

Turning stability from a social value into a productivist and calculative one, Mubarak introduced a politics of *istiqrar* that gives the regime a grip on workers. By making the immaterial labor of expanding networks and relations into a resource that is part of calculations regulating labor regimes, this politics became the norm. Confining new daily and temporary employment to children and relatives of EISCO's permanent workers furthered this politics.

What one may call the politics of *istiqrar*—that is, the contestations over how people ought to live their lives, from the everyday politics from below to the overarching politics of governing regimes—thus perpetuated the capitalist labor regime and values in workers' communities. It also reinforced the representation of the state as a protector. Adequate understanding of stability and why it is such an omnipresent ideal in Egyptian society must therefore take into account the complex ways in which state projects and their imaginative appropriation intersect.

The politics of *istiqrar* manipulates the hopes and aspirations of workers and sets their interests against one another. Permanent workers, who hope to reproduce the conditions of a good life, take on the hegemonic discourse of the state as a provider of stability. This is often at the expense of their solidarity as a group of skilled artisans who control their workplaces. It initiates a long-term distinction between those who become bourgeoisified by securing permanent contracts for their offspring, and those who eventually lose out and face precarious proletarian conditions. A competition also emerges between the daily workers who get into the citadel and those who remain perpetually proletariat.

Labor Struggles post–Mubarak's Ouster

Daily waged workers took advantage of the relaxation of policing at the onset of the revolution to demand permanent work. Cement workers locked the gates of the plant in Helwan and workers in the Sukari gold mine in Marsa 'Alam blocked the highway for five consecutive days. Capital responded ruthlessly. Sumid, a petroleum company in Suez, hired thugs to break a 28-day work stoppage. The police arrested the gold-mine workers who blocked the highway. The daily workers, however, were undeterred and mobilization across Egypt continued nonetheless. Meanwhile, the demands of workers with stable contracts included wage increases or full payment of late wages, setting minimum and maximum wages, the nationalization of privatized companies, abolishing the consultant system for retired managers, ridding institutions of corrupt officials, enabling freedom of association, and reinstatement of workers who were unjustly fired. Permanent employment, however, remained a prominent demand among the most disfranchised, from daily and temporary workers to the unemployed and the families in industrial areas demanding permanent jobs for their precariously employed children.

The government faced immense pressure following the strikes demanding permanent work. It responded by making a small proportion of contracts permanent. These amounted to 10 percent of the estimated 450,000 daily workers. In 2012 it announced that the Ministry of Finance would be appropriating 50 percent of the value of the special funds *(sanadiq khasa)*. In return, more workers were expected to be hired on permanent contracts on state budgets. By 2014 none of these plans had materialized, and the new government suggested a hold on new temporary and daily contracts in an effort to curb the demand of these workers for permanent contracts. A public official warned that the daily workers' saga had become *qunbila mawquta* ('a bomb that will detonate any second'). In both the ministries of agriculture and culture, these arrangements meant that around 10 percent of daily workers got permanent jobs, sometimes through connections without having first worked as daily workers. Ninety percent of the workers weren't hired despite the warnings, pledges, and promises.

The state also used its old tactics to break the solidarity of daily workers. Once again it used workers' dependence on their parents to silence them. In a meeting of daily waged workers with the head of the public authority for culture houses, the manager asked a protesting female worker: "How is your father? Is he good? Please send him my regards." Workers interpreted this as an attempt to keep the protestor from joining others by implying she had better chances of getting a job through her father's connections.

While the documentation of labor mobilization since the revolution focuses on how workers prompted Mubarak's ouster, on the demands of stable workers and the struggle for independent trade unions, the accounts both before and since the revolution have largely ignored the fragmentation of workers, and the way in which this fragmentation takes place mainly along the lines of kinship. Not enough attention has been paid to how mobilization by workers and demands for change continued to be framed by the politics of *istiqrar*.

The Politics of *Istiqrar* and Possibilities for the Future

Returning to the first question of this chapter: Why do daily workers resort to radical actions? The discussion presented above explains how they allocate meaning to their work and the strains they endure. But daily workers opt for radical tactics out of desperation. On the one hand, divisions within the working class make their allies few. Permanent workers rarely join daily workers in fighting for their rights. Many are silenced by the kinship contract. The daily workers' fight is thus a lonely one. Solidarity, a basic precursor to social justice, is scant. On the other hand, daily workers are excluded from the legal justice afforded to stable workers. Without work contracts, daily workers are like ghost workers, unrecognized by the workplaces that employ them. They are also not recognized by the judicial institutions who should guarantee justice to the citizenry. That they continue to make their voices heard and to stand solidly by each other despite the many efforts to break them is inspiring.

This scenario is not exclusive to Egypt. In China, the struggles of permanent workers differ from those of precarious workers, a distinction Lee (2007) identifies as the "rust-belt versus sun-belt" struggles. While the first is waged by workers whom the law acknowledges, and often center on improving their working conditions or compensation for layoffs, the latter is waged by seasonal rural workers who demand recognition by the state. Both are industrial actions, but they vary immensely according to the backgrounds and dispossessions of those involved. Their impacts on politics also could not be more different. While the first strengthens the law as source of justice, the second puts the value of the law in question.

Now turning to my second question: What does the struggle of daily workers tell us about the strategies to control labor and the limits in demanding transformative change? A sad outcome of these inspiring mobilizations is that the labor struggle is taking place on the playing fields initiated by the state as a means of dividing and controlling. By this I mean that, by framing its demands primarily around permanent contracts, the labor movement remains trapped within the politics of *istiqrar*.

By demanding that their work be made permanent, daily workers strengthen the state's grip over the labor movement. The state assumes the role of the 'grantor' of stability and of the good life. In so doing, it gives new life to distinctions between the permanent public-sector workers, whose living and working conditions are akin to those of the middle class, and the perpetually disfranchised workers who are trapped by the "cruel optimism" (Berlant 2011) of a better future. In March 2013, the inhabitants of Shakshouk, a small village in Fayoum, blocked the highway leading to the district of Ibshowy. They surrounded the metallurgical plant, burned car tires, and locked up the workers, preventing their buses from leaving. The neighborhood residents *(ahali)* demanded permanent contracts for their children. This was neither the first uprising by residents of industrial areas nor the most militant. It was a common struggle to which the media had failed to give the attention it deserves. From Alexandria to Suez to Beheira, residents have locked up petroleum, electricity, and textile workers, demanding employment justice. They continue to do so. And they continue to be unheard. Those whose life is an impasse generated by a cruel optimism burst into action to take agency over their lives—actions later deemed 'violent' by the very perpetrators of violence.

Since January 25, 2011, workers around Egypt have followed in the footsteps of the property-tax collectors in setting up independent trade unions. The latter had established theirs in 2008, in a fascinating challenge to the Ministry of Finance. The new unions sprang up among those who were failed by the official Egyptian Trade Unions Federation (ETUF). Their aim was to provide a platform for progressive politics. But they have not always been successful. Clearly the challenges they face in terms of getting legal recognition, in addition to their internal rifts and hierarchical setups, restrain them. But they are also conditioned in their demands by the possibilities enabled by the state and capital—for example, by asking for permanent work rather than challenging the hours of work per day—and have thus not defied the authorities on more structural terms. By not demanding changes to labor regimes, unions risk regressing to the conservative side of the politics of the status quo.

In 2008, at the inauguration event of the first independent union of property-tax collectors, giving priority to the children of permanent workers in the allocation of new jobs was announced as one of the demands on the agenda of the new union. While I tweeted from the launch of this most remarkable event in the recent history of Egyptian labor, I felt a certain unease about the direction in which the demands were leading. Unions have a remarkable history of busting rank-and-file actions and slowing down labor movements. Demands that set workers apart risk making independent trade unions just another elitist, solidarity-busting institution.

Crucially, the demand for permanent work overshadowed new discourses that challenge waged work. Despite the revolutionary fervor, discourses that contest the essence of waged work did not emerge. The productivist regime that evaluates people's lives by their ability to engage in waged labor and abide by a 'work ethic' has not enabled alternative ways to imagine one's life and associate with others. In fact, the politics of *istiqrar* does not challenge productivist regimes; it strengthens them by establishing instead a system where the social values that people hold dear are abused within the labor process to facilitate the continued theft of labor and to eliminate dissent. Instead of freeing ourselves from labor, our factories become bigger and bigger. As Antonio Negri suggests, we are increasingly living in factories without borders (Hardt 2005) where productivism takes over our lives.

While workers' control of production has emerged as an alternative since 2011, when companies that incurred losses were liquidated and run by workers, these alternatives have not been supported and spread to strengthen this model. However, Quta and Al-Araby, two steel factories in the industrial Tenth of Ramadan district that are run by workers, offer the labor movement in Egypt a lot to learn. I am aware that the idea of turning most workplaces where daily workers demand permanent work into autonomous worker-run cooperatives is naive and farfetched in the current context. But suggesting that these alternatives exist and are possible is important to widening the debate beyond mere rights and statist discourses. Like many experiences in the developing world (Bayat 1987; 1991), workers' control in Egypt, with the exception of Al-Araby, has been short-lived. But if supported with the needed legal, economic, and popular mobilization, these models of labor cooperatives could create alternative imaginations that would create new realities in the long term.[14] After all, changing the language of the debate to create new possibilities is probably one of the crucial battles we must engage with, if we are to challenge the divisive strategies of the politics of *istiqrar*.

Perhaps if more work is done to encourage less hierarchical and more autonomous work models, especially in workplaces and enterprises suffering major losses, fewer people will be doing what Tamer did in seeking daily work at the Ministry of Culture when his company went bankrupt. Instead of reinforcing the patriarchal state with tried and tired approaches, we could be opening up the space for more transformational alternatives that expose the roots of exploitation. The alternatives we propose need to always strengthen workers' roles as subjective makers of history rather than passive objects of exploitation. The militant radicalism of daily workers suggests we are off to a good start.

References

Abbas, R. 1968. *al-Haraka al-'ummaliya fi Misr 1899–1952* [The Labor Movement in Egypt, 1899–1952]. Cairo: al-Hay'a al-Misriya al-'Amma li-l-Kitab.

---

14 In 2011 the Egyptian human rights organization, the Egyptian Initiative for Personal Rights (EIPR), issued a report on the experiences of workers' self-management worldwide and how they apply to Egypt. This is a good example of alternative research meant to aid in creating new possibilities.

Abdel Khalek, G. 2005. *al-Sina'a wa-l-tasni' fi Misr: al-waqi' wa-l-mustaqbal hatta 2020* [Industry and Industrialization in Egypt: The Reality and the Future until 2020]. Cairo: al-Maktaba al-Akadimiya.

Bayat, A. 1987. *Workers and Revolution in Iran*. London: Zed Books.

———. 1991. *Work, Politics, and Power: An International Perspective on Workers' Control and Self-Management*. London: Zed Books.

———. 2013. "Revolution in Bad Times," *New Left Review*, 80. http://newleftreview.org/II/80/asef-bayat-revolution-in-bad-times

Beinin, J. 2001. *Workers and Peasants in the Modern Middle East*. Cambridge: Cambridge University Press.

Beinin, J., and Z. Lockman. 1987. *Workers on the Nile: Nationalism, Communism, Islam, and the Egyptian Working Class, 1882–1954*. Princeton: Princeton University Press.

Berlant, L. 2011. *Cruel Optimism*. Durham: Duke University Press.

Braverman, H. 1974. *Labor and Monopoly Capital: The Degradation of Work in the Twentieth Century*. London: Monthly Review Press.

Burawoy, M. 1979a. "The Anthropology of Industrial Work," *Annual Review of Anthropology*, 8(1): 231–266. doi: 10.1146/annurev.an.08.100179.001311

———. 1979b. *Manufacturing Consent: Changes in the Labor Process under Monopoly Capitalism*. Chicago: University of Chicago Press.

Chalcraft, J. 2001. "The Coal-Heavers of Port Sa'id: State-Making and Worker Protest, 1869–1914," *International Labor and Working-Class History*, 60: 110–124, October. http://journals.cambridge.org/action/displayJournal?jid=ILW

De Neve, G. 2005. *The Everyday Politics of Labour: Working Lives in India's Informal Economy*. Delhi: Social Science Press.

Elyachar, J. 2005. *Markets of Dispossession: NGOs, Economic Development, and the State in Cairo*. Durham, NC: Duke University Press.

Foucault, M. 1991. "Governmentality." In G. Burchell, C. Gordon, and P. Miller, eds. *The Foucault Effect: Studies in Governmentality: with two lectures by and an interview with Michel Foucault*, 87–104. Chicago: Chicago University Press.

Goldberg, E. 1986. *Tinker, Tailor, and Textile Worker: Class and Politics in Egypt, 1930–1952*. 1st ed. Berkeley: University of California Press.

———. 1992. "The Foundations of State–Labor Relations in Contemporary Egypt," *Comparative Politics*, 24(2): 147–161.

———. 1996. "Reading from Right to Left: The Social History of Egyptian Labor." In E. Goldberg, ed. *The Social History of Labor in the Middle East*, 163–192. Boulder, CO: Westview Press.

Graeber, D. 2013. *The Democracy Project: A History, a Crisis, a Movement*. New York: Spiegel & Grau.

Handoussa, H. A., and G. Potter. 1991. *Employment and Structural Adjustment: Egypt in the 1990s*. Cairo: The American University in Cairo Press.

Hardt, M. 2005. "Into the Factory: Negri's Lenin and Subjective Caesura (1968–73)." In M. Abdul-Karim and T. Murphy, eds. *The Philosophy of Antonio Negri: Resistance in Practice*, vol. 1, 7–37. London: Pluto Press.

Heydemann, S. 2004. *Networks of Privilege in the Middle East: The Politics of Economic Reform Revisited*. New York: Palgrave Macmillan.

Holmström, M. 1976. *South Indian Factory Workers: Their Life and Their World*. Cambridge South Asian Studies. Cambridge: Cambridge University Press.

Kalb, D. 1997. *Expanding Class: Power and Everyday Politics in Industrial Communities, The Netherlands, 1850–1950*. Durham, NC: Duke University Press.

Kondo, D. 1990. *Crafting Selves: Power, Gender, and Discourses of Identity in a Japanese Workplace*. Chicago: Chicago University Press.

Lee, C. K. 2007. *Against the Law: Labor Protests in China's Rustbelt and Sunbelt*. Berkeley: University of California Press.

Lockman, Z. 1994a. "Introduction." *Workers and Working Classes in the Middle East: Struggles, Histories, Historiographies*, xi–xxxi. Albany: State University of New York Press.

———. 1994b. *Workers and Working Classes in the Middle East: Struggles, Histories, Historiographies*. Albany: State University of New York Press.

Makram-Ebeid, D. 2013. "Manufacturing Stability: Everyday Politics of Work in an Industrial Steel Town in Helwan, Egypt." Unpublished PhD dissertation: London School of Economics. http://etheses.lse.ac.uk/780/

Mollona, M. 2009a. *Made in Sheffield: An Ethnography of Industrial Work and Politics*. New York: Berghahn Books.

———. 2009b. "Introduction." In G. De Neve, M. Mollona, and J. Parry, eds. *Industrial Work and Life: An Anthropological Reader*, xi–xxviii. LSE Monographs on Social Anthropology. Oxford: Berg.

al-Naggar, A. 2010. *al-Inhiyar al-iqtisadi fi 'asr Mubarak* [Economic Collapse under Mubarak]. Cairo: Dar Merit.

Ong, A. 1987. *Spirits of Resistance and Capitalist Discipline: Factory Women in Malaysia*. Albany: State University of New York Press.

Parry, J. (n.d.). "The *Embourgeoisement* of a 'Proletariat Vanguard'?" Unpublished paper.

———. 2005. "Industrial Work." In J. Carrier, ed. *A Handbook of Economic Anthropology*, 141–159. Northampton, MA: Edward Elgar Publishing.

Posusney, M. P. 1997. *Labor and the State in Egypt*. New York: Columbia University Press.

Sanchez, A. 2011. "Capitalism, Violence, and the State: Crime, Corruption, and Entrepreneurship in an Indian Company Town," *Journal of Legal Anthropology*, 1(2): 165–188.

Shehata, S. 2009. *Shop Floor Culture and Politics in Egypt*. Albany: State University of New York Press.

Taylor, F. W. 1911. *The Principles of Scientific Management*. New York: Harper & Brothers.

Toth, J. 1999. *Rural Labor Movements in Egypt and Their Impact on the State, 1961–1992*. Gainesville: University of Florida Press.

———. 2002. *Rural-to-Urban Migration and Informal Sector Expansion: Impediments to Egyptian Development*. Florence: European University Institute.

Uthman, T. S. 1972. "Memoirs and Documents in the History of the Working Class," *al-Katib*, 134.

CHAPTER 5

Islah, from Gift to Right

Yasmine Ahmed

And today, in 1956, following a revolution that rose on your shoulders and the shoulders of your army brothers—who represent no one but you, represent this people—you have finally earned your right to life. Today, fellahin, you must look to the future and envision the struggle that this right requires in order to be preserved. You must hold on to your right to freedom, your right to life, your right to justice, and your right to equality. Work, and only with work can we achieve a good social life . . . work, and only with work can we achieve dignity. . . . Every fellah will work in his field to increase productivity . . . this is your work, this is your duty to protect your rights—your right to life, your right to freedom, may God be with you.[1]
—Gamal Abdel Nasser, January 1956, Cairo

Gamal Abdel Nasser's historic speech in celebration of the 1956 Egyptian constitution was delivered in the presence of more than 20,000 fellahin. Reference to the right of fellahin is made in the first agrarian reform, commonly known as *islah*—a reform that granted them secure access to agricultural lands, subsidized inputs (fertilizers, pesticides), and state markets. Thirty years later, Nasser's social contract with Egypt's fellahin was breached with the issuance of the new land tenancy law—Law No. 96 for the year 1992 (Saad 1999: 388–389). The new law was an integral part of the USAID-engineered structural adjustment program of Egyptian agriculture that began in the late 1970s,

---

1   http://nasser.bibalex.org/Speeches/browser.aspx?SID=430&lang=en. I would like to thank Nariman Youssef for translating this excerpt.

under the directives of the World Bank and the International Monetary Fund. It made tenancy subject to market forces, and gave landowners the legal right to evict almost one million tenants and their families. The implementation of this law also "opened a Pandora's box of claims and counterclaims relating to ownership and control of many types of landholding," including those belonging to the agrarian reform authorities (Bush 2000:239).

One such episode resulted in the eruption of violent clashes between the police and security forces hired by Youssef Waly, who enjoyed the longest-ever ministerial tenure at the Ministry of Agriculture and Land Reclamation (from January 2, 1982 to July 7, 2004),[2] and 245 tenants residing in five villages located in the Qarun region of Fayyum. The two parties were fighting over land that was owned, prior to Nasser's reform, by Muhammad Amin Waly, grandfather of Youssef Waly. Tenants acquired access to the land as part of Nasser's agrarian reform. For 30 years, from 1967 to 1997, they paid dues to the Agrarian Reform Authority, which they thought would render them eligible to own the land eventually. In 1997, however, the police and security forcibly expropriated the tenants' lands, and returned them to the Walys.

The case was exceptional, since the evictions were only made possible by Youssef Waly's grip on power. First, the land was the property of the agrarian reform authorities and not individuals. Hence, it was not subject to Law 96. Yet the law was used here as "a vehicle for misleading farmers and colluding with security forces to dispossess the legitimate farmers of it" (LCHR 2002:126). Second, and more importantly, in 1986, four years into the ministerial tenure of Youssef Waly, the agrarian authority placed the land on sale. Accordingly, tenants asked to purchase the land, and many made a modest down payment to the agrarian authorities. Meanwhile, descendants of Muhammad Amin Waly signed a reconciliation with the agrarian reform authorities, and were re-granted access to land. They also requested the ability to purchase the land. Before finalizing the deal, police and security forces threatened tenants and detained them. After 15 days of continuous torture, the tenants agreed to sign deeds of cessation in order to be released. Meanwhile, the descendants of Muhammad Amin Waly finalized the purchase deal with the agrarian authorities.

---

2   http://www.agr-egypt.gov.eg/En_AllMinisters2.aspx?mid=68

Islah, from Gift to Right

Figure 5.1. Fayyum tenant protesting in front of the Ministry of Justice, Cairo, March 2012

On February 12, 2011, one day after the ouster of Hosni Mubarak, the evicted tenants reclaimed their fields and made a bold move in suing Youssef Waly and his family for evicting them from land that they claim to be their property. The dispute now falls under two legal authorities. The first, in which old tenants filed a series of court cases against 15 members of the Waly family, concerns civil law. The second deals with criminal law: defendants from the Waly family filed accusations against 57 farmers, the plaintiffs of the civil case. Resorting to the courts, however, is not a brand-new experience for tenants. During the evictions, tenants, with the support of farmers' advocacy groups, filed a case against the Walys. However, after a few years of court investigations, the tenants' grievances fell on deaf ears. In 2003, their lawyer died, leaving behind case files locked in his office premises in downtown Cairo.

The tenants are doubtful that the legal arena will bring justice. "*Al-qanun zay al-ghorbal* [the law is like a coarse-meshed sieve]," as Hag Hassan once told me over tea. It is full of loopholes—therefore, it could be easily infiltrated, manipulated, and contested. "The law is not designed to give rights, but to support the powerful. We need political will, we need someone like Gamal Abdel Nasser," he adds. This is not surprising, given that the legal framework that governs reform lands *(aradi al-islah)* is so confusing, imprecise, and dysfunctional in its own terms. These characteristics often produce unresolvable procedural and substantive complexity, not only in cases where disputes occur, but also in regular cases. In such a difficult legal context, tenants pay huge fees to their lawyers and dedicate at least one day a week to attending meetings and court sessions. Furthermore, the judicial system, many tenants argue, was suspected of acquiescing to Waly's political influence. Civil and human-rights lawyers told the tenants that their case will linger in courts for years. Some note that Youssef Waly will probably offer bribes to the legal experts for them to slow the litigation, even while in prison.[3] Furthermore, they anticipate that the first report, which they expect in no less than 15 years, will probably be in favor of the Waly family. Consequently, turning to the legal arena is expensive, time-consuming, and utterly exhausting. This sometimes leads Hag Hassan to rethink the consequences of the reform. On one occasion, he told me "*al-islah damarna* [the reform led to our devastation]." This refers to the fact that *islah* became a burden on the fellah, ever since it lost the essence of Nasser's 'gift' (Saad 2002:190): the guarantee of security.

This situation raises several important questions. How can we interpret the tenants' appeal to law if they think that litigation will not lead to resolution? How can we make sense of the tenants' endless efforts to draw upon national laws, the constitution, and Islamic references—all situated within political and historical specificity—to own property that they think of as a burden? Indeed, this situation leads us to think of the value of reform lands beyond the livelihood framework. This is because most of the evicted tenants for the case I study managed to secure modest livelihoods and to access small parcels of lands elsewhere, primarily through remittances.

---

3   In March 2012, Youssef Waly was sentenced to 10 years in jail for squandering more than LE700 million in public funds in the sale of the al-Bayadeya Island nature reserve in Luxor. Part of the fieldwork for this chapter was conducted when Waly was in jail. Waly was freed on appeal in January 2013.

Answers to these questions are based on participant observation, archival research, and interviews conducted over twelve months, from September 2011 to April 2012 and from November 2012 to April 2013. During this time, I interviewed 30 tenants from four neighboring villages (al-Ab'adiya, al-Khalta, Ahmed Effendi, Quta) in the Qarun region of Fayyum, and their leaders, human rights lawyers, civil lawyers, criminal lawyers, officials from NGOs active in farmers' rights, and legal experts studying the case. In addition to conducting extensive fieldwork in the village of al-Ab'adiya, I observed meetings held between farmers and lawyers and attended court sessions and expert meetings, even if, like the tenants, I was waiting outside the courtrooms and legal offices. In this analysis, I also closely examine petitions written by tenants and a press file of *al-Sha'b* [The People] newspaper, which led a campaign against Youssef Waly's interference, commonly referred to as 'corruption,' in the late 1990s.[4] Among other issues, this campaign covered the Fayyum evictions.

In this chapter, I argue that the legal claims constructed by the evicted Fayyum farmers present a demand for state recognition, rather than a road to litigation. Such a demand is not one that builds on abstract property rights, but rather acknowledges their personal and collective histories as rightful citizens—soldiers of the pan-Arab nation as veterans of the Yemeni war, tillers of the soil, responsible citizens of the state. Thus, I suggest that tenants were seizing the opportunity to take part in a revolutionary movement, and to reclaim their place in what seemed to be the creation of a 'new' republic. These findings support the comparative literature on indigenous property rights (for an overview, see Idrus 2010). Like the Orang Asli in Malaysia studied by Idrus (2010:93), tenants resort to the courts for reasons that go beyond material reward. These reasons are centered around their recognition as rightful citizens. They do so through assembling their war memories, labor histories, a collection of state-endorsed documents, and remembered episodes of Waly 'corruption.' In so doing, tenants expand the meaning of *islah* in a way that captures, even reconciles, competing property regimes that belong to two structural and temporal registers: (1) Nasser's socialist orientation, where secure tenancy was perceived as Nasser's gift to peasants, and (2) the embrace of neoliberalism as a development remedy, in

---

4 I would like to thank Reem Saad for sharing the press file with me.

which private property came to be conceptualized as an individual right accorded to responsible and deserving citizens.

The material in this chapter therefore takes a debate about property conflicts that erupted in rural Egypt over the last 20 years and culminated during the January 25 uprisings as a lens to examine state and citizenship formation in a revolutionary context.

My argument unfolds in the following three sections. In the first section, I locate Nasser's agrarian reform in historical context. Tenants' experience of land occupation is tightly linked to Nasser's agrarian reform; hence, it is important to outline the turning points of land administration regimes, as they serve as a backdrop to the tenants' predicament in the Mubarak, or, more precisely, the Waly era. In the second section, I highlight a tension between tenants and their lawyers, by showing that the lawyers' legal solution (compensation) undermines the dynamism in the historical, political, economic, and social relationships between farmers, land, and the state. Moreover, the lawyers eclipse tenants' critical and changing sentiments in relation to the 1952 agrarian reform offered by Gamal Abdel Nasser. I do so by closely examining the multiple layers on which tenants construct their legal claims, through the mediums of writing (petitions) and oral narration. In the last section, I show that the notion of the 'gift' (Saad 2002:190)—a common reference to the security that Nasser granted to farmers through the agrarian reform—needs to be expanded to include the security of rights and entitlements.

Islah in Historical Perspective

It is impossible to make sense of tenants' views of private property without contextualizing *islah* in Egypt's agrarian history. Scholarship on rural Egypt rightly juxtaposes the logic, ideological foundations, and implications of Nasser's first agrarian reform, implemented in 1952, with the agrarian market 'counter-reforms' announced in 1992 during Youssef Waly's tenure as minister of agriculture and land reclamation. In reviewing this literature, we can easily see that Nasser's iconic status in rural Egypt is acquired by positioning him between two eras of humiliation and exploitation that hailed private ownership first as a modernization and later as a development remedy.

Nasser's debatable version of socialism was based on incorporating citizens into the nation-building project by making them feel that they were benefiting from growth and equity measures introduced to consolidate state power and to ensure national integration (Abou El Fadl 2005:32). The first agrarian reform was a case in point. Ethnographies on this period (Saad 1988; Ghosh 2002) show that the relationship between the fellah and the state was articulated in a way that assigned the former key obligations in reaching the country's development goals in exchange for state support and access to subsistence crops and food security. The stated objectives of the law sought to reduce the gaps among classes, and to improve the living conditions of the fellahin. Its implications for land distribution included regulating landlord–tenant relationships by fixing rent at seven times the land tax, changing the relationship into a contractual one (Saad 1988:3), in effect guaranteeing tenure, and distributing small plots of lands to peasants.

The collectivization of small farmers was a key goal of the first agrarian reform. Although originally introduced long before 1952, agricultural cooperatives increased both in number and in function after the passage of subsequent laws, and played a crucial mediating role between small farmers and the state (Abdel Aal 1998:280). During this period, the cooperatives' financial assets were treated as public assets, their officers as government employees, and their records and stamps as official government paperwork (Saad 1988). The role of the agricultural cooperatives was to distribute agricultural input, and to ensure that farmers abided precisely by the crop rotation system organized by the government, paid taxes and land installments, paid miscellaneous expenses to the cooperative, and more importantly, delivered at a fixed price the required portion of certain crops each season (Saad 1988).[5] Consequently, Nasser's land reform changed the structure of landownership in Egypt in favor of small fellahin, and granted them some welfare benefits and control over the agriculture sector (Ayeb 2012:75).

The introduction of economic liberalization in 1987 was followed by a revision of agrarian policies or 'counter-reforms.' Such reforms were based on a liberal logic that promotes a false developmental promise that is dependent on the integration of Egypt's agriculture sector into world

---

5   It is worth noting that crops differ from one governorate to the other; upper Egyptian governorates were responsible for supplying wheat and wheat seeds at the national level, and Delta governorates were responsible for supplying rice and cotton, and sometimes wheat.

markets (Bush 2002; Ayeb 2012:79). Similar to other contexts, economic crises were invoked to justify the urgency of such proposals. The counter-reform aimed to restore a decline in agricultural growth, to stop deterioration in the agriculture trade balance, and to develop crops for export (Ayeb 2012:84). Land counter-reform was only one dimension of insecurity. The state gradually disengaged itself from the costs of inputs (seeds, fertilizers, pesticides, chemicals, etc.) and passed on these costs to farmers. Over time, the profit from agriculture and the loans intensified the asymmetries. Farmers in turn borrowed money and mortgaged their parcels, and some were tempted into risky projects. The application of the law was justified by perceptions of the peasant population as socially backward, opportunistic, and lazy (Saad 1999), whose (mis)usages of agricultural land are inimical to social progress. Hence, similar to other contexts (Li 2007 on Indonesia and Idrus 2010 on Malaysia), farmers' failure to improve was used as a rationale behind their dispossession and as a justification for transferring ownership to people or institutions who would make better use of the property. Meanwhile, development experts have argued that 'inadequate' land use is a consequence of small landholding. For instance, authors of the 2003 *Fayyum Human Development Report* noted that 83.1 percent of landholdings are less than three feddans while they cover 36.9 percent of the total cultivated area (UNDP 2003:41). Hence, policy debates were restricted to discussions that link property rights to productivity (Berry 2002b: 214).

The counter-reform's most obvious impacts were an abrupt impoverishment of small farmers (Saad 2004:2) and the construction of new capitalist agricultural landholdings (Ayeb 2012:79). Social differentiation in rural areas has significantly increased (Bush 2009). Rural poverty has significantly increased, and many female heads of households were thrown into poverty (Bush 2009:64). Many households not only lost their main source of income and food security, but liquidated their remaining assets to make ends meet (Ayeb 2012:83–84). Inequalities in landholding are well documented by Ayeb (2012); only 3 percent of farmers gained control of 33.5 percent of land, with an average size of more than ten feddans, whereas a mass of small and near-landless farmers became owners of less than five feddans, half of whom live under the poverty line (2012:77). Even worse, tenant farmers became literally invisible to the state, despite their presence in every Egyptian village. They totally

Islah in Historical Perspective

disappeared from national statistics and registers of agricultural cooperatives (2012:81). In an interview with Abdel Mawla Ismail, an advocate for rural and agrarian rights, he told me that a key intentional consequence of the reform is that in the legal arena, discussions on land disputes shifted from exposing failed state policies (liberalization of the agriculture sector) to a question of 'rights,' in which quarrels between individuals—landlords and tenants—occur and become unresolvable. The case that I discuss in this chapter is an example of this situation. However, it also illustrates that this shift did not fully materialize. Because most landlords were members of the government in one way or another (ministers, parliament members, business elites), the tenants are aware that in bringing Waly and his family to justice, they are suing both the 'state' and its oligarchs. Hence, the state is present as a main interlocutor in land disputes.

Based on the above, there are significant parallels that could be drawn between private ownership introduced in pre-1952 Egypt and property rights that were promoted with the shift to liberalization. Both regimes aimed to get rid of an arbitrary system (in the pre-revolution and revolution eras) and an 'archaic' system (in the counter-reform era) of property relations, and resulted in burdening rural subjects with debt. The first was a consequence of the taxation system imposed by the state, and the latter resulted from tenants' loss of their creditworthiness with neighbors and friends as a result of losing the land as "possible collateral for loans" (Saad 2004:9).

My own fieldwork confirms these findings, for tenants' conceptions of property and land are tightly linked to the experience of the land reform. Nasser's era still inspires a wide range of nostalgic emotions in public consciousness that are often contrasted with the rather disappointing eras that preceded and followed it. "We have been devastated ever since Nasser died, may his soul rest in peace," is a concluding sentence in almost any discussion about land issues in al-Abʻadeya. In a mosque built on the reclaimed fields, tenants have pasted posters of their beloved leader on the walls. But this admiration of Nasser should not be read as an attempt to reinvent Nasser's era. As I noted earlier, tenants have realized that the promise of security that was an integral component of Nasser's property regime is no longer firm. Hence, they, too, have internalized the view that private ownership is the guarantee of security in the post-counter-reform era.

Negotiating Citizenship in the 'New' Republic

Sieder (2001:203) has observed that any assumed transition to a more democratic form of governance opens up a space to reflect on state reconstruction, and to negotiate and reinterpret citizenship. He notes that such processes involve a wide range of actors, each attempting to advance his/her competing vision of the state, governance, and citizenship (2001:204). In the context of Egypt's unfolding revolutionary process, protesting has been the most visible manifestation of this negotiation process on the ground. A recent Egyptian Center of Economic and Social Rights report shows the total documented number of protests reached 3,817 in 2012, exceeding all protests between 2000 and 2010 by 500 (ESESR 2013:4).[6]

Another primary site for negotiating citizenship and reflecting on state reconstruction is that of the law. Sieder (2001:204) notes that the primacy of law stems from its very nature as a site setting the framework of rights and obligations. Comparative ethnographies illustrate how ordinary citizens use the legal space to reconfigure and redefine their relationship with the state, with a focus on property rights (for an overview, see Idrus 2010). Based on a case study with an indigenous Malaysian group, Orang Asli, Idrus shows that the group's resort to the courts is a means to voice a vision of inclusive citizenship that recognizes the group's multiple positions in the nation (2010:93). Hence, in addition to the material reward of acquiring property, a major success was to debunk the national representation of the group as a 'development failure' and replace it with other positions—"wards of the state, citizens of the nation, and indigenous people with worldwide recognition" (2010:89).

In many instances, resorting to litigation does not necessarily stem from the plaintiffs' belief in the ability of the judicial process to achieve solutions. On the contrary, in his analysis of a case of land fraud in São Paulo's urban periphery, James Holston argues that law is an "instrument of calculated disorder" (1991:695)—a means "to bring the conflict into the legal arena as a way to keep it unresolved but contained, thus controlling it in a residual sense until the political will is found for solution" (1991:709). As noted earlier, my own fieldwork reveals tenants' critical sentiments toward the law. They mostly view it as a rather slow and biased space of litigation. Furthermore, in the context of a

---

6 http://ecesr.com/contents/uploads/2013/04/Protest-Movement-2012.pdf

dispute over land between tenants and a family of a former politician, the discourse of corruption quickly pops up. Akhil Gupta argues, "One can employ the discourse of corruption to glean what people imagine the state to be, what state actions are considered legitimate, and how ideas of the rights of citizens and subjects are constituted" (Gupta 2005:175). Similarly, Lazar (2005) argues that despite its slippery nature, corruption talk could help us grasp local understandings of the proper use of political power, which Bolivians contrast with the notion of public good (2005:213). She notes that "corruption talk is ... one of the ways in which Bolivians construct a moral public sphere and make claims to the appropriate distribution of resources and to increased accountability" (2005:214).

View of Experts

Civil and human rights lawyers present the case as a classic situation in which farmers claim access to land of which they were deprived during an authoritarian and corrupt rule. Statements drafted by human rights groups in support of tenants frame the problem with a discourse that highlights the very category of the small farmer *(al-fellah al-baseet)* as a victim of the agriculture liberalization policies and the corruption of Youssef Waly, who used his political power for private gain. Furthermore, the legal apparatus should be purified of corrupt clerks so that tenants can claim tenancy rights. But this very concept of 'right' is one that is not shared by tenants. Lawyers perceive 'right' in compensation terms—a plot of land elsewhere or a sum of money. Lawyers do not see reclaiming the original fields as a viable legal option. Many were angry that the farmers did not listen to their legal advice. Some stopped offering their legal support, while others decided not to provide support in the first place. Tenants, on the other hand, draw on multiple kinds of positioning and demand that the state fulfill an obligation to them. In so doing, they reframe the struggle from one of 'victimization' to one of broad rights and entitlement. Thus, I suggest that tenants were seizing the opportunity to take part in a revolutionary movement, and to reclaim their place in what seemed to be the creation of a 'new' republic. An understanding of how tenants assemble their war memories, labor histories, a collection of state-endorsed documents, and episodes of Waly corruption thus becomes crucial.

Fellahin as Soldiers of the Nation

Plaintiffs claim that under the 1971 Egyptian constitution,[7] they should have special treatment as war soldiers. This is in accordance with Article 15, which states, "War veterans, those injured in or because of war, and wives and children of martyrs killed in action shall have priority in work opportunities according to the law." The plaintiffs add that under Article 40 of the Egyptian constitution, "all citizens are equal before the law." They cite three similar cases of compensated war soldiers and martyrs: first, fellahin in other areas, who were granted plots of land under the same circumstances and, after paying the required taxes, were able to enjoy land ownership; second, soldiers who were employed in the public sector because of their participation in the same wars, and are now enjoying pension plans; third, *shuhada' al-thawra* (martyrs of the January 25 Revolution and/or their families), who died or were severely injured during these revolutionary events, and are now in the process of receiving compensation. Hag Ahmed makes the link between his wartime experiences and that of Tahrir martyrs and injured revolutionaries. He claims: "We served this country. The government now is paying incentives to families of martyrs and to injured revolutionaries. We should be treated like them.... Aren't we also heroes of this country?"

To back up their claim, tenants emphasize their military certificates, which display their photograph in an army outfit 50 years ago, and identify the year and place of their service—1964, Yemen. They specifically refer to their participation in the Yemeni Civil War, in which Egypt took part on the side of the Republicans against the Royalists from 1962 to 1970, to identify themselves as *beto' harb al-Yemen* (those who participated in the Yemen war), although references to other wars, specifically the 1967 and 1973 wars, are occasionally made. They use this as a means of differentiating themselves from *muntafi'een* (beneficiaries) who received land from *al-Qanun* (the reform law). This is illustrated in Hag Omar's comment:

> *The other ones got the lands through something called al-Qanun (the Law). And this is a different story, because they did not participate in the Yemen war.*

---

7 Although dissolved at the time of filing the legal claim, it is still the reference for the legal claim.

Fellahin as Soldiers of the Nation

Figure 5.2. Certificate of Appreciation to Soldier al-Sayid Ali Abdel Aziz Ramadan

Documents are used to revive the war as a 'concrete event' (Saad 2000:246). The case of Hag Ali illustrates the point.

> *I was 20 years old and I got married to this woman. We were engaged for two years, then, two months after we got married, the army came and took me. I was recruited for the army on February 2, 1965. My number was 560844, I remember it very well. I was recruited, and I spent eight months at the training center. It turned out that my colonel was in Yemen at the time. So I ended up going to Yemen. At the time, they used to give us 1.98 pounds for serving in the army. We used to call it half a franc then. I spent 10 years in the army. I left on April 1, 1974. I took part in the Yemen war, in the 1967 war, the War of Attrition, and in 1973 . . . . I was injured in Yemen, paralyzed in Port Said during the War of Attrition, and I was injured in the 1973 war.*

References to physical torture, deaths, and long-term psychological trauma are repeatedly made by tenants. The harsher their wartime experiences and the tougher their war days were, the more deserving small farmers are. Hag Karam is a dramatic case that is used as a model story to describe the fellahin's misery during times of war. He joined the army in 1965 and stayed for 10 years, 18 months of which were in Yemen. When he first joined the army, he had just married. His wife gave birth to his first son, Khaled, when he was at war. Since the Yemen war, he has lost his mental and physical abilities, and has stopped working. After a particularly harsh Thursday in his group, 10 of his comrades were shot dead, and he had to stay near them for 10 days because the road was blocked. He stayed awake beside their dead bodies in the mountains. Ghosts of the dead haunted him during the nights, and he became mentally ill. Describing the incident, his wife lowered her voice, saying that since then, has been unable to speak, became half-deaf, and was never able to recover afterward. "Ever since, he cries with no reason," she whispered to me. In addition to the psychological trauma, he was close to death in the 1967 war. As a result of a bullet to the head, he had to go through an operation, and recovered. Furthermore, the health consequences of war transcend generations. His grandson's Down syndrome is also attributed to some mental-health conditions of his son Kareem, who was conceived after Hag Karam's return from war.

The occasion of the families of war veterans receiving land is perceived as a turning point in their perceptions of the state—from a threatening to a rewarding entity. This is illustrated in Hag Hassan's telling of his story.

> *During the time I was in Yemen, the land reform authorities told her [my wife], "We want you." She freaked out and thought they were going to take her to the mayor to tell her I had passed away. But it turned out they wanted to inform her that they were going to give her two feddans, in return for her husband serving in Yemen. So she signed for them and received the two feddans and started cultivating them.*

It is also echoed in the narrative of Hag Moukhtar.

> *I participated in the military in 1965. I completed eight months of training, then left for Yemen. We were surprised to find that the state rewarded us with a plot of islah land.*

The quotations above encompass a number of issues, which provides an understanding of why tenants perceive their parcels of land in terms of rights and entitlement, even though they still express gratitude to Nasser for implementing the reform. Tenants view war as a transformative event that reshaped their relationship with the state and placed them in the domain of citizenship. The effect of war participation in placing the village in a wider national and political framework has been found in Egyptian peasant narratives elsewhere (Saad 2000). This idea of a transaction with the state is often employed to reframe the reform from a mere act of Nasser's 'giving' to an act of compensation or reward. Military service is seen as an obligation to the pan-Arab nation that tenants fulfilled, and for which they were compensated with land ownership. Furthermore, this transaction is seen as exceptional in state–rural subject relations, for it generated fear or surprise at the moment when the recipient was called to receive the land.

Tillers of the Soil

Although any narrative about the land dispute starts with a reference to the Yemen war, it should be noted that not all tenants are war veterans. Some tenants acquired the land because they had no source of livelihood but agriculture. This group emphasizes the amount of labor that they (or their parents) have invested in land. When I asked Ali, a son of a tenant, whether his father participated in the war, he said "no," but quickly added the following:

> My father took the land from Nasser, and invested so much time and effort in it to grow wheat, corn, and clover. When the land was with the Walys, it was not as good, because they did not care about agriculture. They were not fellahin. They came from abroad, some people say from Albania or Turkey. And because they treated fellahin so badly, fellahin, in return, did not care much about the land. But all those who got the land from Abdel Nasser cared so much about the land. They had no other source of livelihood.

It is worth noting that those who were in the Yemen war also stress the labor invested in land. However, due to the absence of men in military service, tenants employ a gendered narrative that highlights the role of women in keeping the land alive until they came back. The following story of Umm Khaled, a tenant's wife, illustrates this point.

> *From 1966 to 1974, I used to farm the land alone. . . . I had my four kids. Was I supposed to let them die from hunger or work to feed them? I used to hire men to plant the seeds and I irrigated it myself. I used to take my few-days-old son Khaled and go to the fields for irrigation and supervision. I did not have anyone to help. His [her husband's] siblings wanted to steal it from me. And my siblings are not fellahin, they are carpenters. I was the one taking care of everything. And then I bought cows, and then I bought a calf for nine pounds. And I bought a house, built it. I built a home with raw brick. . . . I ended up having a home, crops, and livestock. And I became better than a man. It was like that for 10 years when he was absent in the army. When Abu Khaled returned from war, he found a house, a land, livestock, so he shed his uniform and started cultivating with me. We were happy with what we had. He did not have to go here or there.*[8]

The tenants' labor history is backed up with piles of documents. When Hag Hussein heard from Abu Khaled that I was coming to interview him about the land dispute, he asked his daughter Mona to bring his *mostanadat* (pile of legal documents), stored in an old yellow plastic bag that he carefully keeps on top of his wardrobe. During the interview, he constantly used them to prove legal points and review dates, and, at the end, gave me copies in case I managed to meet with concerned authorities in Cairo. He emphasized the importance of documents. "This is my land, because we have its papers. The fellah knows his limits" *(ardi 'alashan ana ma'aya wara' biha, al-fellah 'aref hodoudoh)*— cooperative IDs, agrarian reform contract, tax receipts, he notes. He

---

8 'Here' and 'there' within Umm Khaled's narrative are references to labor migration destinations, specifically Libya and Saudi Arabia. This interview was conducted in a joint collaboration with Habib Ayeb and Ray Bush as part of their 2013 documentary "Fellahin." I would like to thank them for allowing me to use these interviews in my work. I would also like to thank Nada el-Kouny for sharing the transcriptions with me.

started his narration by proudly showing me the first document, a copy of his land contract, signed September 11, 1968, between the custodial official at the agrarian reform cooperative called Qaram and himself. It entitled him to two feddans for a rent amounting to 20 pounds and 580 milliemes. Hag Hussein stressed that the document was stamped and has been signed by four government officers, which he sees as a validation of the document. He went over the documents' articles, which he almost recalls by heart. The contract says the tenant: 1) cannot sell the harvest unless he or she pays the amount agreed upon; 2) should only use the land for agricultural purposes; 3) cannot lower the amount of the rent and has to pay each month on the date agreed; 4) should allow the taxation office to check on land at any time; 5) should protect the land from third parties; 6) should give it back to the government in case of public need; 7) should abide by agrarian policies set by the government according to Law No. 138 for the year 1961. Hag Hussein and others pinpointed the dates in which they were given their shares of subsidized input in exchange for certain crops in order to make sure that I write in my notes the duration of land occupation. They often looked at my notes to make sure that I got the dates right. During tape recording, these were some of the few moments that they looked at the recorder to make sure that it was turned on.

As noted above, tenants view their parcels of land as a material product of their labor—"material objects that connect them with the state as citizens" (Hetherington 2009:225). It is through the reform that tenants acquired full personhood. As echoed in Amitav Ghosh's work in al-Beheira governorate and Reem Saad's ethnography in Fayyum, the peasants regarded reform as a turning point in their relations with the state that resembles the turning point between *jahiliya* (ignorance of divine guidance) and Islam (Ghosh 2002). But to acquire such status, they had to work hard, and in difficult circumstances. Kinship and religious idioms are drawn upon to describe the act of giving life to land—a rich metaphor commonly used to explain the value of the lands.

In a recent visit to the village studied, I asked Hag Sayed, one of my key informants, about the legal case. He told me that they haven't heard anything, but finally managed to get some maps for them to identify the borders of each plot—a requirement for the civil case. His daughter Manal joined the discussion, commenting that he should forget about this case. He doesn't need this particular plot anyway; both of his sons are in Saudi Arabia, and they managed to buy five feddans elsewhere. I reiterated a question that I have been asking tenants who were able to secure a livelihood through other sources over the years: "Why, despite all the hassle, are you insisting on owning this land?" My newborn son was with me. Hag Ali pointed at his thumb and told me, "You have now tasted motherhood. If they asked you to give his thumb away in exchange for all of Fayyum, would you accept?" I replied, "No." Similarly, in several interviews with Abu Khaled, I found him repeating the following sentence: "Land is like my son. So in that case, can someone come and tell me: Give me your son?" This parenting metaphor has been found in other studies on land struggles. For instance, in a discussion on why land continues to be a guarantee for communal struggle, Ray Bush noted that "people see the land like they see their children: it's precious."[9] In terms of religious idioms, Sheikh Hamed, one of the tenants, repeatedly recites two Prophet hadiths that stress ownership by use: "He who gave life to land, it is his," and "He who dug a well is entitled to what is around it." When reviewing these two hadiths, I found that they apply to vacant lands. I went back to Sheikh Hamed and asked him about this paradox, since the land under dispute was previously owned by the Walys. According to local history, it was a Waly who first gave life to this land. Sheikh Hamed confidently responded that the fellahin were the ones farming the land, even at times when a Waly was the official landlord, under the Ottoman system of estate administration. Based on the above, if Nasser gave security as a gift to tenants, they, in turn, gave life to land. Hence, the debt involved in the gift exchange is already settled.

Responsible Citizens of the State

The third claim that tenants make rests in the connection between property owning and responsibility. This connection has long dominated discussions about private property rights in liberal political theory, founded in the work of John Locke (Verdery 2003:16). In this discussion, democracy and property are tightly linked—"the property-owning citizen is the responsible subject of a democratic polity" (Verdery 2003:16).

---

9   Y. Fathi, "When the Strangers Came to Town," *al-Ahram Weekly*, April 21–27, 2005, cited in Bush (2009:67).

Responsible Citizens of the State

In her discussion of land titling in developing African states, Sara Berry argues that the registration of title that accompanied land privatization made it easier to hold owners accountable for the consequences of their actions (Berry 2002b:216), and resulted in intensifying land conflicts and the proliferation of claims (p. 218). Such is the case with regard to the way in which tenants build an image of themselves as responsible citizens. They do so by heavily contesting the ownership of the Walys on the grounds of Youssef Waly's irresponsibility and immorality. Their narratives are shaped by an interplay between their local struggle and broader national concerns *(qadaya qawmeya)*. National concerns revolve around the Walys' misuse of political power to undertake agro-investment projects and making secret deals with foreign importers. They frame their claim in a nationalistic rhetoric that positions the fellah as the main caring food producer for the nation, as opposed to Youssef Waly, whose wealth was accumulated by draining the country's resources and poisoning the nation.

Several social idioms are used to describe Waly's irresponsibility and immorality. The tenants argue that hunger is a consequence of Waly's corruption:

> He *[Youssef Waly]* was the only winner, and his siblings, six in total. Before that, 6,000 families were benefiting from this land ... we were eating from the land. Now many have no land to eat from. Al-gou' kafir *[hunger knows no laws]*, there is no occupation for the fellah but his fass.[10]

Here, hunger is central to the concept of *kufr* ('blasphemy'). It connotes a popular usage of the word that is rooted in Qur'anic teachings and folk narratives, and concerns depriving the poor of food and a means of livelihood (Abu Zahra 1987). In this narrative, studies on the impact of the agrarian counter-reform stress that the reference to hunger is literal, rather than metaphorical. These studies show that evicted tenants have changed their dietary habits following the evictions. For example, Reem Saad (2004:6) argues that the change in eating habits that followed the evictions is "really a euphemism for eating less in both quantity and

---

10 Type of heavy hoe or mattock used in Egyptian agriculture (translated by Hinds and Badawy 2004:637).

quality." Evicted tenants started eating twice instead of three times daily, became dependent on government bakeries for bread consumption, and consumed less meat and no eggs or poultry. Furthermore, "sleeping early in order to avoid feeling hungry" is a common strategy used by tenants to cope with the new situation (LCHR 2003:151, quoted in Saad 2004:6). It is in such a context that Hassan uses the Arabic proverb *al-gou' kafir* (hunger knows no laws) to express the idea that starvation leads to blasphemy, and that those who cause starvation and hunger are considered blasphemous.[11]

Another important criticism against Waly concerns the negative impact of his agricultural initiatives on the health of Egyptian citizens in general, and residents of Qarun in particular. It was during Waly's ministry that chemicals, fertilizers, and pesticides came to be intensively used in rural Egypt. In the Qarun region, one factory was established in the early 1990s by Waly's nephew. A widespread 'fact' among farmers is that Waly deliberately targeted this area by establishing the factory, causing the deaths of many residents, particularly children.

> *He opened a factory here in Qarun, and we knew nothing about its side effects, but when we used it, we realized it was destroying everything. It killed the crops, many of our children were diagnosed with cancer, and five died as a result.*

Consequently, *"Dol 'alam kafara"* ('they are blasphemous people') is a common phrase used by returnee tenants to summarize the corruption of Youssef Waly, which stands as *the* reason for grave consequences that extend even to hunger and death.

In contrast to the arguments made by soldier-peasants, these stories illustrate how evicted tenants collectively imagine themselves as

---

[11] Two examples are worth describing. In his book, Kuwaiti writer Saif Marzouk notes that Bedouins described the British army as *kufar* (blasphemous) because before their arrival in 1919, Bedouins would commute from Nagd to Basra in the south of Iraq for work, and in exchange for their labor, they were given dates. After their arrival, British officers blocked the road, and this cut off the Bedouins' livelihoods. Similarly, in the 1977 bread riots in Egypt, protestors broke alcohol bottles and destroyed cabarets and imported clothing shops, because these were illustrations of excessive consumption in times of hunger, even if they were not blasphemy in the strict religious sense (Abu Zahra 1987:10–11).

"citizens despite the state, rather than citizens who are constituted through a positive relationship with the state" (Lazar 2005:225). This idea is reflected in the scholarship on corruption, in which ordinary citizens "attempt to hold politicians to account" when things go wrong (Lazar 2005:224). In a Bolivian neighborhood, citizens make the claim that Bolivia's underdevelopment is only a consequence of the betrayal of its elite leaders (Lazar 2005:225). Furthermore, an account of the country's rich natural resources and a pride in the masses of the people emerge to maintain this argument (Lazar 2005:225).

The content of this claim often takes a broader and more serious dimension that sheds light on the roles of business elites, US imperialism, and Israel in fundamentally reshaping Egypt's agrarian policies in their own favor, while stimulating a profound sense of political defeat. Tenants make the point that Egypt, a country mentioned in the Qur'an for its resources,[12] imports more than 50 percent of its subsistence crops, including wheat, and exports grapes to Israel, the region's biggest enemy. This is echoed in the statement of Hag Hassan:

> *There is no wheat at all grown by Walys or Abazas. They grow grapes and they make them grow big from hormones, and they sell a kilo for 20 pounds. And they export abroad and bring back in dollar currencies, and then they store the money away. Nothing comes back to the country.*

The intimate business relations between Waly and Israeli businesspersons have been extensively covered in *al-Sha'b* newspaper, occupying several of the newspaper's headlines. This coverage coincided with the US preparations to invade Iraq. The issue of Tuesday, January 5, 1999 has a front headline fully dedicated to uncovering the "Waly–Israel network." Backed up with documents, the story illustrates how Waly and his "normalization network" *(shabaket al-tatbee')* cooperated with "Zionist" businessman Assaf Yagouri to block the delivery of 3,606 tons of potato seeds to the Iraqi population. The blockage occurred in the port of Alexandria, as a result of a secret deal between Youssef Waly, Yagouri, and a Jordanian businessperson. The story reports that Yagouri, an ex-Israeli officer once held as a 1973 war prisoner in Egypt, is now collaborating

---

12 Reference here is made to the verses of Yunus and Yusuf in the Holy Qur'an.

with Youssef Waly against Iraqi (Arab) brothers. This particular detail is of high importance in the narration, as it aims at delivering the message that Waly sacrificed the region's resources and dignity for a Zionist who was once left in jail under the mercy of Egypt's military.

Many of the tenants I interviewed recall some version of this story. By remembering such connections, the tenants bring the battlefront to the national front, maximizing citizens' interests in directly holding Waly (and his colleagues) accountable for subjecting the population to hunger, toxins, and humiliation, while profiteering on a massive scale. Their story aims to mobilize social support and solidarity from ordinary citizens who have suffered from the skyrocketing prices of food staples and bread over the years, while mourning the loss of Egyptian dignity.[13] It also feeds into a profound revolutionary sentiment that seeks to create a sense of vindication for having brought a stalwart of the Mubarak regime to account. For these tenants, putting Waly on trial is as important as bringing Mubarak to trial, if not more. That is why Hag Hassan bought brand-new glasses and ordered a chair from the carpenter nearby in order to follow the trials, specifically that of Youssef Waly.

Islah, from Gift to Right

In his work on the social history of almsgiving in Malaysia, James Scott (1985) differentiates between 'gift' and 'right.' Building on the foundational work of Marcel Mauss, Scott argues that whereas a gift results in a deferred recognition of the favor, a right entails an automatic entitlement without claim (Scott 1985:194). However, he observed that neither notion is static. On the one hand, laborers view the *zakat* bonus as a right they have earned by the hard work they did in the harvest season. On the other hand, farmers gave *zakat* as a way to socially obligate the wage laborer to perform efficiently in the next harvesting season. Consequently, when the farmers decreased the amount of *zakat*, the laborers were not pleased, because for them, it had already been transformed into a right.

Similarities can be drawn between the case described by Scott and that of the evicted tenants. Reem Saad argues that in the post-independence rhetoric, tenants' security was perceived by the peasants as

---

13 Describing how the notion of dignity was revived in the revolutionary momentum is beyond the scope of this paper. It is perhaps enough to mention that one of the revolutionary mottos was "Lift your head up, you are an Egyptian."

Nasser's gift to them (Saad 2002:188). Similarly, Henri Ayrout perceived *islah* as the "revolutionary regime's greatest gift to fellahin" (Ayrout 2005:xi). However, when the gift of security was stolen from peasants, their understanding of it had already been expanded to include that of rights. To distill the argument further, the significant point is that the tenants seem to make an ideological separation between the land as an 'entitlement' and security as Nasser's 'gift.' For them, the gift has a historical significance, but no longer entails a deferred favor. Furthermore, even if this were the case, they have already fulfilled its obligations on the basis of their participation in national wars, the labor they have invested in the land, and the fact that they are more responsible than succeeding owners.

Conclusion

Through an engagement with ethnographic modes of investigation, I have used a discussion of a dispute over land to question the popular and media portrayal of Egypt's countryside as "a bulwark, or strategic reserve for the counter-revolution."[14] This conclusion has been reached primarily through an analysis of voting behavior, whereby rural subjects were mobilized to vote for Islamic and sometimes *feloul* (remnants of the old regime) political leaders. One argument made in this paper is that this conclusion reflects an inadequate depiction of the rural positioning in the revolutionary context. Its inadequacy stems from its being based on a rather abstract and highly contested form of democratic practice. By claiming a right to land, tenants by and large engage in revolutionary events, even if this occurs behind the scenes. However, they, too, have internalized the view that the revolution is centralized in Cairo. Hence, they have to navigate in central offices to make sure that their voice is heard. The legal claims they made were addressed to a particular audience that they view as closer to the revolution. These range from centralized state bureaucracy and parliament members to media, human rights activists, and myself.

The uneven spatial depiction of revolutionary events is not novel to the Egyptian context (see, for example, Bayat 1997 on the Iranian revolution). In a special issue of *American Ethnologist*, several

---

14 http://english.ahram.org.eg/NewsContentP/4/61597/Opinion/Cairo-the-city-vanquished-The-Muslim-Brotherhood-a.aspx

anthropologists noted the urban bias of the media in representing the revolutionary events. Lila Abu Lughod wrote about how the village youth mobilized to address local concerns, directing their efforts to address their community needs, while using "the language of social morality, not the media-friendly political language of 'rights' and 'democracy'" (2012:21). The point made by Abu Lughod is that each group relates to and engages with the revolutionary events in ways that seem relevant to them. My own fieldwork confirms this point, but reveals a different reality. When rural dwellers in the Qarun region mobilized to address the fuel, bread, water, and electricity crises, they, too, borrowed from a citizenship repertoire that emphasized the notion of rights and entitlements.

Through a case of a dispute over land, I have shown how rural subjects hold the state accountable for tacitly abandoning their rights in favor of corrupt political elites during the Mubarak era. I have also highlighted a tension between their views of entitlement and that of legal experts, including their closest supporters—human rights lawyers. Despite the fact that lawyers generally support 'breaking the fear barrier' *(kasr hagez al-khawf)* that dominated the January 25 revolutionary rhetoric, they stick to offering economic solutions to the problem, while relying on a legal framework. In so doing, they do not take into consideration the political subjectivities on which farmers build their legal claims. Furthermore, they obscure the dynamism in the historical, political, economic, and social relationships between farmers, land, and the state. In directing the discussion to the legal/economic terrain, lawyers, including those labeled as activists, reduce the land struggle to a secondary status in the revolutionary context. This situation has been typical in the Egyptian revolution, whereby a schism between the 'economic' and the 'political' took place, rendering the former extraneous to the revolutionary process, while undermining the struggle for economic demands as in itself a political action (AbdelRahman 2012:614).

Last, but not least, this chapter aimed to revisit the meaning of reform, a remnant of Nasser's agrarian policies, 50 years after its implementation, 20 years after the abolishing of its key benefits, and in the context of a revolutionary event. In highlighting people's strong yet changing sentiments in relation to land reform, I conclude by arguing that scholars must move beyond contrasting the 'reform' to the 'counter-reform,' and look instead at the possibilities of addressing new fields of inquiry in agrarian transformation that acknowledge the coexistence of different understandings of property relations in Egypt.

References

Abdel Aal, M. 1998. "Farmers and Cooperatives in the Era of Structural Adjustment." In N. Hopkins and K. Westergaard, eds. *Directions of Change in Rural Egypt*, 279–302. Cairo: The American University in Cairo Press.

AbdelRahman, M. 2012. "A Hierarchy of Struggles? The 'Economic' and the 'Political' in Egypt's Revolution," *Review of African Political Economy*, 39(134): 614–628.

Abou el Fadl, R. 2005. "Rethinking the National Projects of Egypt and Turkey." Unpublished MA thesis, Department of Politics, University of Oxford.

Abu Lughod, L. 2012. "Living the 'Revolution' in an Egyptian Village: Moral Action in a National Space," *American Ethnologist*, 39(1): 21–25.

Abu Zahra, N. 1987. "The Images of Hunger and Plenty in Some Arab Countries," *Alif: Journal of Comparative Poetics, No. 7, The Third World: Literature and Consciousness*, 6–22. Cairo: The American University in Cairo Press.

Aretxaga, B. 2000. "A Fictional Reality: Paramilitary Death Squads and the Construction of State Terror in Spain." In J. A. Sluka, ed. *Death Squad: The Anthropology of State Terror*, 46–69. Philadelphia: University of Pennsylvania Press.

Ayeb, H. 2012. "The Marginality of the Small Peasantry: Egypt and Tunisia." In R. Bush and H. Ayeb, eds. *Marginality and Exclusion in Egypt*, 72–96. Cairo: The American University in Cairo Press.

Ayrout, H. 2005 (1945). *The Egyptian Peasant*. Translated and introduced by John Alden Williams. Cairo: The American University in Cairo Press.

Bayat, A. 1997. *Street Politics: Poor People's Movements in Iran*. Cairo: The American University in Cairo Press.

Berry, S. 2002a. "The Everyday Politics of Rent-Seeking: Land Allocation on the Outskirts of Kumase, Ghana." In K. Juul and C. Lund, eds. *Negotiating Property in Africa*, 107–134. Portsmouth: Heinemann.

———. 2002b. "Negotiable Property: Making Claims on Land and History in Asante, 1896–1996." In G. C. Bond and N. C. Gibson, eds. *Contested Terrains and Constructed Categories: Contemporary Africa in Focus*, 213–234. Boulder, CO: Westview.

Bush, R. 2000. "An Agricultural Strategy without Farmers: Egypt's Countryside in the New Millennium," *Review of African Political Economy*, 84: 235–249.

———. 2002. *Counter-Revolution in Egypt's Countryside: Land and Farmers in the Era of Economic Reform*. London: Zed Books.

———. 2009. "The Land and the People." In R. El-Mahdi and P. Marfleet, eds. *Egypt: The Moment of Change*, 51–67. London and New York: Zed Books.

Ghosh, A. 2002. "Categories of Labour and the Orientation of the Fellah Economy." In *The Imam and the Indian: Prose Pieces*, 134–168. New Delhi: Ravi Dayal Publisher.

Gupta, A. 2005. "Narrating the State of Corruption." In D. Haller and C. Shore, eds. *Corruption: Anthropological Perspectives*, 173–194. London and Ann Arbor, MI: Pluto Press.

Hetherington, K. 2009. "Privatizing the Private in Rural Paraguay: Precarious Lots and the Materiality of Rights," *American Ethnologist*, 36(2): 224–241.

Hinds, M., and E. Badawy. 2004. *A Dictionary of Egyptian Arabic*. Librairie du Liban.

Holston, J. 1991. "The Misrule of Law: Land and Usurpation in Brazil," *Comparative Studies in Society and History*, 33(4): 695–725.

Idrus, R. 2010. "From Wards to Citizens: Indigenous Rights and Citizenship in Malaysia," *Political and Legal Anthropology Review*, 33(1): 89–108.

Land Center for Human Rights (LCHR). 2002. "Farmer Struggles against Law 96 of 1992." In Ray Bush, ed. *Counter-Revolution in the Egyptian Countryside*, 126–138. London: Zed Books.

Lazar, S. 2005. "Citizens Despite the State: Everyday Corruption and Local Politics in El Alto, Bolivia." In D. Haller and C. Shore, eds. *Corruption: Anthropological Perspectives*, 212–228. London and Ann Arbor, MI: Pluto Press.

Li, T. 2007. *The Will to Improve: Governmentality, Development, and the Practice of Politics*. Durham, NC: Duke University Press.

References

Mitchell, T. 2002. *Rule of Experts: Egypt, Techno-Politics, and Modernity*. Berkeley: University of California Press.

Moore, S. F. 1998. "Changing African Land Tenure: Reflections on the Incapacities of the State," *European Journal of Development Research*, 10(2): 33–49.

Nuijten, M., and G. Anders. 2007. *Corruption and the Secret of Law: A Legal Anthropological Perspective*. Great Britain by MPG Books Ltd, Bodmin, Cornwall: Ashgate Publishing Limited.

Saad, R. 1988. "Social History of an Agrarian Reform Community in Egypt." *Cairo Papers in Social Science* 29(1).

———. 1999. "State, Landlord, Parliament and Peasant: The Story of the 1992 Tenancy Law," *Proceedings of the British Academy*, 96: 387–404.

———. 2000. "War in the Social Memory of Egyptian Peasants." In S. Heydemann, ed. *War, Institutions and Social Change in the Middle East*, 240-257. Berkeley: University of California Press.

———. 2002. "Egyptian Politics and the Tenancy Law." In R. Bush, ed. *Counter-Revolution in Egypt's Countryside: Law and Framers in the Era of Economic Reform*, 103–125. New York: Zed Books.

———. 2004. "Social and Political Costs of Coping with Poverty in Rural Egypt." Presented at the Fifth Mediterranean Social and Political Research Meeting, Florence and Montecatini Terme 24–28 March 2004, organized by the Mediterranean Program of the Robert Schuman Centre for Advanced Studies at the European University Institute, Florence.

Scott, J. 1985. *Weapons of the Weak: Everyday Forms of Peasant Resistance*. New Haven and London: Yale University Press.

Sieder, R. 2001. "Rethinking Citizenship: Reforming the Law in Postwar Guatemala." In T. B. Hansen and F. Stepputat, eds. *States of Imagination: Ethnographic Explorations of the Postcolonial State*, 202–220. Durham, NC: Duke University Press.

United Nations Development Programme. 2003. *Fayyum Human Development Report*. Cairo: United Nations Development Programme.

Verdery, K. 2003. *The Vanishing Hectare: Property and Value in Postsocialist Transylvania*. Ithaca, NY: Cornell University Press.

CHAPTER 6

Adapting to Change
Tribal Influence on the 2011–2012 Parliamentary Elections in Aswan Governorate[1]

Hans Christian Korsholm Nielsen

Before the Revolution

Parliamentary elections in Egypt during the decades leading up to 2011 were to a large extent characterized not only by fraud, the tampering with ballot boxes, and the intimidation of voters, but also as being part of a system of "electoral authoritarianism" (Lust-Okar 2006; Schwendler and Chormiak 2006; Koehler 2008), where the elections were characterized by clientelism, lack of political content in the candidates' campaigns, and a wish on the part of the voters to support a candidate with the ability to assure that at least some of the spoils he might gain from his seat in parliament were reaching his constituency, or more correctly his supporters.

In Upper Egypt this system has been developed and refined for decades. Important in this system have been tribes, families, and local forms of association based on feelings of belonging *(qawmiya)*, to which the candidates have appealed for votes and support.

The development and continued importance of these groupings and the ensuing complex of local political traditions should to a large extent be understood as the product of the electoral system itself, characterized by a de facto single-party system, the lack of any substantial political debate, and the lack of real legislative power of the elected parliament.

---

[1] This content of this article is part of the outcome of a research project conducted by the Danish Egyptian Dialogue Institute (DEDI; www.dedi.org.eg) and the Al-Ahram Center for Political and Strategic Studies on the 2011/12 parliamentary elections, covering eight constituencies. Results from the project will be published in Nielsen (forthcoming).

In this system, people often fell back on local forms of organization, such as tribal affiliations, to guide their political action. Tribes (*qabila*, pl. *qaba'il*) in the Upper Egyptian context are groups of variable size, but often quite large, which are united by a belief in their descent from a single ancestor; solidarity is expected between those claiming to be of the same tribe (Nielsen 2004).

These local political traditions were challenged by the new electoral law of 2011, the relatively free access to the registration of political parties, the fall of the "old guard" (who ended up as the despised *feloul*), the general feeling of newly gained freedom, the expectation that the parliamentary elections would be free and fair, without fraud, and not least without intimidation of voters, and that a parliament in alignment with the aspirations of the voters could be elected.

In order to evaluate the outcome of the juxtaposition between the new electoral situation and the tradition of elections it is most illustrative to present the campaigning and voting during the elections for the Majlis al-Sha'b in Aswan governorate, and thereby also to give an insight into what was behind the otherwise rather uniform results of the elections at the national level.

The New Constituency Boundaries

A major challenge to the old local system of rallying behind candidates or organizing followers was the dramatic change of the size of the constituency, which was the product of the new election laws, something that occurred not only in this most southern governorate, but in most parts of the country.

Until the elections of 2011/12, elections for the Majlis al-Sha'b in the governorate of Aswan were held in three independent constituencies, one roughly covering the city of Aswan and the town of Daraw, the second the city of Kom Ombo and the area of Nasr al-Nuba, and finally, to the very north, the area covered by Edfu city and district. Following the new electoral law, these constituencies were reduced to one. Where earlier each of the three constituencies elected two members through the system of individual candidates, one *'ummal/fellahin* and one *fi'at*, in 2011/12 the new Aswan constituency would still elect six members for the Majlis al-Sha'b, but four of them were to be elected on party lists and two by elections between individual candidates, still one *'ummal/fellahin*

The New Constituency Boundaries

and one *fi'at*, and with at least 50 percent of the candidates elected on the party lists also being divided between *'ummal/fellahin*. All party lists were to contain at least one female candidate, but there was no requirement that a woman be elected.

The new constituency included the three former constituencies, and since each of these had somewhat more than 250,000 voters, the new large constituency had altogether around 860,000. The area covered by each of the earlier electoral districts extended between 30 and 60 kilometers along the Nile, while the new constituency extended around 120 kilometers, from the governorate of Qena in the north to the High Dam south of the city of Aswan. The governorate and the constituency stretches farther south along the shores of Lake Nasser to the tourist village at Abu Simbel, and thus makes the length of the constituency more than 400 kilometers, but although some candidates chose to visit Abu Simbel on their election tours, gaining support from this sparsely populated area was not seen as crucial by any of the candidates.

The new large constituency and the large number of voters constituted a severe challenge to all candidates, and limited the number who had a real chance of being elected. The size in itself demanded that serious candidates, both those competing in the elections on party lists and those running as individual candidates, possess financial means and a support apparatus of a certain size. The number of votes needed to win had expanded to an extent that a candidate had to secure support from all parts of the constituency/governorate. Candidates and parties with limited means and a limited group of active supporters had, from the very start, close to no chance of success.

Another factor that changed radically with the newly created constituency was the composition of the group of voters the candidates had to cater to. The former constituencies were in no way homogeneous, but the composition of voters was well known to any candidate of stature.

In the tribal northern constituency of Edfu District, a candidate either had to arrange for tribal alliances or rely on local 'nationalism' *(qawmiya)*, like that in the northwestern area of al-Bussayliya, to be successful. In the central district, covering Kom Ombo and the Nubian area of Nasr al-Nuba, tribal influence is limited because of the character of the city of Kom Ombo, which was originally constructed as a town for workers and technical staff at the Kom Ombo Sugar Factory, and has therefore been a city of immigrants from its very beginning. The elections here thus demanded other strategies; at the same time, one also had to take into consideration the (possible) decisive influence of the Nubian voters. Finally there was the constituency covering the city of Daraw, which to a large extent is tribal, and Aswan itself, the main city of the governorate of Aswan. The city not only contains migrants from all of Egypt, the majority of whom have settled in the city after taking jobs with the High Dam or within the (formerly) thriving tourist industry; it also has a large percentage of people working in government institutions, being the seat of the governorate, and of course the city has large and very visible minorities of Copts and Nubians.

Whereas previously a candidate had only to relate to a limited number of these differences and variations, the new electoral system forced the candidates to take into account a much larger degree of variation. At the same time this reduced the power of the politicians of the older generations, whose thinking was bound up with tactics directed toward securing votes from the immediate surroundings where they maintained day-to-day relations.

The change in the size of the constituency, and the presence of new and in many cases 'foreign' candidates, in the sense that they had no previous standing in the local areas, were also issues preoccupying the voters, and to most of them the overwhelming majority of the candidates were unknown. This was the case for both the elections through party lists and the individual elections. At the same time most people were aware that their local candidate, whom they would traditionally support, probably had a very limited chance of getting elected.

The process of enlarging the constituencies was promoted as a means to break the traditional power bases of the NDP, and to strain alliances between the political figures of the old system and what was understood to be conservative families and tribes. At the same time it was also argued that the political programs of parties would have a greater chance of coming to the forefront during the electoral campaigns, when candidates could no longer rely exclusively on local support.

At a first glance one would say that these changes were successful and created the foundation for nationwide support of a few parties—and thus the development of a national consensus—and in fact only a limited number of candidates from the old guard were successful in gaining seats.

Campaigning in 2011 and 2012 in Aswan

Under the heading "The Elections in Numbers," a local newspaper, *Sawt Aswan*, published an article in early June 2011 preparing for the elections in the governorate. That the traditional logic of elections was still prevalent can be seen from the following section on the District of Daraw, which was previously part of the constituency of Aswan city.[1]

> *The true number [of votes] in the district of Daraw is 59,690. The Ja'afra represents 60 percent of the votes in the District of Daraw, which altogether gives 35,763 votes, and the 'Ababda represents 15 percent, which altogether represents 8,982 votes. The Ansar and the Harbiab in Daraw represent 10 percent, which altogether gives 5,988 votes.* (*Sawt Aswan*, No. 1432, June 2011:10)

And so tribes continued to be of importance, but at the same time the new parties were entering the stage, as many as 50 being registered before the elections were finally up and running. These covered nearly the entire political spectrum, but only a limited number (16) ended up taking part in the elections in Aswan.

The contrasts between three major parties, the Salafi Hizb al-Noor, the Freedom and Justice Party of the Muslim Brotherhood, and the 'liberal' Wafd, are illustrative. Among the parties which were very quick to organize was the Hizb al-Noor. Its campaigns were focused on meeting people in the villages and the neighborhoods of the towns, using mosques for spreading its message, and having smaller political meetings. In addition to this, larger rallies were arranged where leading party members from Cairo spoke in support of local candidates.

As a part of a tour arranged by the party, where the leaders visited different constituencies and met with candidates, a meeting was held in the village area of al-Kelh (al-Kelh covers a cluster of villages and the meeting referred to was held in Kelh al-Gabel). The majority of the people of this village area work either in agriculture or at a local

---

[1] The Daraw District was still expected to be part of the Aswan constituency at the time the article was published, and the author also argued that due to the large number of voters in the District of Edfu (231,741 according to the article), this district/constituency should be divided into two in the coming elections.

industrial complex that combines a sugar factory with the production of pulp for paper. This is a large complex that is one of the main industrial complexes in the District of Edfu, together with the more northern phosphate factory and the ferrosilicon factory located to the east of the Nile. The population of the area is said to belong to the "four tribes of Kelh," smaller tribes that include the inhabitants of both parts of Kelh, on the western and eastern sides of the Nile.

The meeting was inaugurated with a Qur'an recitation, after which the visiting shaykhs and the local candidates gave presentations; of the latter, it was the leading candidate on the party list who made the most substantial presentation, while the other candidates were simply introduced to the public. As the evening went on it became clear that there were two subjects on which the speakers would focus.

First of all the speakers spent much time explaining the role of tribes and tribalism and how it led to discord between citizens and believers. This was something that should be fought. Not only were tribal loyalties and the notion of tribes in general criticized as being un-Islamic; special attention was given to the feuds that these tribes sustain, feuds that may haunt village life and ruin the lives and well-being of families. These remarks, and the detailed references to the feud as a problem of tribes and of the villages in Upper Egypt, were listened to very intensely by the inhabitants of al-Kelh, and many of the visitors from outside were looking at each other, some trying to hide a smile: the area of al-Kelh, not least the village of Kelh al-Gabel, is notorious for feuds running between families for decades. In all of Aswan and the southern parts of Qena Governorate, to be a Kelhi is synonymous with being stubborn, hot-headed, and constantly fighting with one's neighbors. But the feuds in the villages are real, and although many attempts to settle them have been made by local arbitrators, who arranged the traditional Upper Egyptian mediation councils, the *magalis al-sulh* (see Nielsen 2003; 2006), this has most often been in vain. The mentioning of a sensitive local issue—the right-to-the-point approach that the visiting leaders of the Hizb al-Noor took to the problem—was seen as courageous and appreciated by the audience. The idea of combining a confrontation with the tribes and a real but sensitive local problem received applause. The goal of the Noor Party—to denigrate tribes and tribalism—was not just caused by their wish to emphasize the apparent contradiction between tribalism and the form of Islam they advocated. It was also important because their supporters, who came from a large and diversified area, had loyalties to numerous different tribes, which other candidates and also heads of families were expected to try to activate on election day. Therefore, in order to create a corps of supporters and voters, the Noor had a profound interest in reducing the influence of the tribes in the election and instead encouraging loyalty to the idea of the party and religion. This attack on the tribes was also an attack on the old guard who for decades had based their campaigns and power on them.

The other subject that took up time during the meeting—and here it was mainly the local candidates who did the talking—was "the liberals." The liberals, whom the Noor presented as the main political enemy, were described not by their economic policies—which were never brought up—but by their moral deficiencies. Topics were presented and the audience was rhetorically asked whether this was the condition they envisioned for a future al-Kelh or for their children and women. The liberals were described as being basically Western and wanting to impose a Western culture on the people of Egypt, and not least the people of al-Kelh. The Western culture, according to this exposition, contained little but same-sex marriages—"A world like in Britain where men marry men and women women. Do you find this to be a natural thing? Is this what you want in Kelh?"—or adherence to the theories of Darwin: "They think we originate from fish! Here we eat them!" Older villagers were shaking their heads, clearly indicating that the ideas of these liberals (including, it was pointed out, al-Wafd) were not just immoral and against religion, they were outright ridiculous.

Large rallies with dignitaries from Cairo or leading members of the political parties were also arranged by some of the other "big" parties, for instance, the Freedom and Justice Party and al-Wafd Party.

As the elections were approaching the FJP arranged a large meeting in the central square of the city of Edfu, and so did al-Wafd, which pitched a large tent in one of the main streets of Edfu city in order to accommodate the meeting.

The FJP meeting was visited by national leaders from the party, who made their presentations. Qur'an recitation was also featured, and the many people attending were served tea: the large tent that had been raised was incense-scented, and many of the ingredients of a *mulid* were present. The tea-serving and the caretaking of the hundreds of guests were left to a group of young men representing the Brotherhood, all wearing a green scarf across their chests. The main topic reflected the political development in the country at the time of the meeting: the first round of elections had been finalized and the FJP had experienced the first in a series of overwhelming victories. Therefore the most significant topic was a pledge to the idea of parliamentary democracy, and the importance of insuring that the Supreme Council of the Armed Forces (SCAF) would hand over power to the newly elected parliament as quickly as possible, so that a new government could take power, and not least be in charge of drafting a new constitution, without the interference of a "consultative council" appointed by SCAF. The speakers insisted on the necessity of having a parliament and a government supported by the people, in order to be able to initiate the rapid change Egypt so badly needed.

The meeting was well attended, but did not have the intensity of the meeting of al-Noor, which had not just chosen to arrange the event in the rural areas but had also chosen not to discuss general conditions, addressing instead the central problems in the village area hosting the event.

Al-Wafd was the last of the larger parties to hold a public event with any significance on a larger (district) level. This was held on Sunday December 18—the last day the parties were allowed to arrange rallies and other public meetings. Like most of the other parties, al-Wafd had held numerous smaller gatherings in the guesthouses of the different tribes, leading up to this meeting. At the very start of the party's electoral campaign, a meeting was arranged by the main candidate (number one on the party list for the constituency of Aswan) to introduce him and the others on the list, and the political platform of the local branch of the party. The candidate was a lawyer from Edfu city, the leader of al-Wafd, and from a family that had earlier been engaged in elections, as his uncle was an independent candidate in the parliamentary elections of 1995. He was from one of the three tribes dominating the city of Edfu, the al-Marari.

The initial meeting was arranged in the guest house *(bayt)* of al-Marari. The meeting was well attended, but it was clear to all that the majority of those participating were people of al-Marari. Family, colleagues, and friends rose during the meeting to say a few words in praise of the candidate or just to wish him and his campaign good luck. The candidate himself presented his program and some of the history of al-Wafd, depicting the party as the only survivor from the long-gone era of liberal democracy in Egypt, a party that carried a legacy and experience, which would be of great importance for a new parliament. He emphasized that this parliament would be the one to draft a new constitution, and therefore experience was of great importance, especially since many of the candidates and most of the parties participating were without any experience in politics.

The candidate also presented his own program as a list of issues he would fight for if elected to parliament. These were mainly projects to be carried out in the city of Edfu; a few included other parts of the Governorate of Aswan; and even fewer took national concerns into account. It was suggested that a specific area behind a school in Edfu should become a sports field, and that a five-star hotel should be erected on a specific location on the Nile across from Edfu city, which would upgrade the standard of the tourism industry in the district and make it competitive with Luxor and Aswan. He added that new agricultural land should be developed on the west bank of the Nile between Edfu and Aswan, and that the sugar factories in Kom Ombo and Edfu, to which all sugarcane growers of the governorate are connected, should pay a higher price for the sugar cane—here the legacy of al-Wafd as the party of the farmers was stressed. This was applauded by many of the participants. The agricultural area of Edfu is historically one of the large producers of sugar cane, where many farmers depend on cane for cash income. Other suggestions or demands were that a branch of the University of Aswan/Janub al-Wadi should be opened in Edfu, to offer higher education in the area and thereby keep the young people in the city, and also that low-cost housing, especially for the young people, should be built on specific pieces of government land. After the list of projects the candidate would secure for the region, the other candidates of al-Wafd were presented: these were representatives of some of the major groups of the governorate/constituency, including the female candidate, a Nubian. The third candidate was presented not only by his name and place of residence but as a representative of the tribe of al-Ja'afra.

After this, the campaign started in earnest. Besides reminding the public of his candidacy through the use of banners and posters, the candidate visited most of the constituency; still, a major part of his campaign was focused on his home area: the city and district of Edfu.

Just before the elections al-Wafd arranged the large rally previously mentioned, where al-Sayyid al-Badawi from the national leadership in Cairo was present. This in itself attracted many people, but because the meeting was held in one of the main thoroughfares of the center of the city of Edfu, it also attracted many who were just curious about what was going on. The area with the stage was framed by a wall of colorful tent cloth that took up so much space that it nearly caused the traffic in the city to stop. The place selected was in the southern part of the city where the vast majority of those related to al-Marari live: setting up the tent and stage in another, less congested part of the city was unthinkable. Tea and fruit were offered, while again the main candidate presented some of the projects he would start if elected. The other candidates on the party list were also introduced. One by one they entered the stage, and as they entered they were again presented as being Nubian and Ja'fari. While the Noor party was trying to eradicate differences between people by denouncing the tribes (and ethnic groups), the candidate from al-Wafd tried to benefit from involving as many as possible on the list: when all were on stage the "team" held hands in order to express the unity of the group and the unity of the members of the party. Knowing that it was most unlikely that more than one of the candidates would be elected to parliament, this was of course also a way of assuring those spectators who were from the groups represented that the successful candidate would look after the needs of the other groups also, when—or if—elected to parliament.

The visiting leader, al-Sayyid al-Badawi, had been asked to present the political program of al-Wafd as part of his speech: this ended up as a presentation of around ten of the main points found in the program of al-Wafd. This took time, and caused many of the spectators to start chatting with their friends and neighbors attending the event, while others started leaving; the noise and the drifting of people caused the speaker to stop and apologize, saying that he had promised to make sure that the people were aware of what was in the program of al-Wafd and that he would finish shortly, he only had three more points![2]

---

2   See Shehata (2008) for similar descriptions from the 2005 elections in a constituency in Cairo.

While local issues—the promise of projects and changes in the local area—were issues that those attending the meeting that evening could relate to, the more general political ideas of a party, its general demands and its reflections on the importance of a liberal economy for the revitalization of the economy of Egypt, were clearly of lesser interest.

These larger meetings of the parties had large audiences. People came to share in the spectacle and listen to the candidates and the visitors from outside, but even more people were there to enjoy the rallies and parades of cars with photos of the candidates, loud music, and loud voices from the megaphones announcing the names, political affiliations, and symbols of the candidates. The candidates were not being visited by people—they were themselves coming to the voters! Especially in the last few days before the election, the streets of all the cities and provincial towns and the main roads connecting villages in the governorate of Aswan were filled with cars carrying posters and loudspeakers. The last night of campaigning was used to the very end to persuade voters to choose the right candidate.

Individual Candidates' Campaigns

In Aswan, two seats were designated for individual candidates. Individual candidates had in most cases fewer opportunities to arrange for large meetings, but many used the parades—the cars with posters and large loudspeakers—to get to the voters. And all took tours to meet with local groups in their *khema*s (guest houses), trying to persuade the voters that they would be their best representative in the new parliament. The individual candidates who were connected to the larger parties, but who were not running on the party lists, were on the other hand benefiting from the large meetings, being part of panels and being presented as the candidates from the lists at the larger meetings.

A special feature of Egyptian elections is that a number of candidates carry nicknames, which are registered on the official lists of candidates and used on the candidates' posters and banners. These are the names by which the candidates are known among the voters, and they are at the same time used by the candidates to evoke a feeling of belonging to the constituency and closeness to the voters—a son of the people.

Out of the 108 individual candidates and the 64 candidates running on party lists in Aswan Governorate, the names "Kagugi," "Muhammad al-'Umda," and "Klinton" stand out. These three candidates were among the more powerful, all having been in politics for a long time and all having previously been members of parliament.

The candidate called "Kagugi" (Abd al-Mon'em Muhammad Salah) is a contractor from the village of Kagug who allegedly became rich from working in Kuwait. His financial position made it possible for him to support many of the voters in the district and he was especially generous when it came to providing mosques with equipment. Kagugi was an earlier member of parliament for the National Democratic Party (NDP), and although he was therefore accused of being one of the *feloul*, he was still expected to appeal to the older voters. The young, on the other hand, especially the young Islamists connected to al-Noor, ran campaigns against him, as they did against other former NDP members, sometimes spray-painting on walls or hanging up posters with the word "*feloul*" or circulating lists with names of *feloul* candidates on the Internet or Facebook.

Kagugi ran as an individual candidate and also independent of the parties. He chose to start his campaign early, and thanks to his financial resources, his posters could be found from the most northern part of the constituency to the most southern: people had been hired to plaster buildings with his election posters and hang banners from trees and lampposts. Besides that, he was generously handing out gifts; most remarkably, he seemed ready to supply all mosques in the area with air conditioners.

Kagugi had his strong area to the north of Kom Ombo, around his home village. He also belongs to the powerful tribe of al-Ja'afra, from which he hoped to gain his main support. Earlier it had been the Ja'afra of the Kom Ombo constituency who supported him, and although he had to fight strong and more conventional representatives of the tribe (in this area especially from the village of Silwa), he had succeeded. Now he saw that he should build up a base involving Ja'fari votes from the entire governorate, not least the Edfu district, which has a large number of representatives from that tribe. But this was to no avail, as he did not get to the second round of the individual elections. He managed to receive approximately 36,000 votes, which was 5,000 less than what was received by the candidate who entered the second round with the fewest votes.

"Klinton" (Muhammad Abd al-Radi Hamid) had also been a member of parliament for the NDP, as he won a seat during the elections held in November 2010. Although he was not running as an individual but on the list of al-Muhafizeen (the Conservatives), one of the parties created by former members of the outlawed NDP, the list of the al-Muhafizeen was only competing in the elections in Aswan constituency because Klinton expected that it would be an advantage to run on a party list instead of running as an individual candidate.

Klinton is from the northern part of the electoral district of Aswan, from the village area of al-Bussayliya, which had earlier been able to secure itself seats in parliament. This is one of the few areas of the northern part of the constituency where the tribal influence on elections is not dominating, that is, the larger tribes do not have a dominant presence in this specific area. Instead a very strong feeling of local solidarity, presented as 'nationalism,' has developed among the 14 villages of al-Bussayliya. This feeling of solidarity is often seen as similar to the one found within the tribes. Therefore people may also speak of "the tribe of al-Bussayliya," although the solidarity is based on a feeling of belonging to an area rather than on common ancestry. This local solidarity was expected to secure him and al-Muhafizeen the votes needed for a seat in parliament.

Klinton's strategy was based on the calculation that, as he would have to face very strong individual candidates, who could take votes from the entire constituency, he for his part would be able to take nearly all votes in his home area, but not much more. Therefore, although his chances as an individual candidate were limited, if he ran "as a party" he could hope that the other candidates on the list of the Conservatives would be able to attract votes from other areas of the constituency. At the same time, he did not expect any of the other parties to be able to get many votes, except for the Freedom and Justice Party. Therefore the election campaign by the Conservatives was run more or less as if it were the campaign of an individual candidate: posters depicting Klinton were numerous while those of the party were rare. The Muhafizeen was in many ways not a party that ran for elections, but a list through which this former member of parliament expected to be elected and one where some were in doubt whether any of the candidates on the list were aware of what the official party program actually contained!

In contrast, there was the candidacy of "Muhammad al-'Umda" (Muhammad Mahmud Ali Hamid), who, although also a former member of parliament, had been elected as an independent in 2005 and later joined al-Wafd. He lost, to what many saw as an insignificant NDP candidate—a Nubian belonging to the military in the 2010 elections, which was cited as another example of the fraud that occurred during those elections.

During the 2011/12 elections he ran as an individual candidate, independent of the parties. His area was primarily in and around the city of Kom Ombo, very much in what was earlier the constituency Aswan 2, covering Kom Ombo and the Nubian settlements around Nasr al-Nuba. Being young, he often emphasized his rebellious nature and involvement in the demonstrations in Midan Tahrir in Cairo, something that was noted by the younger voters. Al-'Umda was also notorious for his fight for the right—and religious duty—to circumcise girls (in 2008), and for his struggle against foreign (American) influence in Egypt, which he saw creeping in through the NGOs that were allowed to operate in the country (2009). These struggles were fought when he was a member of parliament for al-Wafd (2005–2010).

Although he was a member of the executive committee of al-Wafd, al-'Umda chose to resign from the party as late as October 2011, because the party chose the head of al-Wafd Party in Aswan Governorate (who resides in Edfu City) to be the number one candidate on their list (see below).

The campaigns of the more ordinary and less spectacular candidates, people who had positions as informal community leaders in a neighborhood or in a village area and who had money enough to try their luck in the elections, were run on a smaller scale. Because of the large number of candidates and the size of the constituency, some candidates were rather important as local figures, but seen from outside it was obvious that they had no chance of getting elected. Some still ran efficient campaigns, engaging family, friends, and tribal segments or their neighborhood in the campaigns. From one of these it became clear that they had adopted campaign tactics much in line with what has been described from the elections of 1995, tactics that all candidates used, even al-Noor. For instance, lists were made of guesthouses of the different sections of the tribes, most detailed of course in the candidate's own vicinity, and these were then visited on the campaign tours.

In the hectic days leading up to the elections, young people with computer skills were in demand. They helped out with the computerized lists of voters that were offered by the election committee to all candidates. One young man explained that he had been invited to come and help because of his skills with computers, and he liked the candidate, whom he had known for a long time, but he would not vote for him and he would certainly not have wanted people to find out that he was offering the candidate help—not because of differences in political stands, but because the young man's father was from the 'Ababda tribe and his mother from the al-Marari, while the candidate was from al-Haraiza: he would be seen as a renegade if it were found out that he worked for him and not for a candidate representing his own tribe.

The Election Day

After the conclusion of the first round of elections and the announcement of the sweeping victories of the lists of the Islamic parties, the FJP and Noor, many smaller, especially liberal, parties were more or less forced to surrender to the tsunami of support for those with an Islamic agenda.

The reasons for the success of the Islamic parties are manifold: they are well organized, they are financially well equipped to run elections, and their established presence in the local communities, where they are known for their charity work, are essential. In addition their approach to the world, their insistence on the importance of religion in the everyday life of the ordinary citizen, is in accordance with the beliefs of an overwhelming majority of the Egyptian public. Their actual politics on issues such as economic development, international relations, or the distribution of wealth within the country were of lesser importance, and their (possible) visions or policies on these issues are often shared with a host of other parties.

Besides appealing to a large majority of the ordinary citizens in both rural and urban areas, to many people the Muslim Brotherhood and their party, the FJP, represented an appropriate mix of opposition to the old regime and respect for tradition, of change and continuity, having credentials as an opposition force in relation to the old regime without taking the radical stands of the new revolutionaries. They came to represent a middle-ground position: when it comes to religion, staying free of the extreme views and proclamations of the radical Salafis, and when it comes to cultural change, staying free of the more "radical" demands of the liberal youth.

The results of the elections in Aswan Governorate were a clear victory for the two Islamist parties. Not only did they win three out of the four seats available (the third going to al-Kutla al-Masriya, the "Egyptian Bloc"), they did it with a sweeping majority: the Freedom and Justice Party won two seats with 148,000 votes, the Noor Party two more seats with 104,000 votes, while the seat won by the Egyptian Bloc was obtained with only 40,000 votes. It was only because of an electoral system generous to smaller parties that they succeeded in winning a seat.

The elections were characterized by a relatively high participation rate (54 percent), in stark contrast to previous elections, where participation was continuously falling. The new elections were also marked by enthusiasm and trust in the fairness of the final outcome. The two days of elections were in many ways festive and inclusive, and results were awaited with anxiety.[3]

Individual Candidates' Results

The elections of the individual candidates were followed with great anxiety, not least by the nearly 110 candidates fighting over the two seats available in Aswan constituency. No one had a simple majority, so a runoff was needed between the top two.

Again the FJP and Noor parties were successful: FJP got one individual candidate into the runoffs in each category (*'ummal/fellahin* and *fi'at*), while al-Noor got one candidate, more or less unknown to voters, into the runoffs, as *'ummal/fellahin*. His success was generally ascribed to his party affiliation alone: his candidacy had otherwise hardly been noticed by any of the voters. The last of the individual candidates entering the runoffs was the independent *(mustaqil)* candidate Muhammad

---

3 As Ahmed shows, this optimism evaporated very quickly as the discrepancy between the expected outcome of electing candidates through free elections and the real politics of the winning Freedom and Justice Party became clear. "The fetishized ballot box glosses over the pledges they made to their constituents to address, for instance, deep socioeconomic inequalities" (Ahmed 2013). The "fetishization of the ballot box" is here seen as a strategy of the regime to insist on its legitimacy, not least during the last days of Muhammad Morsi's presidency and when his supporters demanded his return after July 3, 2013.

al-'Umda, who had earlier held one of the seats of the Kom Ombo constituency for the Wafd party, but who had lost in the fraud-ridden elections of 2010. He chose not to run for the party because the position as number one on its list had been given to a more senior member and head of the party from the former constituency of Edfu district. The results of the first round of the elections were therefore in line with the national results: FJP and al-Noor won, with al-Kutla al-Masriya a somewhat distant third, only a few thousand votes ahead of the Wafd. When the above results were unofficially announced there were rumors that the elections might be declared null and void, because of the appearance of the "Free Egyptians" party (al-Masriyin al-Ahrar) on the ballot. (The party did not run in Aswan; in other constituencies the party was part of the Egyptian Bloc, but in Aswan the Egyptian Bloc was only represented by candidates from al-Tagammu' and the Social Democrats.) The ballot should rightly have mentioned the al-Ahrar (Liberals) party.

The main candidate of al-Ahrar, Ruby Gomaa, immediately filed a court case asking to have the election declared invalid. The court agreed, and the verdict was accepted by the Central Election Committee; new runoff elections were then scheduled for January 12, 2012. The Free Egyptians had originally received approximately 2,000 votes out of the 860,000 available. Therefore the error cannot be said to have had a significant influence on the actual outcome of the elections. One could of course speculate that tens of thousands of voters had been looking in vain for the name of the Liberals on the voting list, but this is not very likely.

The results of these first elections, although invalid, may be viewed as quite a good picture of the sentiments of the voters in December 2011. The main results were as mentioned above; al-Wafd was followed by a host of parties that got around 10,000 votes, among these "The Revolution Continues," and then by a group of smaller ones, such as the Free Egyptians, which each received around 2,000 votes.

The runoffs for the individual elections were the place where one could immediately observe the underlying influence of local conditions on the election results, and where ideas about a national ideological or political consensus were of minor importance.

In the Aswan Governorate the independent candidate *(fi'at)*, Muhammad al-'Umda, the former member of al-Wafd, was elected with as many as 160,000 votes against the individual candidate from the FJP, who received around 104,000 votes. His victory was due mainly to his charismatic personality and his unbridled populism:[4] he contacted the leaders of the Christians of Aswan city in order to secure the votes of that community (around a tenth of the votes), and at the same time he struck a deal of mutual support with the individual candidate of Hizb al-Noor *('ummal/fellahin)*, a member of al-Gama'a al-Islamiya who was also running against a candidate from the FJP. The Hizb al-Noor candidate succeeded in gaining 148,000 votes, while his opponent from FJP got around 103,000.

What was most interesting in connection with the local perspective was that the candidate of Hizb al-Noor got into the runoffs mainly with the support of "Noor votes," as he was more or less unknown before the elections, but when the number of candidates was reduced from nearly 110 to two times two, he became a person with a character and the tribal card became central. While the independent candidate, being from the city of Kom Ombo, had no tribal backup to draw upon, the Noor candidate originated from the 'Ababda tribe. As has been mentioned, a central part of the campaign of Hizb al-Noor had focused on denigrating tribalism and all its ways, but this was soon forgotten: "They came from the mountains and the desert to vote for him," a young man said about the support of the 'Ababda for the Noor candidate, referring to the fact that the tribe stems from the Eastern Desert of the southern parts of Egypt. Although the overwhelming majority settled in the Nile Valley more than a century ago, they are still Bedouins and camel herders in popular belief.

---

4   Since the election, Muhammad al-'Umda has moved from being an outspoken but more or less unknown member of parliament from a provincial town in Upper Egypt to one of national fame, partly because he hosted his own television program, "Duwar al-'Umda," on the Muslim Brotherhood channel Misr 25. Through this he became notorious for his style, and not least for a program where he shouted aggressively at— even cursed—the program "al-Barnamig" hosted by the popular Bassim Yusuf, for the way the program (and Yusuf) made fun of president Morsi (May 2013). Among many things he declared that "al-Barnamig" will cause civil war in Egypt, and later he announced that he was able to prove that the program spread homosexuality. After entering parliament in 2012 he remained independent, and although supporting the policies of the Freedom and Justice Party, he also took individual stands such as fighting against women's right to divorce through the so-called *khul'* clause in Islamic law. He became deputy chairman of the parliament's Constitutional and Legislative Affairs Council (being a lawyer by training). All members of this parliament were dismissed in June 2012.

'Ababda support was seen as central to the clear victory of the candidate, and of course this was also seen as having rubbed off on the independent candidate with whom he had struck the deal. The two candidates of FJP both lost, although the party had won a sweeping victory in the party list elections; they could not hold on to the supporters of the party once local political traditions entered the game, and this was so even though they also could rely on tribal support, as they were both from the often politically dominant tribe of Ja'afra.

The power of the local political culture also became visible when the invalidated elections were repeated in January 2012. Here the final result was that four parties—FJP, al-Noor, al-Wafd, and al-Kutla—each won a seat in parliament. In other words, the cancellation of the results of the initial elections on party lists in December 2011 caused the party of the Muslim Brothers to lose a seat to al-Wafd.

The largest difference between the two runoffs was a lack of intensity in the campaigning during the January repeat, so that the number of people turning out to vote was much lower. Whereas 54 percent voted during the initial elections, only around 25 percent chose to come out to vote during the new elections.

The reduction of votes, along with the reductions of candidates in the individual elections, made it possible for candidates to bluntly revert to the old tactics of elections. This was of particular importance for the success of the candidate who happened to be first on the list of al-Wafd.

Expecting that the number of votes needed to secure a seat in the elections would be much lower than during the first, the candidate—Muhammad al-Magheni—focused his new election campaign on a very limited area, primarily the city of Edfu. He knew that if he emphasized local pride and the feeling of the importance of securing at least one member of parliament to represent the city of Edfu,[5] he could limit his campaign visits to other areas of the governorate, especially if he was also successful in striking a deal with the three dominant tribes of the city, the Marari (from which the candidate originated), the Manaqra, and the Haraiza. It is a rule of thumb in Edfu that each of the three

---

5   Of the other candidates expected to be successful and those who had succeeded in the individual elections, none represented Edfu city: this was to be the Wafd candidate's central argument for the tribes of the city to unite politically.

tribes controls around 10,000 votes, and the support of each of them could therefore be decisive. The fact that the three other candidates on the list and the reputation of the Wafd party in general would secure him votes from other parts of the governorate and from other groups was of lesser importance in this connection.

As one of the few parties still in the running, the Wafd, and especially their leading candidate, ran an intense campaign during the days up to the second election, focusing on Edfu city and trying to mobilize the votes of the three main tribes. The other parties and candidates were less active, as most expected the results of the rerun to be a repetition of the results of the first elections.

In the end the tactics of the main candidate of al-Wafd succeeded. With 18,600 votes the party secured a seat in the Majlis al-Sha'b, winning around 1,500 votes more than al-Kutla, which won the last of the four seats available.

While central elements of the election traditions dominant during earlier times, such as local 'nationalism' *(qawmiya)*, tribalism, and ethnicity, appeared on the surface to have been sidelined by national political and religious trends during the 2011/12 parliamentary elections, these same factors stand out as decisive in the two cases described above: the runoffs in the individual elections and the repeat elections following the invalidation of the December elections. Here the electoral tradition developed over decades of authoritarian rule, where the central point was not a focus on selecting candidates who would work for the creation of new national legislation, but candidates with close relations to clients of the constituencies who were ready to serve by diverting the spoils to their supporters, once again became important.

In the early hours of the morning following the second day of the new elections, the sounds of firecrackers and pistol shots rang through the air of the central parts of Edfu city. The Wafd candidate had received the results, and was celebrating the fact that his stamina and his insistence on continuing to fight for the seat had been successful. A large crowd of people wanting to celebrate the victory of the candidate of the city of Edfu congregated, while the results of the elections for Aswan were discussed: the FJP had lost one seat compared to the first elections held in December so that now FJP, al-Noor, al-Wafd, and al-Kutla al-Masriya had each won a seat in parliament based on party lists, and al-Noor and an independent candidate were the individual representatives of the constituency.

While the people were congregating, gifts from the other successful candidates arrived in the alley, where a tent had been erected in front of the *khema* of al-Marari and where the successful candidate greeted and embraced supporters and guests. Each of the other successful candidates had sent a bull, and while the steaming blood from the slaughter of the first bull was seeping into the ground in front of the building, the four others were waiting to be slaughtered and served to the growing crowd of well-wishers.

References

Ahmed, Yasmine Moataz. 2013. "Rural Egypt and Electoral 'Counting.'" *Middle East Institute*, September 19. http://www.mei.edu/content/rural-egypt-and-electoral-%E2%80%9Ccounting%E2%80%9D

Danish Egyptian Dialogue Institute (DEDI). 2012. Reports on the research project of which this article is a part, covering the history of elections in the constituencies, the elections for the Majlis al-Sha'b, and the elections for the Majlis al-Shura, by Abd al-Rahman Muhammad Abd al-Rahman, Hamza Mahmud Husayn, Hana' Ahmad Husayn Ahmad, Muhammad Shehata Yusuf Ali, Nadia Ahmad al-Tayib, Nagwa Muhammad, and Ziyad Akl.

Koehler, Kevin. 2008. "Authoritarian Elections in Egypt: Formal Institutions and Informal Mechanisms of Rule," *Democratization*, 15(5) December: 974–990.

Lust-Okar, Ellen. 2006. "Elections under Authoritarianism: Preliminary Lessons from Jordan," *Democratization*, 13(3) June: 456–471.

Nielsen, Hans Chr. Korsholm. 2003. "Tribes and Tribalism in Edfu, Upper Egypt." In Nicholas S. Hopkins, ed. *Upper Egypt: Life along the Nile*, 73–84. Aarhus: Moesgård.

———. 2004. "Tribal Identity and Politics in Aswan Governorate." In Nicholas S. Hopkins and Reem Saad, eds. *Identity and Change in Upper Egypt*, 213–232. Cairo: American University in Cairo Press.

———. 2006. "State and Customary Law in Upper Egypt," *Islamic Law and Society Review*, 13(1): 123–151.

———. Forthcoming. "Transition through Elections? Parliamentary Elections and the Persistence of Local Political Cultures in Egypt."

Schwendler, Jillian, and Laryssa Chormiak. 2006. "And the Winner Is ...: Authoritarian Elections in the Arab World," *Middle East Report, Year of Elections: Facts and Fictions*, 238 Spring: 12–19.

Shehata, Samer. 2008. "Inside an Egyptian Parliamentary Campaign." In Ellen Lust-Okar and Saloua Zerhouni, eds. *Political Participation in the Middle East*, 95–120. London: Lynne Rienner Publishers.

CHAPTER 7

International Tourism in Post-revolution Egypt
Value Conflict and Economic Pragmatism

Sandrine Gamblin

A Strategic Sector in Crisis

The January 25 Revolution offered to the world a very different picture of Egypt, far from the usual idyllic travel postcards which glorify its unique ancient sites, its sand beaches, and its romantic deserts. More than that, it dramatically affected a strategic sector of its national economy: tourism. On the eve of the uprising, in 2010, 14.7 million foreigners visited the country and generated 12.5 billion dollars of revenue. In 2011, the number of visitors to Egypt dropped to 9.8 million—of which 7 million were European nationals, who generated 8.8 billion dollars of revenue. The hotel occupancy rate decreased in 2011 by 30 to 40 percent at the national level, and by 80 to 90 percent in cultural tourism sites located in the Nile Valley, such as Luxor and Aswan. Political instability and violence scared away European visitors, who, generally speaking, represent three-quarters of international arrivals in Egypt.[1]

In 2012, the number of tourists increased slightly to reach 10 million, generating 9.4 billion dollars, while the first half of 2013 allowed for some optimism, with an increase of 10 percent and 5.7 million visitors. However, massive demonstrations and violence in summer 2013 abruptly halted the tourism sector revival: on June 30, millions

---

[1] All figures are taken from official declarations, referring to the Ministry of Tourism or the Central Bank of Egypt reports. As a matter of fact, tourism figures are controversial: for the year 2011, for instance, a half million Libyan nationals were registered as 'visitors,' while they were mainly escaping from the Libyan conflict. http://english.ahram.org.eg/NewsContent/3/12/31898/Business/Economy/Egypt-tourist-sector-doubts-govt-figures-on-visito.aspx

of Egyptians took to the streets after the Tamarod movement's call for early presidential elections. On July 3, the army intervened to support the popular movement, deposed and arrested the Muslim Brother president Muhammad Morsi, who had been elected a year before, and formed a transitional government, under the presidency of a high-ranking judge, Adly Mansour. Morsi's supporters then took to the streets and occupied squares in many cities until mid August 2013; the most emblematic of these was Rab'a Square in Cairo, where the army dispersed the movement in bloodshed. Hundreds of Morsi's supporters were killed and arrested; a state of emergency and a curfew were imposed.[2] To this dramatic picture must be added attacks against Copts,[3] bomb attacks in Sinai against the Egyptian army and police, and anti-Western propaganda from the regime and the national media. The violence that spread over the country definitely ruined Egypt's hospitality reputation. International travel agencies canceled trips to Egypt for the winter high season; low-cost airlines suspended for the first time their flights to South Sinai and the Red Sea resorts, while European governments such as Russia and Germany, top ranked in visitors to the country,[4] banned their nationals from traveling to Egypt.

Tourism has been a crucial and strategic sector for the Egyptian economy: at the national level, tourism activities in 2010 accounted for 11.3 percent of its GDP and 12.6 percent of the active population (direct and indirect jobs), while tourism revenue contributed 19 percent of the national hard-currency reserve. Tourism revenue has indeed been a strategic asset to finance the import bills, ranking fourth in the balance of payments, after revenue generated by the Suez Canal, the oil sector, and remittances from Egyptian citizens.[5] Moreover, the crisis has affected

---

2 Amnesty International, October 14, 2013, http://www.amnesty.org/en/news/egypt-state-sanctioned-pattern-excessive-use-force-security-forces-2013-10-14; Human Rights Watch, August 19, 2013, http://www.hrw.org/news/2013/08/19/egypt-security-forces-used-excessive-lethal-force

3 Forty-two churches and about 200 Christian assets (schools, shops, etc.) were targeted, and four people killed, during the summer: Human Rights Watch, August 22, 2013, http://www.hrw.org/news/2013/08/21/egypt-mass-attacks-churches

4 Travel bans from most European governments were lifted in fall 2013.

5 See the latest official presentation of tourism figures in Egypt, compiled by the Minister of Tourism: http://dtxtq4w60xqpw.cloudfront.net/sites/all/files/pdf/2_hisham_zaazou.pdf

thousands of households in regions like Luxor, Aswan, the Red Sea, and South Sinai, where tourism and services-related activities represent the sole source of income. Apart from the direct jobs generated by tourism activities (tour guides, hotels, restaurants, and transport), services and productive sectors, such as the food processing industry and contracting companies, have also been affected by the drop of tourist arrivals in Egypt, putting a halt to new projects and investments, especially along the Red Sea coast and in South Sinai.

This chapter aims to offer a comprehensive overview showing how a strategic sector for the national economy, such as tourism, has been managed since 2011, focusing in particular on the Muslim Brotherhood's rule. Tourism is not only a rent to capture, manage, and distribute. Our assumption is that it also implies ideological principles and values that underlie a wider vision of how the country should be ruled, such as liberalism and economic opening, but also regarding values and practices channeled by Western visitors and the inner workings of the global tourism economy. As the Muslim Brothers and radical groups emerged on the political scene, and ruled the country for a year and a half (2012–2013),[6] a crucial question was then raised among tourism professionals and observers: Can a Muslim Brotherhood government pursue, in accordance with its political and ideological project, a tourism development strategy, an engine sector of the national economy, which has been based on values that are a priori incompatible with their political project of an Islamic society? The veil versus the bikini: this is how the question could be formulated.

Islamic Moral and Touristic Values

When the Muslim Brotherhood candidate Muhammad Morsi was elected president in June 2012, tourism professionals and investors worried about the near future of the sector. Egypt had been shaken for a year and a half by violence and demonstrations, offering a negative image on the international market. Now the governing of Egypt was

---

6   It would be more accurate to date this sequence back to March 2011 and the referendum on the constitutional amendments, when discourses from the Muslim Brotherhood and the Salafi groups emerged in the public sphere. Their vision was of an Islamic state *(dawla islamiya)* as opposed to a civil state *(dawla madaniya)*, promoted by secular civil movements (defamed as impious) who participated in the revolution. The March referendum marked a first step toward ideological polarization.

explicitly related to Islam as a societal and political reference, given that Islam as a religion unleashes passions in Western societies and is perceived as a threat.

However, Prime Minister Hisham Qandil's new government reassured the sector and the international market, via his minister of tourism. Appointed on August 2, 2012, Hisham Zaazou, then deputy minister, succeeded Munir Fakhri Abdel Nur (who was appointed minister of industry).[7] Zaazou has worked in the tourism sector for more than 30 years; he started in the 1980s working for a North American hotel company that he established in Egypt. In the 1990s, surfing on the environmentalist wave, he is said to have introduced eco-tourism into the country. He has been a member of many key governmental agencies, such as the Egyptian Tourism Federation, the Egyptian Tourist Authority, and the very strategic Tourism Development Authority in charge of developing the Red Sea and South Sinai region. Zaazou entered the Ministry of Tourism in 2007 as an advisor to the minister.[8]

Hisham Zaazou is both a businessman and a career official, personifying the tight relations between the state apparatus and the private sector in the 2000s, like two previous ministers of tourism under Mubarak's rule: Ahmed al-Maghrebi (2004–2006) and Zoheir Garanah (2006–2011). His profile and professional trajectory show no political affinities with the Muslim Brotherhood; neither did his predecessor's, Fakhry Abdel Nur, a Coptic businessman. The presence of the two men in Qandil's government gave a clear signal from the Muslim Brotherhood to reassure the international community and the private sector on the tourism strategy to be conducted.

Let us step back for a moment. In 2004, Ahmed Nazif's government gave a blessing to the business community as a full partner in public affairs and political decision-making processes. The Ministry of Tourism is a good example of these extensive practices, which we can qualify as convergence of interest (i.e., cronyism), and which have

7 "Egypt Appoints Well-known Tourism Veteran as New Minister of Tourism," *Global Travel Industry News*, August 2, 2012, http://www.eturbonews.com/30450/egypt-appoints-well-known-tourism-veteran-new-minister-tourism

8 *Egypt Independent*, December 2, 2010, "Green Profile, Interview with Hisham Zaazou," http://www.egyptindependent.com/news/green-profile-interview-hisham-zaazou

been implemented since the 1980s, long before it became a quasi-systematic modus operandi in Nazif's government (Gamblin 2007: part 2, ch. 1). Tourism is not only a matter of rent capturing (tourism revenue), but offers opportunities for urban development, investments, and speculation. For instance, Zoheir Garanah, who headed one of the biggest travel agencies in the country, in 2006 succeeded Ahmed al-Maghrebi, the Middle East representative of Accor company (a leading world hotel company), who had been appointed minister of housing. After Mubarak stepped down in February 2011, the first three ministers who were arrested, along with the president and his sons, were the minister of interior, Habib al-Adly, plus Zoheir Garanah and Ahmed al-Maghrebi. That is no coincidence and very symbolic: the two men were accused of embezzlement and selling land in Cairo and the Red Sea area below the market price. However, even if ministers were arrested, their deputies and subordinates remained on duty, like Hisham Zaazou.

For Qandil and Morsi, Zaazou maintained a 'technocratic' continuity with the previous government, but he was also part of a strategy of communication of the new government toward its main institutional partners (European governments) and the international community (tourists and investors). As soon as Zaazou was appointed, in September 2012, he declared that "beach tourism, which represents 70 percent of tourism activities in Egypt," would not be affected by the new government led by the Muslim Brotherhood.[9] In May 2013, the minister, while on an official trip to the United Arab Emirates, reaffirmed his policy in a striking formula: "Bikinis are welcome in Egypt and alcohol is still being served."[10] But despite these two declarations, attacks on tourism actually became more and more virulent and weakened Morsi's team.

In November 2012 a Jihadi sheikh, Murgan Salem al-Gohary, called for the destruction of the Sphinx and the Pyramids in the name of Islam (which prohibits idol worship). The man was invited to a talk show on

---

9 "Egyptian Beach Tourism Here to Stay: Minister," *Ahram Online* and Reuters, September 21, 2012.
10 "Booze and Bikini Welcome in Egypt: Minister Hisham Zaazou," *International Business Times*, May 6, 2013.

Dream TV, a private satellite channel. The veteran,[11] who is said to have fought with the Taliban in Afghanistan and might have participated in the destruction of the Bamian colossus, was debating with the deputy president of the Tunisian party al-Nahda (affiliated with the Muslim Brotherhood), who vehemently defended the ancient Egyptian heritage by referring to historical and Islamic texts.[12] Al-Gohary, who defines himself as a Jihadi, was then unknown in Egypt. His call for the destruction of the Pyramids had an immediate effect, and brought to the front stage a political current, a minor one, but aggressive and threatening to the tourism sector in particular.[13]

We should also note that there is nothing new about Jihadi groups calling for destroying ancient sites in Egypt. Was not Pharaoh in the Qur'an the impious character whom the Prophet defeated? Many local narratives, such as those of the Sufis, refer to this glorious episode and have incorporated it into popular epics: in Luxor, the ancient capital of Thebes, the local saint Abu al-Hajaj vanquished Pharaoh and spread Islam in the region. In a more political domain, Sadat's murderers had claimed during their trial that they had killed Pharaoh. More recently, attacks in Sinai in 2004, 2005, and 2006 were conducted and claimed by a local Jihadi group, al-Tawhid wa-l-Jihad, which condemned archaeological sites as pre-Islamic idol worship, and attacked tourism as being against Islamic values (International Crisis Group 2007).

---

11 Murgan Salem al-Gohary, 50 years old, had been convicted in the 1980s of a 1987 assassination attempt against the then minister of interior, Hassan Abu Basha. Sheikh al-Gohary escaped to Afghanistan, where he stayed in exile for many years, and where he said he met Bin Laden and Mullah Omar. He left Afghanistan after the US military operation in 2003, and settled at the Pakistani border, where he was badly injured. He left for medical treatment in Syria, where he was arrested in 2007 and deported to Egypt. He was freed after the January 25 Revolution. In a long interview which relates his story and ideas, he declared (among other things) that the assassination of President Sadat was a "legitimate duty" and that "democracy is against Islam." *al-Dostor al-Asly*, October 28, 2012, http://www.dostorasly.com/news/view.aspx?id=2f656b8f-ab6a-405c-b6fd-effe313af470. A *Wall Street Journal* investigation mentioned Murgan Salem al-Gohary as a head hunter for the Islamic Jihad movement, but he denied it. "Blowback from Egypt's Released Jihadist Militants," October 2, 2012, http://arabist.net/blog/2012/10/2/blowback-from-egypts-released-jihadist-militants.html

12 To view the debate: http://www.alarabiya.net/articles/2012/11/12/249072.html

13 Interestingly, international media paid more attention to the man than the national ones, contributing a bit more harm to Egypt's image on the tourist market.

If not new, al-Gohary's call for destroying the Pyramids implicitly raised a crucial national identity question: how does a self-identified Muslim nation deal with antiquities as a *jahiliya* (pre-Islamic) legacy? The question became more political and operational while the Muslim Brotherhood was ruling the country after the 2011 parliamentary elections, in coalition with Salafi parties. The Muslim Brothers' popular legitimacy was directly challenged by their main allies, insofar as they claimed that their project for society was based on religious values (with Islam as the reference). Salafi groups were opportunistic allies of the Muslim Brotherhood, who could not have won a parliamentary majority and reached the presidency without them. When the Muslim Brotherhood was ruling the country, the Salafis pressured them on religious values, family law, individual rights, and the private sphere, but also on national identity and the question of what 'Islamic(ist)' governance meant. The tourism sector, as emblematic of the Mubarak regime and its 'Westernization,' was a perfect battleground for the Salafis to test the Muslim Brotherhood's power . . . and its limits.

The coalition of the Salafis and the Muslim Brotherhood started to weaken seriously after January 2013 and the violent commemoration of January 25, followed by weeks of civil disobedience in several cities (in the Canal region, in particular). The divorce was finalized in June; the Development and Construction party (affiliated with the Gamaʻa Islamiya, a radical group in the 1990s) remained the only political ally of Morsi and his government.[14] During the first half of 2013, the Salafis became more virulent and active, calling for more Islamic morals and for the government to act upon them, in the tourism sector in particular. In May 2013, the first *halal* hotel was opened in Hurghada, on the Red Sea, which is a touristic region mainly dedicated to the Western market, especially German and Russian tourists. Alcohol is prohibited, and a section of the hotel and of the beach is reserved for women only. A few weeks before, a hotel announced its intention to conform to Islam, and its manager destroyed dozens of bottles of alcoholic beverages in front of cameras and stupefied foreign tourists. These two events could be regarded as anecdotal, if they were not part of a more general political and institutional process which, firstly, resulted from Salafis' and

---

14 Right after July 3 they founded the Legitimacy Alliance, the main movement that led pro-Morsi demonstrations and sit-ins.

hardliners' pressure on the government by calling for '*halal* tourism,' an expression that had first emerged in the public debate in fall 2011,[15] and secondly, contradicted the Ministry of Tourism strategy, which was desperately trying to reassure the international markets.

In mid June 2013, President Morsi nominated new governors: 11 of the 27 governorates of Egypt fell under Muslim Brotherhood rule.[16] Moreover, Adel Asaad al-Khayat, a founding member of the Gama'a Islamiya in the region of Sohag, was named governor of Luxor. The appointment triggered fierce reactions, in Egypt and beyond. The Islamist group had been found responsible in 1997 for the Hatshepsut Temple massacre, on the west bank of Luxor, in which 57 tourists were killed. Al-Khayat's involvement was never established, and the Gama'a Islamiya officially renounced the use of violence in 2003. However, the consequences of his nomination were quite dramatic: Minister of Tourism Hisham Zaazou resigned, and demonstrations in Luxor became more numerous, in a very sensitive national political context in the approach to June 30. Was it a provocation from the Muslim Brotherhood president? A political miscalculation? Or simply a concession made to his only remaining tangible ally? Questions still remain.

Up to that point, the alliance between the radical groups and the Muslim Brotherhood seemed to be a matter of role distribution. On one hand, the radicals were pushing for more Islam in the society, a demand that the Muslim Brothers could use as part of their capital of popular legitimacy; on the other hand, a supposedly more moderate Muslim Brotherhood government was endeavoring to reassure the international community. However, the 'moralization' process of the state institutions—which many viewed as a 'brotherization'—had already been at work.[17] The wearing of beards was eventually allowed for policemen, as

---

15 Shaykh Yasser Bourhamy, a hardline Salafi, started to advocate '*halal* tourism' in fall 2011. Some Muslim Brothers' voices questioned ancient sites as sites of idol worship, and the Noor Party, the main Muslim Brotherhood ally that won 19 percent of the 2012 parliament seats, called for forbidding beach tourism, which "induces vice." "Egypt's Islamists Offer Controversial Vision on 'Halal' Tourism," *al-Arabiya*, December 13, 2011, http://www.alarabiya.net/articles/2011/12/13/182316.html

16 "Egypt's Newly Appointed Governors," *Ahram Online*, June 17, 2013, http://english.ahram.org.eg/NewsContent/1/64/74199/Egypt/Politics-/Egypts-newly-appointed-governors-A-whos-who.aspx

17 Under Mubarak's regime, governors were mainly army and police representatives.

well as the veil on state television channels, both as concessions made to the more radical groups. This 'moralization' process also affected the tourism sector, in contradiction to the minister's strategy, whose mission was to revive a strategic sector in the national economy: in September 2012, the government allowed the veil for female cabin-crew members in the national company EgyptAir, after a year of pressure and demands.[18]

Under Morsi's rule, the tourism sector faced a two-fold policy: On the one hand, the government, that is, the Ministry of Tourism, tried hard to reassure the international market and its partners; on the other hand, the Muslim Brotherhood, under pressure from their radical allies and/or by conviction, progressively imposed their Islamic and national identity label. In a very tumultuous context of violence and political instability, one still might have been surprised that the government decreed that EgyptAir flights should serve "typical" Egyptian meals rather than international food. Again, such a decision could have been considered anecdotal, had it not raised a broader question: What should a national air company promote around the world as national symbols? The Muslim Brotherhood answered the question: what defines Egyptian culture is food, while the veil defines Islam. Our hypothesis is that this question was related to a broader strategy of political communication which used and overused popular, even populist, symbols in order to 'Egyptianize' the ruling power's image, and to mark a clear rupture with the previous regime.

For instance, at the beginning of Morsi's mandate, the president and his government members used to pray every Friday in a different mosque, around the country. Each time, the prayer was followed by a visit in the region, and a meal taken in the 'Egyptian' way, among the people: the president and his prime minister had lunch, sitting on the floor, eating with their hands, around the traditional *tabliya*, or low table. 'Egyptian' meals were also organized in the prime minister's office, after a cabinet meeting, with media coverage and official pictures. This staging of power, which aimed to establish a clear rupture with the former ruling elite in the official and very formal protocol, had three intricate

---

18 It should be mentioned that Mubarak also made concessions to the conservatives in the 1980s by prohibiting alcohol on EgyptAir. In 2008, the Grand Hyatt Hotel in Cairo, a Saudi property, also prohibited alcohol.

dimensions: Islamic, 'Egyptianist,' and populist. As a result, messages about tourism, which were crucial to revitalize the sector, were caught in the contradictions between redefining state power and international tourism values, which refer to global models and elitism.

Is a Muslim Brotherhood Political Economy of Tourism Possible?

Pressured by their radical allies, in search of popular legitimacy, or simply by ideological convictions, the Morsi–Qandil government was constantly challenged on the ground of morals and identity, especially in the tourism sector and its governance. However, did the Muslim Brotherhood envision a tourism development policy? The Freedom and Justice Party program for the parliamentary elections (to become Morsi's Nahda project) only mentioned the tourism sector three times, one of them (the more consistent one) being part of the chapter dedicated to "Urban Development."[19] Eight measures were proposed for tourism development and air transportation:

1. Protect tourist areas in ancient Egyptian cities, and along the coasts of the Mediterranean and Red Seas.
2. Encourage the private sector and attract foreign investment to effect more development in the tourism sector.
3. Market tourism products on Arab and international levels by working on the revitalization of Egyptian tourism in the main existing markets, and open new tourism markets.
4. Double hotel capacity through the development of existing tourist destinations and the targeting of new tourist destinations, with diversification of tourism services.
5. Provide quality service to tourists, from arrival/reception to facilitation of customs procedures, transportation to suitable hotels, good hotel service, tourist attraction tours, and right up to the moment of departure from Egypt.
6. Promote scientific, conference, cultural, and religious tourism.
7. Fast-track the establishment of a land bridge over the Gulf of Aqaba, linking Egypt and Saudi Arabia, to facilitate the

---

19 Freedom and Justice Party electoral program 2011: http://www.fjponline.com/uploads/FJPprogram.pdf

movement of Arab tourism between the countries of the east and the west—of the Arab world—through Egypt. This should achieve additional economic growth in many areas.
8. Lift all visa, customs, and excise barriers among Arab countries.

It must be noted that these measures were not novelties. To the contrary, they were fully part of the tourism development strategy under Mubarak, such as the Aqaba bridge project and the free-movement zone among Arab countries, which both dated back to the 1990s. Those measures could suggest that economic pragmatism (and a liberal stand) might have prevailed in the Muslim Brotherhood government, especially toward the tourism sector.

Tourism was also briefly, but interestingly, mentioned in two other sections:

- In the section dedicated to "Integrated Development," a summary of objectives to achieve suggested: "Reformulating the tourism industry to support the Egyptian economy in line with our values and moral principles."
- In the section "Budget Management," point 5 mentioned "rationalizing petroleum product subsidies, and eliminating subsidies for energy-intensive industries and some sectors such as tourism, which gets almost 10 million pounds in subsidies."

This last point seemed to be the only one to refer to any sort of economic program. Candidate Morsi had claimed during his presidential campaign that "tourism does not need state funding. Rather, it needs freedom from state bureaucracy. The role of the state should be limited to issuing and enforcing regulations, just like all countries of the world. It should also allow tourist establishments the freedoms they need—without restrictions or conditions except for high quality."[20] This message was delivered—not coincidentally—before the main representatives of the Bedouin tribes of Sinai, who have been largely excluded from tourism development and economic growth for the last 30 years, while the south of the peninsula (Sharm al-Shaykh–Taba) has been

---

20 "Dr. Morsi Assures Tourism Has Priority in Nahda Project," *IkhwanWeb*, May 7, 2012, http://www.ikhwanweb.com/article.php?id=29963

managed by the central administration in Cairo, international development agencies, the army, and a few businessmen.

If the Muslim Brothers actually had a vision for tourism development, it could be summed up as follows: First, the sector had to be morally clean, meaning "being compatible with values and principles" that the Brotherhood believed in and shared with its Salafi allies. Secondly, state action should be limited and subsidies cut, in line with the liberal ideology of the Muslim Brotherhood. This last point may seem paradoxical: tourism has always been carried by the private sector and international companies, and thus incarnated the economic liberalization program that Egypt has pursued since the 1980s.[21] Here, what was targeted was not the former regime's orientation, but the practices of collusion between the ruling elite and a caste of businessmen, in tourism in particular, but more generally, in the speculative and productive sectors—from which the Muslim Brotherhood had been mainly excluded under Mubarak. For instance, urbanization in the Red Sea, South Sinai, and the new settlements in the desert around Cairo was based on dynamics of shared interests (cronyism and embezzlement) between the state (including the army) and the private sector (a selective and exclusive group of businessmen), the latter becoming increasingly important in public affairs management.

We have already mentioned the fact that Nazif's government reflected the tight relations between state power and the business world. Paradoxically, programs of economic reform conducted under Mubarak, which a priori favored the free-market economy and a limited role for the state, actually reinforced the latter, in tourism sector management in particular. In this regard, the state acted not as a regulating institution, but as a provider of services to the private sector in the interest of the businessmen, who had been extensively involved in ministries, agencies, and the parliament:[22] specific legislation, fiscal regime, but above all access to real estate (and related speculation opportunities) in desert regions dedicated to urban development and under the control

---

[21] Since 1990/91, the private sector has constantly represented more than 90 percent of total investment (private and public) in the tourism sector. Central Bank of Egypt, http://www.cbe.org.eg/English/Economic+Research/Time+Series/

[22] Businessmen had started to play a significant role in the parliament since the 1995 elections, as Gamal Abdel Nasser observed and analyzed (Gamblin 1997).

of the army. These measures concerned other sectors besides tourism, but tourism was the engine of urban development in many strategic and lucrative regions. Thus, it is actually no surprise that the Muslim Brotherhood mentions tourism in the "Urban Development" section of their electoral program.[23]

It is tempting to interpret these recommendations as a Muslim Brothers' critique on the negative effects of the free-market economy, and on cronyism practices in the tourism sector.[24] Muslim Brothers are not, generally speaking, against the free-market economy—quite the opposite. However, the tourism sector seemed for the Muslim Brothers more a source of income to cover public deficits, rather than a strategic priority. Apart from cutting state funding, the government program toward the tourism sector was reduced to a pragmatic measure, although a very unpopular one: raising taxes on import goods related to the sector. In March 2013, a presidential decree established a list of 100 consumer goods to be taxed, from 5 to 40 percent, including alcohol, caviar, shrimp, chewing gum, sunglasses, watches, nuts, and yachts. These new taxes would have generated around a billion Egyptian pounds (US $140,000,000), according to official statements. But far beyond the tourism sector, they also concerned goods that the upper Egyptian classes consume. This measure went along with another tax of 20 percent imposed on equipment imported by touristic establishments.[25]

Elhamy El-Zayat, long-time head of Egypt's Federation of Tourism Chambers, remarked that the 2008 financial crisis had already affected the sector, and that tourism facilities had not been upgraded since because of a lack of investment. Not only had tourist arrivals been

---

23 New settlements around Cairo were implied, where legislative tools for real estate and investment were very similar to what had been implemented in the new tourism development zones (the Red Sea and South Sinai, but also the North Coast).

24 In the 1990s, Adel Hussein, a Marxist economist converted to political Islam in the 1980s, chief editor of the bi-weekly *al-Sha'b*, affiliated with the Labor party which at that time hosted the Muslim Brotherhood, used to fiercely denounce the capitalistic dynamic of the tourism economy, the monopoly of international firms, state cronyism and its corruption, and the lack of distribution of tourism revenue for local benefit. Nowadays, Muslim Brotherhood businessmen have been trained in the liberal school and their philanthropic actions are limited to Islamic values *(zakat)* and the charity networks affiliated with the Brotherhood.

25 "Tourism Sector Fears Egypt Custom Tariffs on Imports," *Ahram Online*, March 26, 2013, http://english.ahram.org.eg/News/67802.aspx

decreasing since 2011, but Egypt had been losing competitiveness and service quality in the regional market.[26] Those measures did not revive tourism at all. On the contrary, they increased the touristic establishments' debt, and elicited a general frustration in the sector. Since the revolution, the country had witnessed social movements that grew more numerous under Morsi's rule.[27] Protests hit also the tourism sector: in November 2012, tour guides, who have been dramatically affected by the crisis and whose incomes are mainly related to cultural and urban tourism along the Nile Valley (e.g., Nile cruises), demonstrated and organized sit-ins, demanding a solidarity fund, social insurance, and the independence of their professional union from state control.[28] In December 2012, airports were disturbed by several strikes, especially in Sharm al-Shaykh, mainly demanding better wages. On a political lobbying level, tourism professionals pressured the government to consider tourism as a national priority in Article 17 of the 2012 constitutional declaration, connected to the broader general industrial policy. Whether they were political or corporatist, claims from the tourism sector were framed into the general post-January socioeconomic demands, underlining the role of the state as a regulating and protective body.

Fiscal measures and higher taxation on import goods in the tourism sector were not at all in line with the social and economic demands which the people had expressed. However, Egypt was then (and is still) under pressure to find cash assets, preferably in hard currency, to pay the import bills. Since 2011 the government had been negotiating an IMF

---

26 According to the *Travel and Tourism Competitiveness Report 2013* published by the World Economic Forum, Egypt was ranked 85 in 2013 among 140 countries, whereas it was ranked 75 in 2011, and 66 in 2008 (among 130 countries). *Travel and Tourism Competiveness 2013*, http://www3.weforum.org/docs/WEF_TT_Competitiveness_Report_2013.pdf; *Travel and Tourism Competiveness 2008*, http://www.weforum.org/pdf/Global_Competitiveness_Reports/TTReport/TTfullreport.pdf

27 A report from the Egyptian Center for Economic and Social Rights (ECESR) on labor movements during 2012 shows that most of that year's 3,817 labor strikes and economically motivated social protests happened following Morsi's election. "Labour Strikes and Protests Double under Morsi," *Daily News Egypt*, April 28, 2013, http://www.dailynewsegypt.com/2013/04/28/labour-strikes-and-protests-double-under-morsi/

28 In the year 2000, the Ministry of Tourism managed to take over the Tour Guides Union, after decades of political independence. On this issue, see Gamblin (2007, part 2, chapter 3).

loan, worth $4.3 billion, to no avail. The country was technically bankrupt, hit by a deep economic crisis which called for cuts in subsidies and economic reforms that no one has dared to initiate because they are too unpopular in the electoral context. Whether or not the Muslim Brothers had an economic program and the skills to implement it, their action was narrowed to fiscal pressure, with no real measures to contain the crisis that harmed tourism professionals in particular, and with no incentive to attract visitors.[29] Tourism—in its dominant trend, that is, western tourism—was not a priority for Morsi's government, but a profitable sector which generated hard currencies and tax revenues. The result was the growing discontent of a major part of the active population and the business community. The Muslim Brotherhood did not have a vision of a tourism policy to be conducted in Egypt, and the consequences were costly, on both the political and the human levels.

Containing the Crisis, or, When Tourism Serves a "Pan-Arabo-Islamist" Diplomacy

As mentioned above in the Muslim Brothers program (point 8), part of the crisis was to be solved by increasing 'Arab' tourism, and opening tourism to other Muslim countries. Under the suggestion of the Ministry of Tourism (February 2013), visa procedures for North African countries were lifted. It must be recalled that promoting 'Arab' tourism was not a novelty, and has been regularly put forward as a solution to the crisis of the sector, such as in the years 1994–1997.[30] During that period, Arab nationals (mainly coming from the Gulf countries) represented more than 40 percent of total arrivals in Egypt. In 2011–2012, although they were increasing by 6 percent compared to the previous year (2010–2011), they only accounted for 22 percent of total tourist nights and 15 percent

---

29 In March 2013, the Central Bank of Egypt announced, with no conviction, and in contradiction to the Muslim Brotherhood stand on state disengagement, a plan to revitalize the tourism sector, assuming that "the banking sector has a 'national' duty to support Egypt's economy and help preserve the tourism sector, which is one of our main sources of foreign currency." "Egypt Central Bank Launches Tourism Initiative," *Ahram Online*, March 14, 2013, http://english.ahram.org.eg/News/66846.aspx

30 Egypt's tourism sector was hit by the attacks of radical groups, targeting international visitors but also Copts and state representatives. The Luxor massacre in 1997 (62 dead in the Hatshepsut temple) was the peak of this violent cycle.

of total arrivals.³¹ Beyond the statistics, visitors in Egypt from the Gulf countries have mainly gone to urban areas (Cairo and Alexandria), renting flats or villas for long-term stays. These specific leisure practices involve economic activities which have very limited additional distributive effects on the local level (income generation, job creation, services), and have no substantial economic effect on touristic sites (museums, historical sites). In the 2000s, Gulf countries' investments in the tourism sector have increased, especially on the northern Mediterranean coast, between Alexandria and the Libyan border. Although this region has witnessed tremendous urban/tourism development, the number of Gulf nationals visiting Egypt has decreased. Gulf investment trends over the last 15 years have shown that they are not aimed to promote Arab tourism, but to speculate on new economic development zones dedicated to the European market and the Egyptian upper class.³² Concerning potential visitors from North Africa (Morocco, Algeria, Tunisia, and Libya), it must be underlined here that the upper classes from these countries cannot supply a substantial market which could replace European demand: their number and their purchasing power are limited, and these countries have also been hit by the economic crisis and political instability.

However, the government thought that rescue could come from the east: Iran, as a new tourism market to be promoted by the Muslim Brotherhood, and above all, as a tool to promote the new Egyptian–Iranian diplomacy. Egypt and Iran had halted their relations since the 1979 Camp David agreements and the assassination of Sadat.³³ In April 2012, Iran eventually appointed a representative to Cairo, reestablishing diplomatic contacts, and Morsi paid an official visit to Tehran two months after he was elected. The new friendship between Egypt and Iran was sealed in February 2013, with the visit of then President

---

31 Central Bank of Egypt, http://www.cbe.org.eg/English/Economic+Research/Time+Series/

32 For instance, Qatar had planned to invest US $18 billion (in loans and grants), from which $10 billion was supposed to be dedicated to tourism projects, mainly located on the northern Mediterranean cost. "Qatar to Invest $18bn in Egypt over Next 5 years," *Ahram Online*, September 12, 2012, http://english.ahram.org.eg/NewsContent/3/12/52169/Business/Economy/Qatar-to-invest-bn-in-Egypt-over-next--years.aspx

33 Islambouli, one of Sadat's murderers, was considered a hero in Iran, while Egypt hosted the Iranian royal family in exile after the 1979 revolution.

Ahmedinejad, on the occasion of the Organization of Islamic Cooperation Assembly in Cairo. The first commercial flight between the two capital cities, carrying a first group of Iranian tourists, was planned for the spring, and at the end of February, the Egyptian minister of tourism flew to Tehran to sign a bilateral agreement, aiming to attract 200,000 Iranian visitors annually who would generate $250 million of income.[34] As a principle of reciprocity, the visa requirement was lifted for Egyptians visiting Iran.

The new Egyptian foreign policy toward Iran, and especially the announcement of a first visit of Iranian tourists in Egypt, triggered such virulent reactions that the minister had to announce that the agreement was not aimed to promote Shi'a tourism, despite the fact that Cairo possesses major Shi'a religious sites.[35] Salafi groups, especially the Noor party, a main electoral ally of the Muslim Brothers, initiated violent anti-Shi'a propaganda, calling again, but in a different context, for *halal* tourism. Neither booze nor bikinis were the target here. Boundaries in defining tourism and the notion of Otherness shifted with violence to the Shi'a/Sunni confrontation. Ahmedinejad's visit was disturbed by a few incidents and demonstrations turned into clashes, while the Iranian representative's villa was attacked by Salafi groups. The first and last Iranian tourist group (about 50 people) eventually landed in Cairo on April 1, under very tight security conditions, and their visit was restricted to pharaonic sites.

This sequence marked a clear rupture between the Muslim Brothers and their Salafi allies. In addition, several close advisors to Morsi resigned, such as Fu'ad Gadallah, who declared that the visit of Iranian tourists to Egypt was "the return of the Fatimid state and an infiltration of Iranian money and interests in the service of their goal of eliminating the Sunni sect from Egypt."[36] By reestablishing relations with Iran, Morsi sent contradictory signals to other countries in the region and to his allies. Egypt's government supported the Syrian regime (as the army had done), when the Syrian Muslim Brothers were fighting in the

---

34 It must be noted here that the income generated by Iranian tourists cannot compete with the expenditures of Europeans (about $5 billion in 2010).
35 Notably al-Husayn's and Sayyida Zaynab's tombs in Cairo.
36 "President Muhammad Morsi's Efforts to Befriend Iran Upset His Other Allies," *The Economist*, May 4, 2013.

opposition. Saudi Arabia, Iran's major foe, has been a key sponsor of the Salafi groups in Egypt, and saw in the new Egyptian–Iranian friendship a threat to its regional ambition and interests. Last but not least, Qatar and the United Arab Emirates decided to suspend their financial aid to Egypt.[37] The Iranian policy, in which tourism was a tool of communication, definitely branded Egypt as an 'Islamist' country worldwide, siding with the 'rogue' countries such as Iran. As a result of this initiative, a few dozen Iranian tourists increased Morsi's unpopularity in the country, speeded up his divorce from the Salafis, and froze Egypt's relations with its main sponsors. Even worse, Morsi's diplomatic policy revived a latent and very violent anti-Shi'a sentiment, which culminated with the killing of four Egyptian Shi'a in June 2013.[38]

Conclusion

This chapter describes events that happened before June 30, 2013, during a year of Muslim Brotherhood government. The exercise has been challenging for several reasons: the complexity of events, the multiplicity of actors, the swings of alliance and misalliance, the ideological polarization, and the 'conspiracy' tendency. The Muslim Brothers' detractors, among them many intellectuals and businessmen, claimed the government had no economic vision, while sympathizers of the Brotherhood argued with the best free-market instruments to justify the government's economic policy. In practice, and in its defense, it must be admitted that the government had a very narrow margin of action: in order to tackle the economic crisis and the structural public deficit, they were strongly pushed to initiate unpopular economic reforms (subsidy cuts in the energy sector, for instance) that would have harmed the Muslim Brothers' popular legitimacy that they had gained through elections. Besides, the government was acting under pressure: on one hand, from its Salafi allies and the more radical component of the Brotherhood, who aggressively challenged the government on the ground of values

---

37 "President Muhammad Morsi's Efforts to Befriend Iran Upset His Other Allies."
38 Egypt is home to a small Shi'a community. After the revolution, some of its members funded a political party and tried to organize. Anti-Shi'a propaganda had started before the revolution, but was amplified in the last months of Morsi's rule when Shi'a members were arrested or tried for insulting religion. "Egypt: Lynching of Shia Follows Months of Hate Speech," *Human Rights Watch*, June 27, 2013.

and morals, requiring to some extent the 'halalization' of the tourism sector; on the other hand, from the professionals of the tourism sector, who had largely benefited from Mubarak's regime (and some of them remained faithful to the old regime), and have been struggling with the crisis in the sector. Lastly, Morsi's government had to deal with the army, which remained a major political and economic actor.

Managing the tourism sector under Morsi's rule pinpointed the contradictions of the Muslim Brotherhood as a political and ruling organization. Tourism was not an economic priority for the Muslim Brothers, but only a rent to capture (via taxation). However, it was a fierce opportunistic confrontation ground of values with respect to religion, morals, and even identity, where the Salafi allies appeared much more efficient in assuming and promoting their own vision. Lastly, tourism was used as a tool for diplomatic communication in the Iran–Egypt rapprochement which rapidly proved to be politically counterproductive, although the first intentions were based on a very common (and somehow naive) conviction shared and promoted by international development agencies: tourism as a bridge between peoples and cultures. More generally speaking, tourism (mis)management by the Muslim Brothers sheds light on their contradictory policy-making, on the limits of their political alliances, and on their lack of economic pragmatism.

References

Gamblin, Sandrine, ed. 1997. *Contours et détours du politique en Egypte: les Elections parlementaires de 1995.* Paris: Cedej/L'Harmattan.

———. 2007. "Tourisme international, Etat et sociétés locales en Egypt: Louxor, un haut lieu disputé." PhD dissertation: Ecole Doctorale de Sciences Politiques, Paris. http://www.fasopo.org/reasopo/jr/these_gamblin.pdf

International Crisis Group. 2007. *Egypt's Sinai Question.* Middle East/North Africa Report 61, January. http://www.crisisgroup.org/~/media/Files/Middle%20East%20North%20Africa/North%20Africa/Egypt/61_egypts_sinai_question

CHAPTER 8

Militarism, Neoliberalism, and Revolution in Egypt

Zeinab Abul-Magd

In the Nasr City area of northeastern Cairo, the heavy presence of the military institution cannot be missed. The visible signs of the Ministry of Defense are atop vast hotels, wedding halls, large parking lots, supermarkets that sell foodstuffs from the military farms, fast-food places that offer sandwiches and French fries, gas stations, a domestic cleaning company, outlets for mineral water and olive oil, and gigantic advertisement boards for Queen pasta on the Sixth of October Bridge. Even the roads carry the institution's imprint—"Field Marshal Tantawi's Central Highway," to name one example. Moving to the south of Cairo, the Maadi area, the picture is no different. Many military social clubs and wedding halls occupy the Nile Corniche and are open to the public at affordable prices. One of them is the club of the Ministry of Military Production's factory number 54, which manufactures many civilian products, including aluminum kitchenware. Moving farther south into the Helwan area, one encounters the giant industrial complex of the same ministry, mostly now engaged in civilian production. This is where things such as televisions, pots, pans, appliances, kitchen stoves, and butane gas cylinders for these stoves are produced.

The Egyptian military institution surrounds Egyptians of all social classes, and it intensively occupies the urban social and economic spaces across the country. In the postcolonial Egyptian state, the army decided to intervene and take down existing regimes three times: once over 60 years ago, in 1952, and two more recent occasions in 2011 and 2013. In all three cases of intervention, the military institution deployed the same nationalist rhetoric about its duty as the 'guardian' of the nation and the protector of national security and unity. However, the new army of the last three years is not the same institution that existed 60 years ago. This chapter argues that a new military institution was born in Egypt in the 1980s, after the country fought its last war with its traditional enemy and signed a peace treaty. It is an army that owns vast business enterprises in a neoliberal milieu, enjoys financial autonomy beyond public scrutiny, and intervenes in politics with heavy leverage for reasons different from those of the old army while using the same nationalist rhetoric.

This chapter argues that a fundamental rupture took place in the Egyptian military institution in the 1980s, and this rupture gave birth to the new army that the country has today. The old and new armies differ in their socioeconomic composition, doctrine, and the way they militarized society.[1] Whereas the old army was composed of lower- to middle-class soldiers who rose into an affluent ruling elite and militarized society through wars and socialism, the new army is controlled by a class of managers of military business enterprises and militarizes society through economic dominance. Whereas the old ruling army's ambitious doctrine adopted an Arab nationalist identity and a socialist ideology, and was externally oriented to regional affairs, the new army's less ambitious doctrine focuses on narrow Egyptian patriotism and is internally oriented to domestic matters. On the eve of the two recent interventions, the Egyptian army was no longer the 'vanguard' of progressive forces and modernization—as Nasser described it in the past—but it was another economic player and competitor in an open market.

The existence of military business is not unique to the Egyptian army. In fact, it is a global phenomenon born in many other countries during the last three decades, before and after the end of the Cold War. Most Arab and world armies, with the termination of the Cold War, grew less relevant in their respective states, had to face budget cuts, and militarism faded away in most developed countries. Economic reform

---

[1] 'Militarization' is derived from the term 'militarism.' According to Ayse Gul Altinay, militarism as an ideology is intertwined with nationalism and shapes identities. It is "a set of ideas and structures that glorify 'practices and norms associates with militaries.' In this sense, militarization is 'a step-by-step process by which a person or a thing gradually comes to be controlled by the military *or* comes to depend for its well-being on militaristic ideas.' Militarization is successful when it achieves a discourse of 'normalcy' in public discussions surrounding the power of the military in civilian life, politics, economics, and people's self-understandings" (Altinay 2004:2–3).

plans in socialist regimes transitioning to a market economy required substantial public spending cuts, including in military budgets. During the last two decades, the militaries of most European countries moved from 'modern' to 'postmodern' armies, as they gave up large sizes and huge budgets to become smaller-sized professional armies that rely on high technology and occupy themselves more with peacekeeping activities. However, many Third World militaries still preserve themselves as oversized modern institutions, through the continuity of compulsory conscription of male youth, and, more importantly, by creating profitable business enterprises that compensate for budget cuts and allow them to enjoy privileged status within their respective states (Brommelhorster and Paes 2004).

Both the old and the new Egyptian armies resemble many other global militaries that followed similar courses of intervention based on parallel nationalist discourses. In the immediate postcolonial era, Third World armies in general perceived themselves as vanguards of modernization and the vehicles of progress in their respective developing states. In the Latin American and Turkish experiences, for instance, armies assumed the position of the 'guardians' of their nations and protectors of national values and unity. They often interfered through coups or heavy political influence to fulfill these self-assigned duties. These armies acted as 'political arbiters' who carried the patriotic mission of resolving disputes among civilians and ending social polarization, and claimed to be neutral mediators defending the public good. During interventions, these armies invoked their historical contributions in building modern governments in order to justify their superior status in the political order. Whereas in many Latin American cases armies often ruled directly for decades, in the Turkish case the army returned quickly to the barracks, but after amending the constitution in a way that preserved a superior status for the officers (Pion-Berlin 2011).

There are different theoretical approaches to explain why the military intervenes to depose an existing government. One approach emphasizes the rational interests of individual officers; another looks at the structure of the military institution as a whole, seeking its own interests against existing civilian powers. The latter approach argues that more united, cohesive, and autonomous armies are more likely to launch coups. United armies might intervene to protect their very autonomy against civilians inciting internal division within its structure. Some scholars within the same approach affirm that intervention might take place to protect the military's corporate interests, or positions and resources, against threats of civilians in power. Other approaches consider the culture of the officers, and the culture of the country as whole: some countries have sets of beliefs that expect the army to interfere to resolve internal conflict between civilian forces, and some military institutions hold norms that make it their mission to intervene in times of national disunity. The history of the country and the institutional history of its army shape this culture, which places political expectations on officers. Other approaches argue that domestic factors, namely the political structure and culture of the country, provoke intervention: militaries are more likely to intervene in weak states that are culturally accustomed to broad military influence in politics. Another approach asserts that external factors, namely international threats, lead to military intervention to defend the security of the nation.[2]

The Egyptian cases of military intervention, especially the two recent incidents, could be analyzed by more than one of the above theoretical approaches. Every incident of intervention of the old and new Egyptian armies had its own unique drives—despite using the same nationalist rhetoric that was forged by Nasser decades ago and invoked twice during the last three years. This chapter argues that military business managers intervened in 2011 partially to protect their economic interests. When they interfered again in 2013, it was in response to perceived internal and external security threats, but on that occasion they actually risked their own economic interests. In addition, the chapter indicates that while institutional interests have heavily influenced the army's political actions, entrenched popular perceptions about the officers' patriotic heroism, weak regime structure, and perceived internal and external security threats still informed their behavior to a great extent.

This chapter traces the rupture that took place in the Egyptian military institution in the 1980s, and the birth of a class of military entrepreneurs who enjoy considerable leverage in domestic politics today. It starts with a historical background of Nasser's military institution in the 1950s and 1960s and economic militarism in its socialist form, and alludes to Sadat's brief attempt at 'demilitarizing' the Egyptian state in

---

2 For elaborate details of these theoretical approaches see Taylor (2003:6–26).

the 1970s. The chapter then moves to the birth of the new army under Mubarak from the 1980s onward. In the 1990s and 2000s, the class of military business managers took advantage of Mubarak's neoliberal reform to amass profitable enterprises, without necessarily believing in the dicta of the market economy. Finally, the chapter investigates the role of the new army in the 2011 and 2013 uprisings, emphasizing its economic interests and security threats.

Militarizing the Nation (1952–1970)

On July 23, 1952, a group of young officers launched a coup that deposed the monarch and kicked out the British colonizer, and within the course of only a few weeks they turned this coup into a 'social revolution.'[3] On September 9, in response to the long-standing demands of the lower classes, the new military regime issued the land reform law, Law No. 178, which resulted in the confiscation of thousands of feddans from the landed aristocracy and their distribution to impoverished peasants. This was soon followed by other measures affecting the industrial properties of national and foreign capitalists in the country, gradually nationalizing many of them.

In their quest for modernization, postcolonial societies placed high expectations on their armies, and officers responded by 'revolutions from above.' Nazih Ayubi explains that in developing countries in the 1950s and 1960s, military institutions tended to be the most organized, educated, and technologically advanced groups in the nation, and thus the best able to carry out such a task. He adds that they "tended to justify their intervention either by citing nationalistic reasons (fighting colonialism or confronting a foreign threat), the need for national unity above ethnic and tribal lines, the need for order, discipline and organization, or the need for prompt socio-economic reform" (Ayubi 1996:258). Ayubi invokes Gramsci's concept of 'revolution from above' to describe the action of many Middle Eastern militaries that appropriated politics in the name of 'development' and applied "radical socio-economic reforms" (Ayubi 1996:259).

The leaders of the army's revolution came from middle- to lower-class social backgrounds. General Muhammad Naguib, the old general among the young revolutionary officers and the first military president

---
3   For the definition of a classical 'social revolution' see Skocpol (1976).

after 1952, explained that aristocratic families had long avoided military service and left it to "the sons of civil servants and soldiers and the grandsons of peasants" (Berger 1960:20). From the late 1950s onwards, the new regime militarized the Egyptian economy by installing officers and 'military technocrats'—officers who had studied civilian subjects such as economics, law, journalism, engineering, and political science in the public sector and the high administrative levels of the socialist state (Abd Allah 1990:35).[4] The president and all prime ministers were military, and "of 131 ministers who served under Nasser, 20.6 percent were officers and 13.9 percent were officer technocrats" (Cooper 1982:208). Furthermore, the tradition of appointing officers as governors of provinces started in 1961 with the first application of the new local administration law. Out of the 21 governors appointed, 11 were army officers and five were police officers (Abd Allah 1990:36).[5]

In 1962, the military ruling elite issued a new constitution stipulating that socialism was the official state ideology. The state came to own all economic assets through nationalization, and then built numerous public enterprises, aiming for an ambitious plan of 'import substitution industrialization' (ISI). Army officers installed themselves as the managers of these state-owned enterprises. In 1964, Nasser issued a new socialist constitution that stated that "the people control all means of production," and army officers were the self-appointed deputies of the people in controlling these means. Corruption and mismanagement proliferated throughout the public sector, and Nasser's project ultimately failed to deliver the promise of economic prosperity. As a result of the army's neglecting its main task of defending national security, Egypt suffered the 1967 war defeat. After the defeat, the years between 1967 and 1970 were a period of gradual demilitarization, and the state took steps toward economic liberalization (Cooper 1982:204–205).

Between 1970 and 1981, Anwar Sadat applied radical measures to demilitarize the Egyptian state. In order to consolidate his authority against the remaining influential figures from Nasser's years, Sadat marginalized the officers in politics and reduced their economic

---

4   For tables of names of military officials and ministers see Abd Allah (1990:40–50).
5   In 1964, 22 governors were officers, according to Robert Springborg, "al-Ra'is wa-l-mushir: al-'alaqat al-madaniya al-'askariya fi Misr al-youm," cited in Abd Allah (1990:66).

influence. He increased the number of civilian technocrats in the cabinet and the bureaucracy. "With the January 1972 cabinet, the military declined to a level below any other cabinet since 1952 and it continued to decline. . . . Lawyers grew to considerable prominence in the cabinet by the later Sadat cabinets . . . as did business professionals and engineers. . . . Under Sadat, of 127 ministers, 7.5 percent were officers and 7.5 percent were officer technocrats" (Cooper 1982:208, 210). Every time an officer retired from civil service, Sadat appointed a civilian in his place. In addition, Sadat radically reduced the number of military governors. In 1980, only five governors out of 26 were military (Springborg, in Abd Allah 1990:66). Moreover, the army's economic control over the public sector declined with Sadat's 'open door' *(infitah)* policy, as he privatized parts of the state-owned enterprises that officers had previously managed. The army now had to share its influence with a rising community of crony capitalists.

After this brief period of demilitarization of the Egyptian state by Sadat, economic militarism returned intact under Mubarak—albeit in a novel form.

Birth of Military Entrepreneurs (1980s–2000s)

Everything changed in Egypt after Mubarak ascended to power, including the Egyptian military. During the 1980s, the internal and international milieus changed, and the military had to reposition itself within the new political, economic, and social arrangements that rapidly unfolded during these years. These were the years of the expansion of private businesses, the oil boom and migrant labor, political pluralism, and the weakening of the Soviet Union. Moreover, the 1980s were the Ronald Reagan years, seeing the rise of neoliberalism as a hegemonic global doctrine, and Mubarak was under constant pressure from the International Monetary Fund (IMF) to apply economic reform schemes that included reducing military spending. Furthermore, during these years Egypt had the heavy presence and activities of USAID, whose mission was to manage US economic aid and exert pressure for deeper market reforms. Amid these developments, the army lost much of its stature after fighting its last war against its traditional enemy and signing a peace treaty, and had to reinvent a new role of dominance for itself and a nationalistic discourse to support this role.

Field Marshal Abd al-Halim Abu Ghazala, Mubarak's minister of defense, who enjoyed close ties with the US and was vocally anti-Soviet, strongly believed that *infitah* should be applied to the Egyptian military, not just the civilian economy, and adopted every policy that ensured such openness. Part of the 1979 peace agreement pertained to redirecting the energy and human resources of the Egyptian military to economic activities, and Abu Ghazala exerted every effort to usher in this radical transformation. The Ministry of Defense created the National Service Products Organization (NSPO) to be its arm for civilian production and public works. Abu Ghazala was in favor of liberal reforms, and the officers involved in business activities favored dealing with multinational corporations and with the private sector over the public sector (Springborg 1989:261).

From the 1980s onward, the military disappeared from movies and songs that celebrated their heroism in wars, especially the 1973 war, and the officers replaced this by celebrating their contributions to 'economic development' in the postwar country. In order to justify penetrating into new civilian realms, the army forged a new discourse based on its role in price controls and the welfare of the lower classes.

Abu Ghazala's army asserted that it aimed to help the government with the five-year plan, by accepting conscripts who were not "medically, culturally, technically, or psychologically fit" for military service and putting them to work in 'national service,' *al-khidma al-wataniya*, in lighter duties, especially in producing food for the army's self-sufficiency and for the Ministry of Supply (Abd Allah 1990:96–99). Abu Ghazala started the army's involvement in the economy with humble projects such as building subsidized apartments for officers in the Nasr City area. He used conscripts as free labor in these projects, explaining that they received training to become skilled workers and technicians after they left service (*al-Malaff* 1981–1989, part 1). Using the same free labor of conscripted soldiers, he ventured heavily into the field of construction, as the army assumed the role of a major contractor for government infrastructure projects. He also expanded considerably into the field of food security, establishing self-sufficiency for the army and providing for the state. While the NSPO occupied itself extensively with 'food security' *(al-amn al-ghitha'i)* (Abd Allah 1990:81–82), the organization of military engineers *(al-hay'a al-handasiya)* busied itself with public works. On the side of the government, civilian officials justified relying on the military by arguing that the army had been successful in self-sufficiency and it would be useful to transfer its experience to civilian sectors (*al-Malaff* 1981–1989, part 2:494).

Asserting that its production was primarily to achieve self-sufficiency and provide the government with the surplus, Abu Ghazala built bakeries for subsidized bread, factories for frozen vegetables, mechanized slaughterhouses, chicken farms, fish farms, pasta factories, textile factories for military uniforms, and a furniture factory. The army constructed thousands of apartment buildings for officers who in turn sold their subsidized apartments to civilians; constructed roads and bridges for the government; renewed the infrastructure of national telephone lines; erected water desalination plants; renovated public schools and erected new ones; built sporting clubs, halls, swimming pools, and the Nasr City international conference center; constructed new urban areas in the desert; and developed water resources in Sinai. For example, the army built up to 2,600 bakeries to meet the combined needs of the armed forces and the Ministry of Supply. Furthermore, the Ministry of Defense established military vocational schools to train conscripts and workers for military and civilian sectors, and built military hospitals and supporting nursing high schools. The Ministry of Military Production expanded military factories and increased services for civilian workers in them (*al-Malaff* 1981–1989, parts 2 and 3).

The Egyptian military formed business ties with US capital, especially General Motors. Robert Springborg states, "The army has also moved into civilian manufacturing, symbolized by the deal it negotiated with General Motors in 1986 to manufacture passenger cars. Under pressure from the US Embassy, USAID pledged $200 million from its aid budget to subsidize this project" (Mitchell 1991; Springborg 1989:110). In addition, the shipping of items of US military aid to Egypt took place through certain companies that collaborated with the Egyptian army to establish monopolies in this profitable realm, and when leftist media raised a controversy, Abu Ghazala denied accusations of favoritism and asserted that the agreements had been arranged with selected shippers through public tenders in Washington, DC (*al-Malaff* 1981–1989, part 1:51).

The military budget during the 1980s was kept secret, unreported to the monitoring authorities of the Central Bureau of Auditing

(Abd Allah 1990:15). Opposition newspapers raised a controversy about large and unjustified military spending, as well as the military's engagement in economic and commercial activities and privileges. In 1984, a retired general, Ibrahim Shakib, responded to the criticism of leftist newspapers by asserting that the military did not enjoy "privileges" but "services" that it deserved like other global armies. He added that army officers who serve as business managers should be judged only on their efficiency in such work, and that they did not desire to isolate themselves from society and leave it to the market forces (Abd Allah 1990:21–24).

In 1992, Egypt finally responded to US pressure to apply economic reform à la 'Washington Consensus' model. After Mubarak applied a full-fledged economic liberalization plan, he allowed the military to expand its business enterprises by creating new companies and factories—in competition with the expanding private sector. In addition, Mubarak assigned a large number of retired generals and colonels to high administrative positions in the state bureaucracy and the public sector. During the last 10 years of his reign in particular, Mubarak granted the generals this type of entrenched economic and political influence in order to appease them and secure their approval of the succession plan of his son, Gamal.

Two years after Mubarak sacked the ambitious and charismatic Abu Ghazala in 1989, he replaced him with the low-key Field Marshall Husayn Tantawi for the following two decades, until the 2011 uprisings. During the 1990s, Tantawi continued what his predecessor started, with the military as a dominant food security producer and government contractor. The army reclaimed thousands of acres of desert land for commercial agriculture, such as the Sharq al-'Uwaynat and Nubariya farms. The army also built more public schools, stadiums, affordable housing, roads, water and electricity plants, and sewage systems, and erected sawmills and brick factories for construction. In addition, Tantawi ventured into new fields, producing chemicals, optics, plastic, and mineral water, and created companies for mining, petroleum, cleaning and maintenance, and much more. The Arab Organization for Industrialization (AOI), originally created in the 1970s for military manufacturing, recreated itself during this period as a growing manufacturer of civilian goods, such as polyethylene pipes for water, sewerage, gas pipes, and fertilizers.

Birth of Military Entrepreneurs (1980s–2000s)

The AOI opened projects for the treatment of drainage/sewerage water, produced computers, and manufactured fire engines.

Mubarak reversed Sadat's administrative demilitarization, as he appointed retired army generals and colonels to numerous bureaucratic positions. While former army officers occupied high positions in every part of the country, they preferred certain locations where influence and wealth were concentrated. For example, the majority of governors of provinces were retired army generals, and if they did not succeed in becoming governors, they served as governors' chiefs of staff, or as directors of small towns *(marakez)*, or heads of both the wealthy areas and the poor but highly populated districts in Cairo. They ran administrations in key places such as the tourist regions of Upper Egypt, all the Suez Canal provinces, the two Sinai provinces, the major Nile Delta areas, and Alexandria. The state-owned oil sector also became highly militarized as retired generals were put in charge of many natural gas and oil companies. They also controlled parts of commercial transportation. The head of the Suez Canal was always a former military chief of staff. The heads of the Red Sea ports were retired generals, as was the manager of the maritime and land transport company (Abul-Magd 2012a; 2012c).

The birth of military corporate entrepreneurs in effect took place during the 2000s. The army started to engage in business ventures with a capitalist and globalized orientation, in competition with Gamal Mubarak's patronage circle of business tycoons in the National Democratic Party's *lagnat al-siyasat*, the supreme Politics Committee responsible for designing the party's high policies. The military invested in heavy industries in collaboration with global capital, and in export-oriented agriculture. At the opening of every new economic enterprise, official statements of military managers of the enterprises filled national newspapers with claims of how this project would improve military self-sufficiency to make the military less of a burden on the state budget, help the state with its developmental plans, serve the welfare of the masses by providing them with cheap goods, and contribute to price control.

For instance, in 2004, AOI purchased Simaf, the railway wagons factory located on the outskirts of Cairo, from the state; in 2005, the Ministry of Military Production opened a steel factory in Qalyubiya that competed with the private Ezz Steel; in 2011, the NSPO opened a complex for chemicals—including fertilizers—in Fayoum; and in 2012, the same organization opened a cement factory in North Sinai. The NSPO invested in export-oriented farms in Toshka along with other foreign and local capitalists, and created a Nile transportation company in Aswan to ship the commercial produce of the Toshka farms. The army transformed regular roads into toll highways for its benefit. The AOI collaborated with the Ministry of Health to produce mobile clinics, with the Ministry of Communication to assemble computer printers, and with the state oil companies to manufacture turbines. The AOI also recycled agricultural waste to produce organic fertilizers.

The army collaborated with the new market regime that Gamal Mubarak installed—based on his circle of business clients and his father's authoritarian rule—and Field Marshall Tantawi was a member of the state privatization committee.[6] While military enterprises asserted that they were contributing to price control and the welfare of the middle and lower classes, the reality was different: they were competitors in the neoliberal market, yet with exceptional privileges. The army's untaxed, unaudited enterprises distorted the free market in their own interest rather than correcting it in the interest of the masses.

For instance, the cement factory of al-'Arish— erected on free state land in Sinai in collaboration with a Chinese company and using German technology—claims to help control prices, but the price of the military cement is almost the same as that of other public and private factories, or sometimes higher. In fact, cement prices have skyrocketed ever since the military factory was opened in April 2012. Newspapers celebrate the cheap prices of the military cement, but the reality is otherwise. Similarly, the Simaf railway wagons factory does not provide its products to the government at affordable prices in the interest of the working masses who use railways; if they had, the Ministry of Transportation could have renewed the whole railroad system at reduced prices and saved the lives of thousands who die in train accidents annually.

Another example is related to the work of the military's Engineers Organization *(al-hay'a al-handasiya)* in the construction of affordable

---

6 Walid Magdi, "Da'wa tutalib bi-l-tahqiq ma'a 50 mas'ul baynahun Tantawi wa-l-Ganzuri wa-Musa fi fasad al-khaskhassa," *Al-Masry Al-Youm*, January 8, 2012.

houses. The EO presents itself as the most efficient and disciplined contractor in the country, and it always won government contracts without entering into free and fair tenders where other private contractors could compete. This kind of direct agreement with the government is called *bi-l-ittifaq* or *bi-l-isnad al-mubashir* and the EO constantly exploits the public tenders law that permits this as an exceptional means to hire contractors. After obtaining a government contract, the EO uses subcontractors from the private sector to execute the project and ultimately the state foots the bill. More importantly, the EO charges the government far above the market price. Although the government pays the bill, the military propaganda brags in the media about how the army kindly builds projects for the people. Every year, the army holds Engineering Organization Day, *Youm tafawwuq al-hay'a al-handasiya*, to celebrate its excellence. On this day, Tantawi used to praise the organization's contribution to economic development and the welfare of the lower classes, and he also watched a documentary on the fundamental role of the organization in designing a historic bridge to cross the Suez Canal in the 1973 war.

The enterprise of building affordable public housing (or subsidized social housing) for the middle and lower-income classes—*masaken al-shabab*, for example—was in the hands of the EO, in collaboration with the Ministry of Housing and its Organization of New Urban Communities. Retired army generals and colonels dominate high administrative positions in the Ministry of Housing and the organization. Without public tenders, the ministry and the organization directly grant contracts to the EO to build middle- to lower-income suburbs on the outskirts of Cairo. Evidently, the work of the EO is not the most efficient: the public complains about extensive delays and corruption, and private-sector contractors have accused the EO of stealing their designs.[7] Employees inside the ministry and the organization have called for the dismissal of the corrupt retired officers there.[8]

---

7   Iman Ibrahim, "al-Mugtama'at al-'umraniya tatala'ab fi makittat al-iskan al-'a'ili," *al-Dostor*, February 16, 2014; Maha Salim, "Mamduh Hamza yattahim al-hay'a al-handasiya bi-sariqat tasmimatuh," *al-Ahram*, March 7, 2012.
8   For example: Amina 'Abd al-'Azim, "I'tilaf al-mugtama'at al-'umraniya yutalib bi-iqalat al-qiyadat al-'askariya min al-hay'a," *Sada al-Balad*, August 19, 2012.

Military Entrepreneurs and Revolution (2011–2013)

In February 2011, after a sit-in of 18 days, the protesters in Tahrir Square celebrated deposing Mubarak and aborting his son's succession plan. They carried banners calling for social justice against Mubarak's destructive market transition. The Supreme Council of the Armed Forces (SCAF) immediately offered its help to run the country for a short transitional period of six months. Grateful for such support, the Egyptian masses chanted "The army and the people are one hand," and state-owned media played the 1960s national songs of Nasser's era. SCAF stayed in power for a full year and a half, until they turned over power to an elected president from the Muslim Brothers in June 2012. One year later, as this president—who soon sacked the old SCAF—drastically failed in running the country's distressed economy and mass protests emerged again in numbers much larger than those of 2011, the new SCAF decided to intervene once more to overthrow him. Cheerfully expressing their appreciation of this military action, the celebrating masses filled Tahrir Square with posters of Nasser and General Abd al-Fatah al-Sisi, the new minister of defense appointed by the deposed president Morsi. The army's public relations department funded the production of a song, titled *Tisalm al-ayadi*, praising the soldiers' hands that saved the nation and invoking the 1973 war victory. The song quickly became so popular among Egyptians of all social classes that it was played at weddings.

After decades of non-intervention in domestic politics, the Egyptian armed forces returned with fundamentally decisive roles. During the last three years, military business managers in Egypt have deployed the old nationalist rhetoric invented by Nasser to present themselves as the 'guardians of the nation,' but in order to reach different ends. Whereas the 2011 intervention took place against a weakened ruling elite and was done partially to protect the military institution's economic interests, the 2013 case was to face internal and external security threats and, on the contrary, posed a risk to these economic interests.

After the 2011 intervention, SCAF formed a close alliance with the Muslim Brothers and other Islamists, who happened to win the majority in the subsequent elections that were supervised and provided with security measures by the army soldiers. In return, the army was granted exceptional status in the Brotherhood's constitution, which protected the secret budget and civilian enterprises of the military. On the other hand, after the 2013 intervention, the army largely withdrew from the political scene after taking the Islamists out of it, and occupied itself with security matters, especially in the Sinai Peninsula. It is not clear yet whether the military would fully retain its privileged status in the new constitution. There is public debate about keeping the military budget secret, shielded from parliamentary oversight, and about the institution's right to choose the minister of defense. Furthermore, because the United States disapproved of the 2013 intervention to depose the Muslim Brothers—who functioned as allies of the Obama administration during their brief time in power—the military risked losing its annual US military aid. The Obama administration made a decision to cut military aid to Egypt, and the Pentagon suspended scheduled shipments of equipment to Egypt.[9]

After deposing Mubarak, the old SCAF formed a conspicuous marriage of convenience with the Muslim Brothers based on power sharing. After assuming power, this SCAF voluntarily adopted a democratic discourse and oversaw many elections. The Egyptian people went to the ballot boxes to vote four times under the old SCAF: in a referendum on a constitutional declaration drafted by a committee chosen by SCAF to include Muslim Brothers leaders and be headed by Islamist judges; two parliamentary elections; and one presidential election. In every election, the ballot boxes were in favor of the Islamists—particularly the Muslim Brothers and the Salafis. In March 2011, the Islamists were very helpful in using religious slogans to mobilize the masses to vote in favor of SCAF's constitutional declaration, and SCAF repaid the favor. The soldiers protected the polling stations, but they allowed the Islamists to violate electoral rules by using religious slogans and distributing publications with religious signs inside and at the doors of electoral commissions. In addition, civil society organizations that monitored elections recorded cases of buying votes from rural and

---

[9] See Zeinab Abul-Magd, "US Military Aid to Egypt Lost Value," *Jadaliyya*, July 25, 2013, http://www.jadaliyya.com/pages/index/13186/us-military-aid-to-egypt-lost-value-; Fox News, "US Cutting Military Aid, Hundreds of Millions in Cash Assistance to Egypt," October 10, 2013, http://www.foxnews.com/politics/2013/10/10/us-cutting-hundreds-millions-in-aid-to-egypt/

urban lower-class citizens.[10] In the presidential elections, the electoral violations on the part of the Muslim Brothers in favor of Morsi were evident, but the army turned a blind eye to them.[11]

The Muslim Brothers returned the favor. In June 2012, when Muhammad Morsi of the Muslim Brothers won the presidential election, he began his first national address by thanking the armed forces. He saluted the Egyptian military and added, "Only God knows how much love I have in my heart [for it]."[12] Morsi maintained the privileged status of the army in the bureaucracy, by hiring ministers, governors, and other top administrators from among the army officers. In August 2012, he sacked Tantawi and replaced him with General al-Sisi, after a grave incident in Sinai where terrorist groups killed a number of conscripts. As rumors spread about al-Sisi that he was a closeted Muslim Brother, he engaged in full cooperation with the Morsi government.

The Muslim Brothers granted the military a semi-autonomous status in the constitution that they issued through a public referendum in December 2012. Article 197 of this constitution kept the military budget—even the parts pertaining to revenue from civilian businesses—above state oversight and public scrutiny. It placed the oversight of the military budget in the hands of the National Defense Council, a governmental body consisting mainly of military officers internally nominated. The parliament was obliged to consult the same council about any proposed laws relevant to the armed forces before they were issued. Furthermore, Article 195 in the same constitution stipulated that the minister of defense should always be

---

10 Safa' Surur, "Taqrir huquqi: shira' aswat wa-bitaqat dawwara wa-qudah yuwagihun al-nakhibin fi awwal ayyam al-marhala al-thalitha," *Al-Masry Al-Youm*, January 3, 2012; al-I'tilaf al-Mustaqil li-Muraqabat al-Intikhabat, *Taqrir al-marhala al-ula li-intikhabat maglis al-sha'b 2011. November 28-29, 2011. Taqrir al-Muraqaba al-Midaniya* (Cairo: al-Gam'iya al-Misriya li-l-Nuhud bi-l-Musharaka al-Mugtama'iya, December 2012), http://www.mosharka.org/index.php?newsid=417

11 "Hurra naziha: Mursi yatasaddar intihakat al-yawm al-awwal bi 57%...," *al-Badil*, May 23, 2012; Khalaf 'Ali Hasan and Mu'tazz Nadi, "Hurra naziha: ansar Mursi fi Qina yuwazzi'un zayt wa-lahma wa-sukkar 'ala al-nakhibin," *Al-Masry Al-Youm*, May 24, 2012.

12 Al-Arabiya, "Awwal khitab li-l-ra'is al-misri al-muntakhab Muhammad Mursi," June 24, 2012, http://www.youtube.com/watch?v=pzs7R3lUeUQ

chosen from ranking officers, that is, no civilian could be appointed as the minister of defense.[13]

SCAF expanded its business empire during this period. Morsi and the Brotherhood government granted the military extensive advantages that overstepped sound civil–military relations (see Abul-Magd 2012b; 2013). The Shura Council, under Muslim Brotherhood control, helped the military expand its business empire in collaboration with Morsi's cabinet. This council's Committee of Human Development transferred the property rights of a state-owned car factory to the Ministry of Military Production.[14] The same ministry invested in assembling computer tablets, and other ministries in the Brotherhood cabinet placed orders to buy thousands of these items outside competitive public tenders.[15] In addition, the military was allowed to acquire more land to build new malls,[16] and received a state permit to establish a medical school to train staff for its profitable hospitals that admit civilians.[17] As the budget of the army's civilian enterprises remained secret, the head of the state's Central Auditing Organization complained that he had no access to the accounts of military-owned businesses.[18]

Although the new SCAF of al-Sisi collected numerous favors from Morsi and the Brothers, it perceived them as a threat to national security. Besides suffering from severe economic failure and crushing public discontent because of police brutality, the government of the Muslim Brothers supported jihadist groups inside and outside the country. After marching in massive protests of tens of millions across the country on June 30, 2013, most Egyptians expected the army to carry out its

---

13 For the full text of the constitution see http://www.almasryalyoum.com/node/1283056
14 Rami Nawwar and Kamil Kamal, "Na'ib al-Nur yaltaqi wazir al-intag al-harbi li-bahth tashghil al-Nasr li-l-Sayyarat," *al-Youm al-Sabi'*, February 10, 2013; Muhammad Abd al-'Ati, "Tafa'ul bi-intiqal sharkiat bi-qita' al-a'mal li-l-intag al-harbi," *Al-Masry Al-Youm*, April 15, 2013.
15 "Wazir al-intag al-harbi: 'urud kharigiya dakhma li-shira' al-tablit al-masri," *Rassd*, April 23, 2013, http://rassd.com/3-59838.htm
16 'Ammar al-Nisr, "Bi-l-suwar: mul tigari kabir l-gihaz khadamat al-quwwat al-musalaha bi-Bilbis," *Sha'b Misr*, March 18, 2013.
17 "al-Shura yuwafiq niha'iyyan 'ala insha' kuliyat al-tib tabi'a li-l-quwwat al-musalaha," *al-Youm al-Sabi'*, June 27, 2013.
18 "Ra'is al-markazi li-l-muhasabat: ma 'alaqat aa'at afrah al-quwwat al-musalaha bi-l-amn al-qawmi?," *Sada al-Balad*, November 4, 2012.

'traditional' duty of protecting national security by saving the country from an economically failed government that had ties to international jihad. The military institution responded to the people's demands, and formed a coalition with several political parties and public figures that deposed Morsi on July 3.

Two weeks before his ouster, Morsi gathered tens of thousands of Islamists from different factions in Cairo Stadium in order to declare international jihad in Syria. Without military approval, Morsi announced that the "Egyptian people and army" together were going to help free Syria from its tyrannical regime by supporting the militant rebels there. Within this large meeting, many extremist Sunni clerics made strong sectarian statements with Morsi's consent, and this was followed a few days later by the massacre of four Shi'is in a village near Cairo.[19] In his meeting with US Secretary of Defense Chuck Hagel in Cairo in April 2013, al-Sisi expressed deep concern that the severity of the situation in Syria might spill over into other countries in the region.[20]

Three weeks before the stadium incident, terrorist cells in the Sinai Peninsula kidnapped seven Egyptian soldiers. Morsi interfered to stop a planned military operation against the kidnappers, who eventually released the soldiers and escaped without being arrested or identified.[21] After the end of this crisis, many former military generals asserted that the Muslim Brothers sponsored the Sinai jihadists and facilitated the criminals' escape from security forces. The former founder of the counterterrorism unit in the Egyptian military, Team 777, claimed that the brotherhood and Hamas were responsible for many other incidents of kidnapping army soldiers in the troubled peninsula.[22]

For many Egyptians from different generations, the dark memories of the 1990s when there was widespread terrorism in the country are still vividly alive in their minds. During this period, the military played little to no role in arresting dangerous jihadists who committed

---

19 Bassam Ramadan, "Muhammad Hassan yunashid Mursi alla yaftah bab Misr amam rafidat Iran," *Al-Masry Al-Youm*, June 15, 2013; "Maqtal 4 baynahum za'im Shi'i fi hugum ganub al-Qahira," *BBC*, June 23, 2013.

20 Adam Entous, "US Defense Chief Mans Hot Line to Cairo," *Wall Street Journal*, July 11, 2013.

21 "Mursi mana' al-hugum 'ala musallahi Sayna'...," *al-Ahram*, July 29, 2013.

22 "Mu'assis al-Firqa 777: ikhtitaf al-gunud musalsal batalahu al-Ikhwan wa-Hamas," *al-Arabiya*, May 22, 2013.

atrocities against tourists and Egyptians; other security forces took on this difficult duty. The January 2011 uprisings fundamentally weakened those security forces and left them impotent to perform such vital tasks. Thus, the military, already humiliated by jihadists kidnapping its soldiers in Sinai, probably realized it had to carry the responsibility this time. Only one week before the June 30 uprisings, al-Sisi asserted that the army would not tolerate those who try to "scare and terrorize" the Egyptian people.

The Egyptian military decided to oust Morsi, despite the fact that this act put their economic advantages at risk. For many long months, al-Sisi was content with these advantages and he invited Morsi to many military ceremonies, where the deposed president saw the graduation of new officers and the opening of new military projects. Al-Sisi publicly asserted on several occasions that the army would not interfere in politics and would only put its efforts into protecting the country internally and externally.[23] Thus, for the military to side with youth and opposition groups who had long chanted against such privileges could result in significant future losses. There is an ongoing tense debate between the military and the committee set up to draft the new constitution over the articles that pertain to the army. In addition, the military lost US aid when the Obama administration suspended parts of it to sanction the Egyptian military for undertaking a 'coup' against her allies in the Brotherhood.

Conclusion

Since the 2011 revolution, the memory of Nasser has been intensively revived throughout the country. Pro-military protesters carry portraits of the charismatic leader, next to those of al-Sisi, in Tahrir Square, and state-owned television stations screen old movies and documentaries that glorify his legacy. In a large national celebration attended by al-Sisi, many popular singers patriotically performed in an operetta to celebrate the 1973 war victory once again. In the absence of a functioning government, the army's Engineering Organization rescued a Giza village drowned under sewage, al-Sisi decided to cancel small peasants' debts owed to state banks, and the armed forces announced their contribution to paying taxi drivers' loans to the Ministry of Finance. Militarism

---

23 "Al-Sisi: wala' al-quwwat al-musalaha li-l-sha'b wa-l-dawla," *El-Watan News*, November 27, 2011.

is clearly back and growing more entrenched in Egyptian culture and society, with the Egyptian people's full desire and consent. The future of democratic transition in Egypt is not clear yet, but clearly the military will always play key roles in the unfolding processes. Regardless of public controversy over the military's business enterprises, it is obvious that the army does not plan to give up such privileges—which only means the continuity of its domineering leverage in politics. It is also obvious that the army will continue to maintain the superior status of a state within a state.

References

Abd Allah, Ahmad, ed. 1990. *Al-Gaysh wa-l-dimuqraitiya fi Misr*. Cairo: Sina li-l-Nashr.

Abul-Magd, Zeinab. 2012a. "The Egyptian Republic of Retired Generals," *Foreign Policy*, 8 May.

———. 2012b. "Egypt's Politics of Hidden Business Empires: The Brotherhood versus the Army," *Atlantic Council*, October 5.

———. 2012c. "Understanding SCAF," *Cairo Review*, 6 (Summer).

———. 2013. "Chuck Hagel in Egypt's Economic Chaos," *Atlantic Council*, April 29.

Altinay, Ayse Gul. 2004. *The Myth of the Military-Nation: Militarism, Gender, and Education in Turkey*. New York: Palgrave Macmillan.

Ayubi, Nazih. 1996. *Over-Stating the Arab State: Politics and Society in the Middle East*. London: I.B. Tauris.

Berger, Morroe. 1960. *Military Elite and Social Change: Egypt since Napoleon*. Princeton: Princeton University Press.

Brommelhorster, Jorn, and Wolf-Christian Paes, eds. 2004. *The Military as an Economic Actor: Soldiers in Business*. New York: Palgrave Macmillan.

Cooper, Mark. 1982. "Demilitarization of Egyptian Cabinet," *International Journal of Middle Eastern Studies*, 14: 203-225.

al-Malaff al-watha'iqi li-l-mushir Muhammad 'Abd al-Halim Abu Ghazala. 1981–1989. Parts 1–3. Cairo: Markaz al-Ahram li-l-Tanzim wa-l-Microfilm.

Mitchell, Timothy. 1991. "America's Egypt: Discourse of the Development Industry," *MER* 169(21). http://www.merip.org/mer/mer169/americas-egypt

References

Pion-Berlin, David. 2011. "Turkish Civil–Military Relations: A Latin American Comparison," *Turkish Studies*, 12: 293–304.

Skocpol, Theda. 1976. "France, Russia, China: A Structural Analysis of Social Revolutions," *Comparative Studies in Society and History*, 18: 175–210.

Springborg, Robert. 1989. *Mubarak's Egypt: Fragmentation of the Political Order*. London: Westview Press.

Taylor, Brian. 2003. *Politics and the Russian Army: Civil–Military Relations, 1689–2000*. Cambridge: Cambridge University Press.

CHAPTER 9

Affordable Housing Policies in Egypt after the 2011 Revolution
More of the Same?

David Sims

Introduction

This chapter makes an assessment of how and to what extent housing policies of the government, aimed at addressing housing needs of the majority of Egyptians, changed in the two years following the revolution of January 25, 2011. The government has had a long history with directly providing housing to citizens in need, and there has been a succession of regulations controlling housing production and markets. The results have been disappointing, to say the least.

Some would have thought that the revolution's principles of basic needs, democracy, and social justice would lead to a fundamental rethinking of what has gone on in the past, especially compared to the record during the Mubarak regime. Of course, over the two chaotic years following the revolution it is unfair to assume that far-reaching and comprehensive housing sector reform would be achieved by the military or the Muslim Brotherhood governments, but at least there should be some indications of the beginnings of such policy shifts. This chapter attempts to feel these out, by reviewing both new government policies and legislation and official pronouncements.

This chapter first gives the general reader a very short background on the nature of housing in Egypt as of 2010—its modes of production, type of housing produced, market dynamics, and the thorny issue of housing affordability. Then the reader is presented with a synopsis of both explicit and implied housing policies as they had evolved in Egypt up to the 2011 revolution and who had been the main winners and losers. This sets up the framework for a comparison with what happened in the following two years, to attempt to identify important emerging housing policy changes if they exist, or to confirm if blind adherence to past approaches continues. Finally, a few tentative observations are made about what might be some emerging characteristics of Egypt's post-revolutionary political economy in the light of what can be uncovered from the housing sector.

A Brief Background on the Nature of Housing in Egypt

Housing in Egypt is a complicated subject, and only major features of housing systems can be noted here. The focus will be on housing in urban areas, since it is in urban areas that housing needs are most acute, and also it is urban housing toward which practically all government programs and policies are directed.

Overwhelmingly, urban housing in Egypt is produced by families and small informal contractors. The most comprehensive study of the sector, carried out in 2008,[1] shows that corporate and government housing systems account for only about 25 percent of recent production. Also, it is through individuals and informal brokers that most housing is bought and sold. In addition, rental housing, which has come to be the dominant form of housing tenure since the New Rent Law of 1996 came into force, is exclusively the domain of individual landlords and renters. And a sizable portion of housing exchange among individuals and families is through mechanisms other than the market, such as gifts, free rents, and inheritance.

Comparing census figures between 1996 and 2006, there was an increase of 4.6 million housing units, or a percentage increase of 56.2 percent. Over the same period the urban population grew by 24.6 percent and the number of households by 34.3 percent. Thus the production of housing units exceeded the growth in the number of households and greatly exceeded that of the population. This excess of production of units over households was also very apparent in the 1986–1996 period. As a result, in urban areas in 2006 there was an excess of 4.9 million housing units over households (or an excess of 38.2 percent). From a purely quantitative perspective, these figures suggest that there should not be a housing shortage in urban Egypt,

---

1 USAID (2008). Other volumes on Egypt's regions and on the study methodology are also available.

A Brief Background on the Nature of Housing in Egypt

and this points to a peculiar feature of urban housing: a very high rate of housing unit vacancies, one of the highest in the world.

Who produces housing in urban Egypt? There are three main modes of production: the government (under a number of agencies and programs), the formal private sector both corporate and individual (measured by the issuance of building permits), and the informal sector (built without permits and thus unrecorded). According to a World Bank study, it is estimated that over the 1982–2005 period, production shares by mode were 22 percent by government, 33 percent by the formal private sector, and 45 percent by the informal sector.[2] The informal-sector share of total production is actually much higher, especially if urban and urbanizing areas presently classified as rural by the census were to be included.

What kind of housing is being produced? By far the dominant type of building is the small-footprint, multi-story apartment block (four or five floors is average, although tower blocks are becoming more common in both formal and informal areas). For example, practically all housing units surveyed in the 2008 survey were single apartments in buildings (85 percent), and only 8 percent were classified as either villas or rural houses. Single-room units represented only 4.5 percent of the urban housing stock. Contrary to the impression one might get from advertisements for projects in the new towns around Cairo, urban housing units are quite small. The median gross housing area of occupied housing units was 75 m^2 and the median net area was 70 m^2. Only 10 percent of housing units had gross areas in excess of 120 m^2. Smaller housing units (less than 40 m^2) represented 5.6 percent of the total units. Overall, the average net area in a housing unit per person was 23.2 m^2, and the average number of persons per room was 1.21.

Almost all occupied units had a private kitchen, a bath and toilet, and running water and sewer systems, even in informal housing. And the quality and durability of buildings was mostly good—especially for buildings constructed in the last 30 years—with the dominant form of construction being reinforced concrete frame and slab flooring, with brick infill walls. However, in informal areas where there is no control, most streets are very narrow and a number of housing units suffer from lack of light and ventilation.

---

2   See World Bank and USAID (2008:3–4). It would seem that the percentage figure for government production is too high.

Is there a housing crisis in Egypt? The answer is certainly yes if you are a family below the median urban income (at the time of writing some LE1600 per month from all sources) and have no equity. And if you are a bachelor seeking an apartment for marriage and must rely on your salary (assuming you are employed), you will have very few choices other than renting a tiny unit in an informal area, unless you can manage to queue for government units. In other words, in terms of access to decent housing, affordability remains the key issue in urban Egypt, even though housing markets present a remarkable array of choices. And this issue is unlikely to go away any time soon.

Egypt's Housing Policies as They Had Evolved Up to 2011

In past decades and up to 2011, the Egyptian government had no explicit national housing policy, nor had it adopted anything like a comprehensive housing policy document. The government's approach was dominated by one single feature: the production by the state of housing units ostensibly for families of limited income.[3] It is this program that has preoccupied national and local state agencies dealing with housing, has claimed virtually all of the state budgetary allocations to the sector, and takes priority for access to public lands. However, it must be recognized that there have been a number of laws issued that attempt to regulate the wider private housing sector. These together can be considered expressions of an implicit housing policy, and they are briefly addressed at the end of this section.

Social housing programs. Government-provided, subsided public and cooperative housing in Egypt has a long history, starting in the early 1950s. Various government-financed and government-implemented housing programs were ostensibly aimed at lower-income households, and the main types were small apartments in walk-up housing blocks. The serviced land upon which this housing has been built was, without exception, state-owned land provided at no cost, increasingly in remote desert locations. Thus in addition to subsidies inherent in low rents or low installment payments, land and its associated infrastructure were also heavily subsidized.

---

3 In Arabic *mahdudi al-dakhl*, but never defined. As recently as 2011, to qualify for the National Housing Program a family's salaried income must not have exceeded LE2,500 a month, which implies that over 75 percent of urban families were of 'limited income.'

Over the period 1952–1982, a total of 1.1 million units of government housing were built throughout the country, at an average rate of 37,790 units per year (not counting military housing). In 1981 the prevailing subsidized rental system was changed to one of *tamleek*, under which beneficiaries paid very low monthly installments and, after 30 or 40 years, would become owners of their units. Over the 1982–2005 period, production totaled 1.26 million units, with an average annual production of 54,700 units. These government programs were under different authorities (mainly governorates, the housing cooperative authority, and the new-town agencies), but the housing models and payment conditions remained remarkably similar, at least up until the introduction of the National Housing Program (2005–2011).

Although theoretically government housing is aimed at households with limited income, as far as is known there were no attempts to target beneficiaries based on income or wealth thresholds or means tests. In fact, in most government housing programs the required qualifications are of the most rudimentary, with available units being distributed by lottery if demand exceeds supply.

State subsidies in housing production have been large. For the typical Mubarak Youth housing unit (1997–2002), at least 68 percent of every pound directly invested by the state was never recovered. And the true subsidy element is much higher, since calculations assume perfect repayment, no cost overruns, rapid construction, and timely allocation.

Since land for government housing must be costless state land, the result is that almost all government housing is located either in the new towns or on local government desert lands which are also far from existing urban agglomerations. This makes it difficult for beneficiaries, especially those of limited income, to pursue normal livelihoods. It is no wonder that in more recent government housing programs vacancy rates exceed 50 percent.

Given the high subsidy element in past government programs, both the down payments and installment payments could be considered affordable by at least 75 percent of urban households. But were lower-income households the main beneficiaries of government housing programs? It is extremely difficult to answer this question because the targeting/assignment system is dependent on an 'application regime' which is executed partly on a lottery basis, and partly rationed by the small size of the unit and the unattractiveness of certain locations. In any event, resale of units is very common although forbidden, making acquisition of a government unit a potential speculative monetary windfall more than anything else.

In 2005 the government of Egypt launched an initiative called the National Housing Program (NHP), which aimed to construct 500,000 subsidized housing units over six years spread throughout the country, a level of production never achieved before. The program coincided with Hosni Mubarak's new presidential term and in fact was referred to by many as "the president's promise" *(wa'd al-ra'is)*. The main features of this program, which represented some improvements from past practices, were:

- Engaging the private sector in the construction and marketing of some units.
- Introducing new housing models, particularly systems for housing sites and services.
- Replacing the old unclear financial subsidy mechanisms with a straightforward up-front cash subsidy for each unit. The remaining financing comes from beneficiary down payments and mortgage loans made under Law 148 of 2001 and the institutions created under this law.
- Introducing more choice in equity down payments by beneficiaries to better fit household finances.
- Reintroducing heavily subsidized rental tenure into the product mix, mainly for resettlement cases.
- Improving financial management of housing projects through greater involvement of banks and mortgage institutions.

In October 2010, the Ministry of Housing presented numbers that showed the NHP was moving towards realizing its target of 500,000 units. As of that date, 322,284 units and land plots had been completed or delivered to beneficiaries, while 211,579 units were under construction/allocation. The program was being implemented through seven schemes, three of which—Ibni Beitak (Build Your House) land plots, home ownership, and private developers—are considered the most important and widely applied, as shown in table 9.1.

Table 9.1. NHP housing units built/under construction or land plots delivered/to be delivered (as of October 2010)

	Scheme	Total number of units completed and delivered	Total number of units completed and being currently delivered	Number of units currently under construction
1	Home ownership (governorates/new cities)	129,794	50,077	115,350
2	Provision of small land plots for individuals in new cities (Ibni Beitak)	90,993	1,873	1,682
3	Provision of land for private developers in new cities to build 63-m^2 housing units	16,940	3,884	43,112
4	Family home ownership in Sixth October City *(beit al-aila)*	1,750	1,270	0
5	Rental units of 42 m^2 for the most deprived groups *(al-awla b-al-re'aya)*			
	Units for *al-awla b-al-re'aya*	4,581	7,123	22,113
	Most needed villages in governorates	132	932	15,128
6	Rental units of 63 m^2 in governorates, new cities, and by *awqaf*	3,879	2,412	9,546
7	Rural home ownership in governorates and desert hinterland	4,797	1,847	4,648
	Total	252,866	69,418	211,579

Source: Translated from Agence Française du Développement 2011, Tableau 5.2

Actually, these figures showed a certain creative manipulation to present numeric achievements of the program in the best light. For example, the Ibni Beitak targets were simply delivered land plots, upon which few houses had been finished and none occupied. And even among "completed and delivered housing units," practically none were actually lived in. It is understood that by mid 2012 a sizable portion of the NHP units were still unfinished or undelivered. It should be mentioned that such a preoccupation with achieving quantitative production targets was a common feature of the Mubarak regime, and any actual assessment of impacts and lessons-learned was practically never carried out.

Criteria for selecting beneficiaries under the program were only the most rudimentary. Applicants had to furnish documentary proof that their salaried income did not exceed LE1,750 per month if single and LE2,500 for a married couple[4] (meaning that at least 80 percent of all households in Egypt would qualify). In addition, the applicant (and the members of his nuclear family) must not already have acquired a housing unit or land from the government anywhere in Egypt, and he/she must sign a declaration to this effect.

The housing units produced by the NHP (except rentals) were less affordable than older programs, especially for households who were equity-poor and whose incomes were not buoyant.[5] In addition, the NHP continued many of the drawbacks of previous supply-side subsidized housing systems. The most serious of these were:

- Locations of new housing at sites which were remote and unattractive to limited-income families.
- High and rising infrastructure costs which were not accounted for in calculations and represented an additional burden on the state budget.
- Persistent cost overruns and delays in housing production, which further compromised the NHP's financial viability and added to the subsidy burden.

---

4   The ceiling for monthly incomes until 2008 had been LE1000 for singles and LE1,500 for married couples.

5   The installment payments for unit ownership were set at only LE60/month but had steep escalator clauses that rapidly made these payments very burdensome, and for the rental schemes the low initial rents of LE60/month were valid for only seven years, after which it was anyone's guess what they would be.

- No explicit attempt at internal cross-subsidization to reduce overall costs of housing estates.
- No attempt at specifically targeting the poor was made, with units distributed randomly by luck and rationed by unattractiveness.
- The phenomenon of unoccupied and vacant units would probably exceed the already embarrassing rates of previous programs.

A couple of years before the 2011 revolution, the government and its backers began to prepare for a second National Housing Program (NHP2) that was to produce a similar volume of housing units (500,000) under a similar time frame (six years). This program evaporated after the revolution, although some of its concepts were carried into new programs, as will be seen in the next section. Among these was a loan from the World Bank of US $300 million called the "Affordable Mortgage Finance DPL," signed in 2009, which was to be pumped into housing programs to strengthen mortgage-backed loan systems and thus mainstream mortgage financing for government housing.

Implicit housing policies under Mubarak. As mentioned above, there is nothing in Egypt that could be called a 'national housing act' or that specifically aims at regulating the housing sector. The social housing programs, including the 2005–2011 NHP, had been based on presidential or prime ministerial decrees and had been incorporated into state budget planning. However, there are a number of laws that have had some impact on the wider urban housing sector in Egypt and together can be considered an implicit expression of housing policies. These are:

1. The New Urban Communities Law (Law 59 of 1979), which created the New Urban Communities Authority (NUCA) under the Ministry of Housing and gave it extensive powers to develop state lands and generate revenues from this development. These powers meant that NUCA was able to create urban areas in ways that neither governorates nor even other ministries could. It also gave NUCA the authority over all aspects of development in the new towns, including a direct role in housing provision, where over the years a very substantial amount of social housing (over 50 percent) has been located. Not only do the new towns created

over decades under this legislation underpin national urban spatial planning policy, they also imply that new housing estates should be of very high modern standards, with low densities, spacious landscaping, and none of the informal economy that dominates existing cities.

2. New Rent Law (No. 4 of 1996). For rental contracts made after this date, a new system of term-limited, contractual rents was established. This greatly improved rental markets, allowing the landlord and tenant to come to contractual agreements which set the rent and the period of validity, and also allowed for special conditions. Long overdue, it replaced the previous rental control regime. The effects and popularity of this new form of rental relations between landlord and tenant have been considerable, although some landlords remain hesitant to use it. In 2002 a presidential decree was issued which modified some aspects of the old Rent Law, such as limiting inheritance of fixed rent contracts to one generation.

3. The Mortgage Law (No. 148 of 2001) introduced, for the first time in Egypt, a system of property loans from banks and mortgage finance companies in which collateral for the loan was the property itself. The law allowed for foreclosure of the loan and repossession of the property for delinquent payment, enforceable through civil courts. Basically, it is similar to enabling legislation for mortgage lending as found in most countries, and it reflects the neoliberal policies of the government during the 2000s. Due to a number of structural problems, until 2011 the volume of housing financed under this law was restricted to a few thousand new upscale housing units as well as some units of the NHP.

4. Property Tax Law (No. 196 of 2008), which replaced the inefficient 'awayid building tax, had been under preparation by the Ministry of Finance for years. It was finally approved by Parliament in 2008. Even so, by 2011 its executive regulations were still being modified, and considerable confusion remained as to applicable rates, coverage, and implementation procedures. Populist calls for exceptions were many, and eventually properties with a market value of LE500,000 or less were considered exempt, which meant that the exemption covered over 90 percent of urban

residential units. The main logic of this legislation was to uncover a new and buoyant source of government revenues, but it also was to discourage holding housing in a vacant state. It remains unclear whether it should be applied to vacant and unfinished units, and the law specifically does not cover vacant urban land. Thus what is probably the greatest arena for pure property speculation—that on land—can continue happily, since there are no recurrent costs associated with holding such land parcels.
5. The Unified Building Code of 2008 (Law No. 119 of 2008 and its executive regulations of March 2009) became the core legislation for both urban development and housing construction, having amalgamated previous legislation. Although many observers hoped that the law would permit more local control of planning and allow for more flexible and realistic standards for subdivision and building in popular areas, the law and its executive regulations actually seem to impose even stricter, more rigid control. Thus subdivision and building regulations continue to impose high-end standards that make the construction of low-cost housing very difficult. The law gives the impression that the already onerous, bureaucratic, costly, and ineffective building-permit regime present over decades will become even more entrenched.

Absence of effective housing policies. It should be clear that up until 2011 affordable housing policy in Egypt was restricted to government social-housing programs. And while there had been a number of reforms and adjustments over the years, the stark fact is that, even if production targets are met and only the intended low-income households benefit (both of which are very doubtful), the programs could only reach between 20 and 35 percent of annual housing needs for the lower income strata. Moreover, the past programs, including the NHP, have taken a largely supply-side approach, aimed at increasing the production of new housing units either in the new towns or in governorates, always on state land and increasingly in remote desert locations poorly integrated with existing urban agglomerations.

Other housing policies are implicit in legislation which affected the whole housing sector, as pointed out above, but none of these laws tried to make housing more accessible or affordable to the poor or even the average-income household. In fact, most of this legislation had the effect of making housing more expensive and less accessible.

As shown above, urban Egypt has a very large and dynamic housing market, at least half to two-thirds of which is informal. This wider housing market is, by and large, untouched by current government housing policies and is dismissed as illegal, even though this huge subsector includes both the majority of new housing and the vast majority of housing affordable to limited-income groups. There has been a total reluctance on the part of government to try to make informal housing systems and markets function more efficiently and to be more responsive to demand by those in most need of housing.

Such an unbalanced and restrictive 'supply-side' approach by government toward the urban housing problem has been recognized in the last few years by both Egyptian and foreign housing specialists. They have posed the question: How might interventions be devised which would influence the existing market to remove or reduce current distortions and to stimulate more affordable housing solutions? Over the period 2006 to 2008 a series of policy studies were carried out for the ministries of housing and investment under the sponsorship of USAID and the World Bank, and these were presented to the government in 2007 and 2008.[6]

Some of these proposals included recommendations for improving the NHP itself, but the proposals also presented a wide range of measures which could be relatively easily adopted, to begin to make Egypt's huge existing housing markets more efficient and more responsive to those most in need. Some of these proposals were purely regulatory, procedural, and institutional. Others tried to apply small government subsidies to improve affordability, especially to stimulate the demand side. Proposals focused on a number of housing issues, including:

- Unlocking the stock of vacant housing by providing incentives and guarantees to owners of vacant units to encourage them to market such units, including small loans for finishing units.

---

6 The two main documents were World Bank and USAID (2008) and World Bank (2008).

- Creating more efficient rental markets by strengthening regulations for fair and transparent dealings between landlord and tenant and accelerating rent decontrol.
- Enhancing affordability of housing options by including informal housing units as qualifying for financing and for subsidies in certain cases.
- Improving the targeting of public subsidies to ensure that they are provided to (1) the lowest-income households, who require them in order to obtain adequate shelter, and (2) specific market segments to assist in clearing well-defined market blockages.

Unfortunately, these proposals seem to have fallen on deaf ears. The government in 2008 seemed preoccupied with completing the production targets of the first NHP and preparing for the second. Reforms and improvements within these programs were being considered, but stepping outside the NHP envelope was perceived as either legally too difficult or politically unacceptable. None of these proposals had stimulated any interest up until January 2011.

Housing Policies in Post-revolutionary Egypt

Since the January 2011 Revolution, little has changed in Egypt in terms of housing policies. There have been no legal reforms or innovative schemes to address housing affordability and housing for the poor, which might have been expected to follow on from revolutionary rhetoric. More than ever, most housing in urban Egypt (and practically all suitable affordable housing) is being produced out-of-sight by the informal sector. As yet, the post-revolutionary governments have continued the old regime's approach to these areas—neglect, marginalization, and failed proscription. The government's social housing schemes have largely stagnated, even though grand pronouncements have been steady fare in the media. Although most of the electoral programs of the main political parties participating in the 2011 parliamentary elections—including the Freedom and Justice Party—called for affordable housing for the poor, these were vaguely worded populist slogans that have not been repeated.

The story, or rather non-story, of housing policies in Egypt in the first two years after the revolution can be pieced together as follows:

On April 11, 2011, only two months after the fall of Mubarak, the minister of planning and international cooperation sent to donors a proposal for a "National Social Housing Program."[7] This new program called for building a colossal amount of low-cost housing—some one million units in five years, a level of annual production more than twice that of the unachieved 2005–2011 NHP target, and four times the average national annual production in the 1982–2005 period. The estimated program cost was $3.3 billion per year. The Ministry of Housing, the Housing Development Bank, and NUCA would be the implementing agencies, and housing projects would be in the new towns as well as in governorates. The minister called for international donors to contribute some 50 percent of total costs, equaling a total grant commitment over the life of the program of over $8 billion, more than any previous donor-financed development program in Egypt and completely eclipsing all previous donor support for the housing sector.

The donors huddled together and came up with a polite, dissimulating response that called first for a national housing strategy which would set the parameters for any subsequent housing programs. The fact that the proposed program would repeat and even exacerbate the problems of the earlier NHP—being very expensive, financially unsustainable, ill-targeted, and creating thousands of units in remote new-town locations that would remain mostly empty—could be read between the lines.

In any event, the new National Social Housing Program has remained a very visible government priority, at least in terms of pronouncements. In 2012 the Ministry of Housing announced 62 tenders for contractors to build 27,100 apartment units of 70 m² surface area each in seven new towns around Egypt.[8] By March 2013 none of these had been completed. In addition, it is understood that over the last two years the armed forces have delivered perhaps 20,000 apartment units to the Ministry of Housing for distribution under the program, presumably using its own military

---

7   Arab Republic of Egypt, Ministry of Housing and Utilities and Urban Development, National Social Housing Program, March 31, 2011.
8   http://www.newcities.gov.eg/about/Projects/Housing_projects/SocialHousing/default.aspx.

budget and land.⁹ These two small projects are, so far, the only concrete evidence of the one million units scheduled to be built by 2016. On the other hand, a list prepared by the Ministry of Housing of the distribution of the program across 27 governorates appeared in July 2012, showing that the new towns surrounding Greater Cairo are to capture over 25 percent of the total one million units.¹⁰ Interestingly, a new classification has been included in the list called *istibdal al-'ashwa'iyat* (replacement of informal housing), amounting to 150,000 units. This is an ominous sign that the government intends to begin informal housing clearances and resettlement in practically all governorates.

Of course, to reach anywhere near its targets the Social Housing Program will need huge amounts of financing, and as is well known the central government's budgetary resources are practically depleted, with stiff competition to capture whatever discretionary development funds still exist. In this light it would seem counterproductive for the current government to maintain the fiction that the program remains on track, but admissions of failure or even unavoidable delays are evidently not part of its vocabulary.

Another component of the one-million-unit Social Housing Program appeared in October 2011, with the announcement by the then minister of housing of a scheme to release 100,000 plots of land in new towns "for those of limited income."¹¹ Plots average around 260 square meters and up to four floors can be built. Plot layouts show that quite spacious three-bedroom apartments with 2.5 baths can be built on each floor, in addition to off-street parking and a little garden. Prices for plots range from LE60,000 to LE150,000, and can be paid over three years. Practically any citizen can register for these plots, and group applications of four for one plot are allowed. Controls are to be put in place

---

9   It is difficult to pin down details of this army housing. On August 28, 2012 a newspaper article reported that the armed forces had completed 90 percent of a social residential project for low-income citizens of some 6,000 units located in Helwan, presumably part of the 20,000-unit total. The project was expected to be completed by the beginning of 2013, with units of 90 m². This is hardly low-income housing. See http://www.dailynewsegypt.com/2012/08/28/armed-forces-low-income-housing-project-near-completion/

10 http://www.youm7.com/News.asp?NewsID=737181&

11 "Al-iskan: tarh 100 alf qta'at aradi li mahdodi al-dakhl bidayat 2012," *al-Masry al-Youm*, October 23, 2011, 4.

to force construction and dampen speculation and resale.[12] Presumably enough raw land will be found in the new towns, but the component implies that some 10,000 hectares will be provided with infrastructure, services, and landscaping. According to the Ministry's website, by the end of 2012 only 22,665 plots of land had been put up for sale by *qur'a* (lottery). Very small numbers of these plots are available in some new towns around Cairo, but the majority will be created in the other new towns in Upper Egypt, most of which appear to be ghost towns.

It is absurd to call this program "land for those of limited income,"[13] considering that the outlay for land alone can exceed LE100,000 and that a single apartment unit will cost at least LE250,000 to build in remote locations that require private vehicles. And it is ironic that this type and standard of housing plots are precisely those for which there is already the biggest glut on the Egyptian housing market. But it is an indication that the government desperately needs to be seen as active in the housing sector and needs to generate hope among the middle classes, and since funding for the new National Social Housing Program is practically nonexistent, the carving up of unserviced desert land, which costs almost nothing now, was seen as a brilliant intermediate solution that also could quickly be added to the one-million-unit count.

Another government housing land scheme, not actually part of the Social Housing Program, was announced in March 2012. Some 8,000 plots of land in various new towns around Cairo are to be made available by NUCA for Egyptians working abroad.[14] These plots are for luxury housing and range from 700 m² to 1200 m², with the price per m² ranging from $250 to $675 (which in Egyptian pounds represents some of the highest land prices in Cairo). This scheme is purely a money-spinner, and it could generate over $3 billion to replenish the government's coffers, assuming overseas Egyptians will actually pay such exorbitant land prices. In the year since this initiative was announced, there has been no further information on how it is proceeding, and the Ministry's webpage for the program is currently not accessible.

---

12 Based on a 33-page *daftar shurut* issued by NUCA (in Arabic, no date).
13 In fact, according to the Ministry's website, this housing-plot scheme has been redesignated "middle-income housing," even though it is clearly labeled as part of the one-million-unit Social Housing Program.
14 http://bouportal.com/en/Categorydet.aspx?id=105

What about other initiatives that could be considered to reflect the government's post-revolutionary housing policies? After the election of President Muhammad Morsi and the formation of the new cabinet in the summer of 2012, little was heard of housing initiatives. The Ministry of Housing and the new minister, Dr. Tarek Wafiq, seemed mainly preoccupied with advancing the Suez Canal corridor development concept, which has little to do with housing, and with reinvigorating the depressed real-estate market in the new towns, which certainly has nothing to do with affordable housing.

As reported in February 2013, the government sees revitalizing the private real-estate sector as a key to economic recovery.[15] Thus it is revamping the rules of the New Urban Communities Authority (NUCA) that govern corporate property investments, aiming to replace controls and penalties with "incentive-based regulations" that will attract new investments and create a more business-friendly environment. It will replace the well-known Law No. 89 of 1998 that requires competitive bidding for lands *(qanun al-munaqasat wa-l-muzayadat)*, and which has led to the imprisonment of a number of prominent Mubarak-era businessmen. And it will also revise Law 59 of 1979 (the new-communities law) to remove obstacles to "serious investments," especially in the new urban centers that it hopes to create in such locations as al-'Alamein and Wadi al-Natrun. To attract private capital to these new areas, it is even mentioned that new land-release mechanisms are being considered to give usufruct rights to investors without any initial payment. These new megacities (with target populations of four million each) follow pronouncements made just before the revolution for the creation of a number of million-population urban centers in desert locations, *mudun al-milyuniya*. Little has been heard of these lately.

It seems from these announcements that the Muslim Brotherhood government continued the previous regime's preoccupation with grand urban schemes in the desert that, in the current absence of state funds for investment, will somehow miraculously materialize through a new partnership with private corporations. The fact that there are already some 25 new towns in the desert and that most are embarrassing failures seems to have been forgotten. But generating the chimera of grand

---

15 "Al-mugtama'at al-'umraniya tuwafiq 'ala laiha l-tanshit al-iqtisad al-'aqari," *al-Masry al-Youm*, February 14, 2013, 6.

projects, which one would have thought had been dismissed as part of the Mubarak regime, is evidently alive and well.

And where does this leave affordable housing policies? Except for the feeble, mostly unaffordable, and increasingly off-track Social Housing Program, housing initiatives that attempt to influence wider urban housing markets, mobilize the dynamic of the informal sector, and assist poor families are totally absent. Attempts to introduce interventions which would influence the wider existing market to remove current distortions such as were proposed in 2008 continue to be ignored. The new towns as embodiment of Egypt's urban future continue to dominate urban planning policy, attempts to stimulate the tiny and largely irrelevant housing mortgage finance system continue to be pursued, and the imposition of the new property tax system continues to be tinkered with.

Political Economy Generalizations

Of course 26 months is far too short a time to identify patterns in state behavior that indicate concrete political economy shifts in Egypt. The following are only some speculative hints of this, as reflected in government approaches toward the housing sector.

First, populism and its underlying state paternalism seem alive and well, as evidenced by the government's announcement of the huge Social Housing Program 2011–2016. This program continues and even expands the philosophy of the Mubarak period that "the state shall provide" housing for those in need, in spite of all evidence to the contrary. It is interesting to note that a similar large national housing program was announced in early 2012 by the transitional government in Tunisia.[16] Relative to Tunisia's population, this social housing program implies a level of state housing production that is even larger than the program in Egypt and one that eclipses all other previous programs.

Secondly, if the housing issue is any indication, the 2012–2013 Egyptian government was more opaque than ever, presenting no hard information about the location and details of schemes being formulated,

---

16 "Tunisie—Construction de 150 mille logements sociaux sur 3 ans," *Business News*, February 14, 2012, http://www.businessnews.com.tn/details_article.php?temp=1&t=520&a=29331#?

and maintaining a total lack of transparency about budget allocations, actual expenditures, and availability of land for projects. Instead, the only information comes from vague and contradictory pronouncements by state officials.

Thirdly, the bankrupt concept of 'high-modernist' government continues unabated from the Mubarak era, especially as evidenced by the continued ignorance and denial of the huge informal housing sector, which paradoxically has been and is now more than ever the main source of affordable housing in Egypt. Most Egyptian architects, engineers, and planners both in and outside government seem stuck on believing Egypt can emulate the West (or more likely the Gulf states) when it comes to both the standards and designs for housing and the preference for a mix of state and corporate modes of housing production.

Finally, it appears that the current government, in the ways it approaches both housing production and the shaping of its new cities, is continuing the love affair with the private (usually foreign) investor as the *deus ex machina* that will magically rush in to fulfill dreams for Egypt's new built environment. This thinking was a hallmark of the last 15 years of the Mubarak era, and if anything it has since increased, in spite of the avalanche of scandals and theft of state wealth relating to businessmen that have appeared since 2011.

To be fair, two years is a short time, and, given the nation's downward spiral in economic, political, and security terms, the current government could be at least partly excused for not attempting to set new directions for housing and not giving affordable housing the priority it deserves. Perhaps more practical and realistic housing policies will eventually emerge, but if current trends are any guide, don't hold your breath!

References

Agence Française du Développement. 2011. *Égypte: Étude relative au panorama des secteurs du développement urbain et du logement social.* Final Report, January 6. Cairo: Agence Française du Développement.

United States Agency for International Development (USAID). 2008. *Housing Study for Urban Egypt.* Technical Assistance for Policy Reform II. Final Report, December 24. Authors David Sims, Hazem Kamel, and Doris Solomon. Washington, DC: USAID/Egypt Policy and Private Sector Office.

World Bank. 2008. "Egypt—Next Step Recommendations for Affordable Housing Policy and the National Housing Program: Mortgage-Linked Subsidies and Housing Supply Considerations." June 2. Washington, DC: World Bank. https://openknowledge.worldbank.org/handle/10986/7956

World Bank and USAID. 2008. *Egypt—A Framework for Housing Policy Reform in Urban Areas in Egypt: Developing a Well Functioning Housing System and Strengthening the National Housing Program.* Washington, DC: World Bank. http://documents.worldbank.org/curated/en/2008/06/15961811/egypt-framework-housing-policy-reform-urban-areas-egypt-developing-well-functioning-housing-system-strengthening-national-housing-program

CHAPTER 10

Islamic Finance in the New Egypt

Clement M. Henry

As of the end of June 2013, the political economy of the new Egypt seemed incoherent amid widespread perceptions that the economy was "Going to the Dogs," as *The Economist* headlined it.[1] Well-intentioned government efforts in December 2012 to demonstrate fiscal responsibility to the IMF by raising various taxes lasted about six hours, until President Morsi or his minders from the Muslim Brotherhood changed his mind. This perception of external influences on the president reinforced the opinion of many observers that he continued after his election to be the "spare tire" of the Brotherhood (substituting for Khairat al-Shater, disqualified from running in the presidential elections) rather than the president of all Egyptians.[2] The story about the new taxes is actually a bit more complicated: the measures, announced on Sunday afternoon, December 12, and repealed at 2 a.m. on Monday, had been scheduled weeks earlier and were on automatic pilot, implementing an understanding already reached in November between the government and the International Monetary Fund (IMF).[3] Despite the political angst caused by President Morsi's assumption of full powers on 22 November,

---

1 *The Economist*, March 30, 2013, http://www.economist.com/news/middle-east-and-africa/21574533-unless-president-muhammad-morsi-broadens-his-government-egypts-economy-looks
2 Many advisors appointed by the president shortly after he took office had resigned within months. Fu'ad Gadallah cited as one of his reasons for resigning "the overweening influence of Mr Morsi's fellow Muslim Brothers in devising policy." *The Economist*, May 4, 2013, http://www.economist.com/news/middle-east-and-africa/21577117-president-muhammad-morsis-efforts-befriend-iran-upset-his-other-allies-pious
3 IMF press release No. 12/446, November 20, 2012, http://www.imf.org/external/np/sec/pr/2012/pr12446.htm

the apolitical, inexperienced government, flying blind, kept on schedule; ironically, then, Morsi's assumption of full powers actually lessened his authority and compromised any capacity to support the new taxes: he quickly had to reverse the tax measures in the face of a constitutional crisis and bloody street battles.

This episode encapsulates the economic dilemmas of the Morsi regime: there were no policies. The Brotherhood's Renaissance Project remained a mystery, and President Morsi's master plan, promised in January 2013, was never launched. Ikhwanweb, the Muslim Brotherhood's official English website, described it as "based on four axes, namely integrated development, economic development, urbanization—out of the narrow Nile valley, and building a modern State"—a work in progress, in short, but hardly a presidential initiative. It was up "for public discussion soon," so Ikhwanweb claimed,[4] but political discord apparently ruled out any public dialogue on serious economic policy matters. One of Egypt's opposition leaders, Nobel Prize winner Mohammed ElBaradei, deplored the political gridlock on an independent TV channel:

> *The ability to run the state is missing, especially after the revolution [because of] difficult and exceptional circumstances. This is not related to the Muslim Brotherhood or a certain current.... I spent two years defending the Muslim Brotherhood before the revolution and I still defend their rights.... Egypt is at war with itself, and the world turned from admiration of the revolution to that of concern and pity because we are mismanaging the revolution.*[5]

While the country remained polarized and economic decision-making was apparently paralyzed, however, private sectors may be reforming themselves in anticipation of new Islamic financial markets. Dr. Mohamed Gouda, spokesman of the Freedom and Justice Party (FJP) Economic Committee, was in denial as late as December 2012

---

4   "Four-Axis Presidential Project to Build Modern Egypt," Ikhwanweb.com, January 21, 2013.

5   "ElBaradei Says Political Gridlock is Blocking Recovery," *Egypt Independent*, February 12, 2013, http://www.egyptindependent.com/news/elbaradei-says-political-gridlock-blocking-recovery

concerning any Egyptian economic crisis,[6] but perhaps closer to the mark when he projected an increase in the market share of Islamic sharia-compliant assets to 35 percent of the total assets of Egypt's commercial banking system within five years, once the necessary bank legislation in preparation since April 2011 is enacted. Meanwhile the transitional government did not await a new parliament to pass legislation concerning *sukuk* (Islamic bonds).

Indeed, whatever the outcome of the clash of pro- and anti-Morsi forces, Islamic finance capital coming from the Gulf Cooperation Council (GCC) is bound be a major driving force underpinning the political economy of the new Egypt. Just as Qatar helped to finance the Morsi regime, so Saudi Arabia, Kuwait, and the UAE financed the transitional government of July 2013. Any economic policy is in fact bound to include more Islamic financial cosmetics, whether managed by Muslim Brothers, Salafists, liberals, or social democrats. Egypt's economic situation is reminiscent of the late 1970s, when spectacular oil revenues in the Gulf elicited the dream articulated by Saad Eddin Ibrahim (1982) and others of a new prosperity in Egypt founded on Gulf Arab capital, Western technology, and Egypt's strategic location and manpower. Similar opportunities await Egypt today. Arab oil revenues may be peaking in the face of slowing world demand and alternative supplies of oil and gas, but considerable private as well as public Gulf capital is available. One difference between the 1970s and the current decade is that privately held capital accumulation in Saudi Arabia and its little neighbors exceeds that of the public reserves and Sovereign Wealth Funds (SWFs, Luciani 2005). Capital in private GCC hands is in the trillions of dollars, whereas the SWFs are only in the hundreds of billions. Differences concerning Egyptian and Arab appropriations of Western technologies are another story (Zahlan 2012) beyond the scope of this work. The point to be stressed here is that private capital in the region is the driving force behind Islamic finance. Consequently this chapter will first examine the emergence of this peculiarly modern form of finance before discussing the current controversy in Egypt about sovereign *sukuk*—hyperventilated by the specter of a mortgaging of the Suez Canal—and more general concerns raised by Islamic financial practices in Egypt.

---

6   See his statements on Ikhwanweb of December 25 and December 27, 2012.

Islamic Finance Capital

Officially the Conference of Islamic States, flush with rising oil revenues (fig. 10.1), launched a consortium bank in 1975. As proposed by the heads of state of Algeria, Saudi Arabia, and Somalia, the bank was not only to be named the Islamic Development Bank (IDB), but to be managed "in accordance with the Islamic shar'ia" (Kahf 2004:20). At about the same time Prince Muhammad al-Faisal and Sheikh Saleh Kamel were entertaining the idea of establishing Islamic banks, and a pious businessman close to Dubai's ruling family decided to establish the Dubai Islamic Bank, based on Islamic principles as he understood them. As a pioneer of interest-free banking in rural Egypt, Dr. Ahmed al-Naggar was called in as a consultant, and various 'Islamic banks' took off in the late 1970s. The 'Islamic' label drew in substantial savings deposits ('investment accounts') in countries such as Egypt and Sudan, where Prince Muhammad gained ready access. Converting savings into prudent and profitable investments, however, presented serious problems. The IDB, for instance, quickly learned that literal profit-sharing through equity investments was too risky: their portfolio of equity-like *mudaraba* was rapidly reduced, whereas *murabaha*, credit sales, could be safely expanded as techniques of artificial sales were fine-tuned.

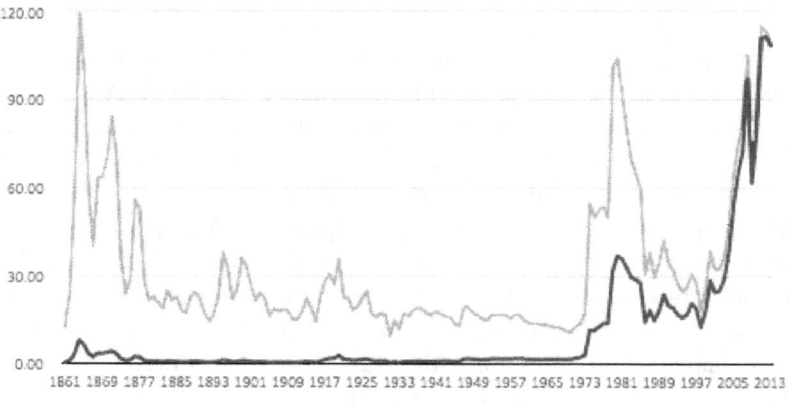

Figure 10.1. Oil prices, 1861–2013. (Source: BP Statistical Review of World Energy 2014)

The first wave of Islamic banking lightly penetrated much of the Muslim world. In Egypt the Faisal Bank, joined in 1980 by Al Baraka, garnered close to 10 percent of the deposits of the commercial banking system at their peak, in 1986, before steadily declining to about 5 percent in 2000 (Soliman 2004:275). In Kuwait Islamic banking fared better, with some 18 percent of the market (Henry and Wilson 2004:7), but in Saudi Arabia, the epicenter of Islamic finance, there were no officially recognized Islamic banks because any such recognition might imply that other banks were not sharia-compliant, to the detriment of the kingdom's legitimacy.

The start of the new millennium coincided, however, not only with the beginning of another surge in oil prices (fig. 10.1) but also a new wave of Islamic finance, this time in the form of bonds to develop Islamic capital markets and complement the banks. Bahrain introduced the first Islamic Treasury Bill, a non-tradable *sukuk al-salam*, followed in 2001 by a *sukuk al-ijara* that securitized leases. Malaysia developed the first internationally tradable *sukuk* in 2002, and the Islamic bond industry subsequently blossomed. Despite some setbacks associated with juridical differences as well as the financial crisis of 2008, the Islamic bond market continued to flourish, attracting interest in Egypt as in other countries desiring financing from GCC investors. Worldwide sales reached $138 billion in 2012, including "an unprecedented $46.5 billion" in corporate bonds.[7] While Malaysian issues were almost three-quarters of the total, Arab *sukuk* markets seemed bound to grow. Conditions seemed so propitious that Turkey, too, was developing plans to complement its active capital markets with extensive issues of sovereign and corporate *sukuk*.[8]

The other striking development paralleling the new oil boom has been the steady growth of the 'Islamic banks' and Islamic windows of conventional banks in domestic Gulf markets. By 1999, the year the current surge in oil prices began from historically rock-bottom

---

7   The data were compiled by Bloomberg in Kinibiz, March 26, 2013, http://www.kinibiz.com/story/corporate/11305/sp-sees-malaysia-leading-sukuk-as-poll-nears.html

8   Nevzat Devranoglu, "Turkey Steps Up Islamic Finance Push as Sensitivities Ease," Reuters, May 29, 2013, http://www.reuters.com/article/2013/05/29/turkey-islamicfinance-idUSL5N0E91SP20130529

prices (slightly lower in November 1999 than fig. 10.1 indicates), sharia-compliant finance was already penetrating Saudi retail markets to such an extent that even its premier commercial bank, Saudi American (SAMBA), opened a window to sell sharia-compliant products in response to its customers' demand. The kingdom had rejected earlier formal applications of Islamic banks for commercial banking licenses. Although the two principal Islamic bank groups, Dar al-Mal and Al Baraka, were respectively headed by Saudi Prince Muhammad al-Faisal and a self-made Saudi businessman, Sheikh Salah Kamel, the Saudi Monetary Authority (SAMA) turned down their applications for licenses in the kingdom to avoid any implication that other banks were less than Islamic, as mentioned above. In 1988 SAMA did grant a commercial banking license to al-Rajhi, a money changer, because it was too big to abolish along with all the other money changers liquidated that year in the wake of a financial scandal. Although al-Rajhi unilaterally proclaimed itself Islamic to justify not paying interest to its depositors, SAMA did not recognize it as anything other than a conventional commercial bank. Its success, however, undoubtedly whetted the appetites of the other commercial banks, which, like SAMBA, established Islamic windows to keep their customers. By 2008 a Hongkong Shanghai Bank survey indicated that 38.4 percent of Saudi Arabia's financial assets in commercial banks were sharia-compliant (*The Banker*, November 2009, in Henry and Springborg 2010:246). The kingdom's biggest bank, the National Commerce Bank, had meanwhile been restructured so as to deal exclusively with sharia-compliant financial instruments on the retail level. Not so coincidentally, Muhammad Gouda, the economic spokesperson for the FJP mentioned above, had served as one of the bank's advisors in the transition process and supervised the transition, as well, of its Lebanese subsidiary.

These developments in Saudi Arabia, largely echoed in the smaller GCC city-states, should have a significant impact upon patterns of foreign direct investment in Egypt. Private-sector foreign direct investment (FDI) may well become a major driver of economic development, and GCC sources of private capital are likely to buy into corporate private rather than sovereign *sukuk*. That is why Egypt's new *sukuk* law, like Turkey's, is designed to regulate corporate as well as sovereign bonds. Earlier drafts of the Egyptian law promoted by the Ministry of Finance under the Mubarak and SCAF regimes had dealt exclusively with sovereign *sukuk*.

Sacking and Recovering the *Sukuk* Law

The Finance Ministry's fascination with *sukuk* well predates the January 25 Revolution, as these bonds were viewed as a convenient way of accessing GCC funds. Islamic financiers who had pioneered them since 2000 seemed to have developed ways of packaging these financial instruments that squared the circle, acting like regular interest-bearing bonds while yielding streams of sharia-compliant profits. Through complex designs of special-purpose vehicles (SPVs), lawyers in New York and London could engineer *sukuk* to meet the specifications of a club of specially qualified Islamic jurists. They usually securitized bundles of receivables in the form of accounts payable *(murabaha)* or leases *(ijara)*. Figure 10.2 shows an example of one of the first sovereign *sukuk* utilized by Bahrain, Malaysia, and Qatar.

As the author of the diagram explains,

> *The underlying assets were bought from the seller and immediately leased to the lessee based on the principle of* ijara muntahia bi-tamlik *(lease ending with purchase). The SPC will act as the trustee for the* sukuk *holders and will distribute to the* sukuk *holders the rental proceeds of the leased assets in accordance with the terms of the trust. At the end of the lease period the SPC will sell the assets to the original seller for a sum equal to the original sale price, which the SPC will distribute to the* sukuk *holders to redeem the* sukuk. (Haneef 2005)

My favorite example is less conventional but apparently also satisfied the Islamic jurists. It involved the financing of a South Korean real estate project that required fixed interest payments by Korean law. The financial engineer relied on the contingent residual value of the project to junior debenture holders as a way of legitimating the investor's fixed returns as sharia-compliant. The financial flows were detailed in an elaborate series of diagrams (McMillen 2005).[9] In Mubarak's Egypt,

---

9 Dr. McMillen was originally an obstetrician before becoming a lawyer and financial

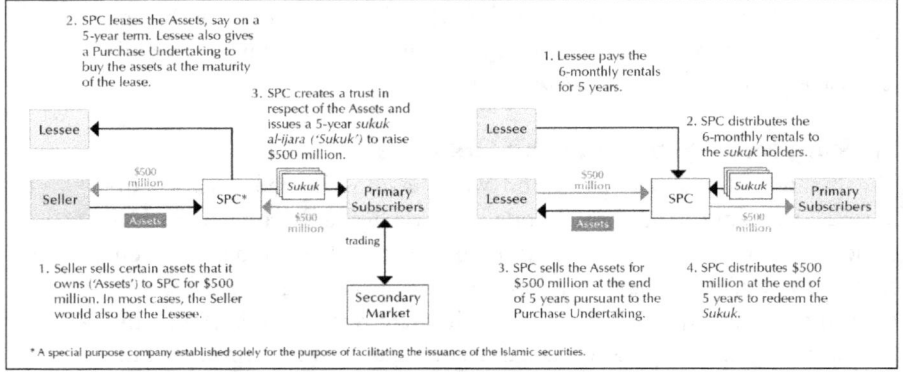

Figure 10.2. A typical *sukuk al-ijara* structure (Source: Haneef 2005)

however, any *sukuk* would have been designed along the more conventional lines developed in Bahrain and other states of sovereign rather than corporate bonds.

After the Revolution one of a succession of finance ministers, a technocrat, resuscitated from his ministry's files a draft law to this effect. But other figures close to President Morsi's new government had other ideas that might better serve the business community as well as the government. The FJP, enjoying its control over the newly elected People's Assembly in 2012, killed the ministry's draft. Sheikh Hussein Hamid Hassan claimed in mid February that the government was planning to raise $2 billion by issuing *sukuk* after first rejecting IMF overtures for a similar amount.[10] Close to government circles, he also sits on seven sharia boards of Islamic financial institutions, including the Accounting and Auditing Organization for Islamic Financial Institutions (AAOIFI), Bahrain, which sets the accounting rules for Islamic financial institutions. More recently this highly respected sharia scholar, an appointed member of the Shura Council, claimed that Egypt could raise at least $200 billion in *sukuk* to fund viable economic projects as well as finance government debt.[11] After all, as he had explained already

---

engineer.

10 *Egypt Independent*, February 14, 2012, http://www.egyptindependent.com/news/government-prepares-sell-us2-bn-islamic-bonds-says-scholar

11 *Amwal al-Ghad*, December 24, 2012, http://www.amwalalghad.com/en/business/banks/12646-egyptian-jurist-says-sukuk-can-bring-egypt-us-200-bln.html

in 2007, "When we built the first Islamic bank in 1975, it was easier to say Islamic whisky than Islamic bank. I myself could not imagine that the Islamic banking industry would grow that fast."[12]

In February 2012, shortly before the Finance Ministry's effort to pass a *sukuk* law failed, the Egyptian Islamic Finance Association (EIFA) was founded. Presided over by Dr. Muhammad Beltagi (no relation to the FJP's leader in the 2012 People's Assembly), it served as a neutral legal forum for Islamic finance, associating financial and legal experts independent of existing banks, parties, and government ministries. In early November 2012, for instance, EIFA assembled representatives from the Ministry of Finance, the Dar al-Ifta, the FJP, the Noor (Salafi) Party, and other interested legal experts to design a new *sukuk* law defining the guidelines for both corporate and sovereign issues. EIFA also strongly opposed a subsequent effort by the Ministry of Finance to pass another version of its sovereign *sukuk* law, published on December 19, 2012, just as presidential authority was being vigorously protested in the wake of Morsi's power grab of November 22.[13] In response, the Egyptian Financial Supervisory Authority presented yet another draft covering corporate as well as sovereign *sukuk*.

In the face of criticism from the (Salafist) Noor Party, the Muslim Brotherhood propelled the more general legislation dealing with both sovereign and private-sector Islamic bonds through the Shura Council on March 19, 2013, after almost two years of discussion and debate.[14]

---

12 http://ifresource.com/2007/12/03/dr-hussein-hamid-hassan-all-arabs-will-prefer-islamic-banking/. His curriculum vitae shows several sharia board memberships, including the Dubai International Bank, founded in 1975 without a sharia board but required to appoint one in 2009, when it needed a government bailout. Sheikh Hussein was educated at NYU as well as Cairo University and al-Azhar. He is fluent in Russian as well as English and French and has served as a financial consultant to Kazakhstan as well as GCC states. He supervised the conversion of the National Bank of Sharjah into a purely Islamic one and presumably is positioned to offer similar advice to Egyptian banks. His vita is available at http://www.irf.net/index.php?option=com_content&view=article&id=190%3Abiodata-hussein-hamed-hassan&catid=57%3Aorators-international&Itemid=174

13 Scholars objected to loopholes in the law that might allow bondholders to gain state property rights. See Alaa Shahine, "Pasha's Legacy Haunts Egypt amid Sukuk Law Push," *Bloomberg*, January 7, 2013.

14 For a close analysis of the issues, see the January 2013 commentaries of Walid Hegazy (no relation to the finance minister) on the website of his law firm: http://www.hegazylaw.com/Sukuk.html

Even so, the *sukuk* law awaited presidential ratification. Although the Muslim Brotherhood counselors rode roughshod over Salafist objections in the Shura Council and demands that any legislation await approval from al-Azhar, the constitutional interpreter of sharia (Article 4), President Morsi relented and sent the bill to al-Azhar. Once again, on April 30, 2013, after further consultations with al-Azhar, the Shura Council adopted its proposed amendments and passed the bill unanimously. *Sukuk* seem central to any Muslim Brotherhood strategy of economic survival. The new finance minister selected in January, after all, had been named for his expertise in managing these financial instruments. Although he was removed from office in the cabinet reshuffle of May 5, after the passage of the law, the way was now open to engineer sovereign as well as corporate *sukuk* to alleviate Egypt's serious cash flow problems. If "Islam is the solution" for Islamists, the praxis of any distinctly 'Islamic economy' seemed to be Islamic finance, spearheaded by *sukuk*.

Even al-Azhar had not raised any objections to the law, at least not publicly, concerning the techniques of securitization that the tight little international community of sharia scholars accepted. The only objections concerned any potential claims of *sukuk* holders on state assets such as the Suez Canal or the Pyramids, objections that the proponents of the *sukuk* law dismissed as misunderstandings of the legislation.[15] Other more independent scholars could view these bonds having fixed returns as yet another illustration of the 'sharia arbitrage' that pervades the Islamic finance industry, enabled by a self-selecting nucleus of sharia experts who monopolize the boards and define the accounting standards of the new financial instruments.[16]

Sheikh Hussein Hamid Hassan's visions of $200 billion worth of *sukuk* will not materialize any time soon, however. Although the Finance Ministry announced plans in late May 2013 for an eventual $12 billion sovereign *sukuk* issue, Egypt still cannot dispense with the stamp of approval that the IMF will offer if negotiations for an extended standby facility succeed. Even potential bondholders will need assurance that the government is engaged in sustainable policies, notably with respect to fuel subsidies and budget deficits. The *sukuk* law was still under government review in November 2014.

---

15   See Article 3 of the Sukuk Law, *Official Journal*, No. 18 of May 7, 2013.
16   On sharia arbitrage see El-Gamal (2005; 2006).

Public Opinion versus *Riba*

Islam's solutions of *sukuk* and other financial instruments nevertheless seem very much in keeping with public opinion. The sheikh did have a point about whisky. Generic conventional banks are viewed by most Muslims as at least as unacceptable as whisky; in fact, debt hangovers may last much longer. In an Arab Barometer poll conducted in Egypt during the summer of 2011, a representative sample strongly affirmed the following proposition: "Bank interest is against the teachings of Islam."[17] A strong majority (71.6 percent of the 1124 respondents giving definitive answers, out of a total sample of 1220) agreed with the proposition. The results may surprise some Egyptians but are also very much in keeping with responses to the same question recorded between 2006 and 2008 in the first wave of the Arab Barometer, which did not include Egypt. Algerians, Jordanians, Kuwaitis, Moroccans, Palestinians, and Yemenis all scored well over 72 percent in favor;[18] only the Lebanese, with 68 percent, were slightly less sympathetic to interest than the Egyptians. The substantial majority of Egyptians who apparently rejected conventional interest-based banking might prefer to join the groundswell of Islamic finance surging from the GCC. A second Egypt survey conducted in 2013 confirmed these findings, as table 10.1 indicates. An even smaller percentage of Egyptians disagreed with the proposition that interest was *haram* (religiously forbidden), although fewer *strongly* agreed and over 20 percent confessed ignorance or refused to answer the question.

In Egypt in 2011 differences between urban and rural populations were statistically significant, although not as any crude modernization theory might predict; the urban populations were more opposed to conventional interest-based banking than the rural folk ($r = .09$, $p < .002$).

---

17 The question was introduced as follows: "The opinions of Islamic jurists and religious scholars differ and I want to ask to what extent you agree or disagree with some of these issues? 'Banks charging interest contradict the teachings of Islam'" (www.arabbarometer.org). Only a small number of items of the Egyptian second-wave data was available for the analysis developed below in table 10.2. A third wave of data collected in 2013 was published online in October 2014, in time to be reported in table 10.1.

18 Positive responses (of those expressing an opinion) ranged from 88 percent in Algeria to 81 percent for all the others except wealthy Kuwait, where only 76 percent opposed interest.

Table 10.1: 'Banks charging interest contradict the teachings of Islam.'

Year of survey	2011	2013
strongly agree	485	275
	39.8%	23.0%
agree	329	388
	27.0%	32.4%
disagree	183	200
	15.0%	16.7%
strongly disagree	129	74
	10.6%	6.2%
don't know	92	247
	7.5%	20.7%
declined to answer	0	12
	0.0%	1.0%
Total	1219	1196
	100.0%	100.0%

Source: Arab Barometer, Waves 2 and 3.

Looking more closely at the 2011 data, it seems that it was primarily males from the countryside who were the most tolerant of conventional banking practices, perhaps because they were in more need of any form of financing. Only 63.7 percent of rural men rejected interest, compared to 74.2 percent of their urban brothers, whereas women, always more conservative than the men, did not vary significantly with respect to their habitat. In the sample, age and education made little difference, apart from the small numbers of university graduates and postgraduates who tended to be a bit more tolerant of interest.

In light of the June 30 uprising against the Muslim Brotherhood, it is interesting to speculate about possible opinion shifts with respect to Islamic finance. With the limited data made available to me at the time, it was possible to construct two factors, "Political Islam" and "Prescriptive Tolerance."[19] Table 10.2 shows a logistic regression of our dependent variable, the view that "Bank interest is against the teachings of Islam," on urban/rural, gender, Political Islam, and Prescriptive Tolerance.

Table 10.2. Logistic regression of bank interest opinion on urban, male, Prescriptive Tolerance, and Political Islam

		Estimate	Std. error	Wald	df	Sig.	Odds ratio
Threshold	[bank *haram* = 1.00]	.861	.311	7.672	1	.006	
	Urban	.333	.142	5.457	1	.019	1.395
	Male	-.441	.140	9.951	1	.002	.643
	Prescriptive Tolerance	-.249	.070	12.466	1	.000	.780
	Political Islam	.132	.070	3.583	1	.058	1.141

The logistic regression estimates the difference in the odds of affirming that bank interest is against the teachings of Islam, holding all other independent variables constant. For instance, living in a city increases one's chances of affirming the proposition. The coefficient (estimate) is a natural log, e to the power of .333, or a 'log likelihood,' in this context of

---

19 "Political Islam" was a factor score generated from responses to three propositions: "Men of religion should have no influence over the decisions of government"; "Religious practice is a private matter and should be separated from sociopolitical life"; and "It would be better for our country if more people with strong religious beliefs held public office." Mark Tessler used the same variables to generate his "Political Islam" for the entire second wave of the Arab Barometer, which was not yet available to the public in June 2013. See Mark Tessler, "What Do Ordinary Citizens in the Arab World Want: Secular Democracy or Democracy with Islam?," http://www.arabbarometer.org/sites/default/files/files/wtkindofdemocracyppt.pdf). "Prescriptive Tolerance" was a factor score I generated from "Difference and variation between Islamic scholars with regard to their interpretation of religious matters is a good thing"; "There should be one interpretation of Islam and numerous interpretations should not be allowed"; and "Disagreement with some scholars in religious interpretation should not be used to label them as non-believers."

affirming the proposition. If living in a city had no independent effect, the log likelihood would be 0, and e to the power of 0 would be 1, or even odds, 50-50. In this case the log likelihood translates into an odds ratio of 1.395. In other words, all else equal, you are 40 percent more likely to affirm the proposition. If, on the other hand, you are a male, you are less likely, the odds being only .643 (the natural log of which is -.441, the coefficient in table 10.2), roughly two-thirds to one, that you will affirm the proposition.[20] Obviously, too, respondents who were 'prescriptively tolerant,' believing that people may differ in their understandings of Islamic teachings, were less likely to affirm that bank interest ran against them.

In this sample, however, the attitudes of the political Islamists appeared to be relatively flexible. The direct correlation between Political Islam and opposition to bank interest was weak ($r = .042$) and insignificant. Moreover, political Islamists tended to be significantly more 'prescriptively tolerant' than others ($r = .17$; $p < .0005$). Only by holding gender, geography, and toleration constant were they slightly (with marginal statistical significance, $p < .058$) more likely, the odds increasing by 14 percent, to affirm the proposition and presumably favor Islamic (interest-free) finance. The change of regime in July 2013 seemed unlikely to have much impact on public opinion, which generally seemed favorable to Islamic finance.

The Evolution of Islamic Banking in Egypt

The Mubarak regime had tolerated but deliberately contained and limited the growth of Islamic banks. Faisal Islamic Bank of Egypt, the first to open its doors, in 1978, enjoyed a hospitable climate, along with a special tax-free status for five years, because of good relationships between Saudi Prince Muhammad al-Faisal and President Anwar Sadat. Efforts in the 1980s to open more branches beyond the 16 or so then in operation were discouraged. The Al Baraka group also came to Egypt, but a third initiative backed by local prospective Islamic financiers collapsed.

---

20 It is also possible to add log likelihoods. Thus the coefficient of an urban male would be 0.108 and the odds reduced by only 10.2 percent that he will affirm the proposition (women being more conservative). Odds do not directly convert into probabilities, but as mentioned earlier, 74.2 percent of the urban males affirmed the proposition, compared to 63.7 percent of the rural males.

The Evolution of Islamic Banking in Egypt

The Mubarak regime attempted to control the rise of Islamic finance by enabling Banque Misr to open Islamic branches. In safe state-run hands, these branches succeeded by 1997 in accumulating more deposits than Faisal Islamic Bank, but meanwhile Islamic banking peaked in the mid 1980s, when it held up to 10 percent of the deposits of the commercial banking system.

They subsequently lost momentum as other 'Islamic investment companies'—the infamous *sharikat tawzeef al-amwal*—bought the approval of some religious *sheikh*s to market them. These upstart enterprises were a by-product of Egyptian government efforts to keep its currency inflated at an artificial rate. The most famous of them, Rayan, consisted of a family of money changers, uneducated for the most part, working on the parallel market and able to offer higher rates of return than conventional banks for remittances. As long as they could rely on the steady depreciation of the Egyptian pound on the parallel market, these upstart companies enjoyed a competitive advantage. But they lost it once an IMF standby agreement stabilized the pound in 1987. To keep up with clients' expectations, they built pyramid schemes that subsequently collapsed, discrediting 'Islamic' forms of financial marketing. By 1996 the official Islamic banks held only 5.1 percent of the deposits of the banking system, down from 9.7 percent in 1986 (Henry and Wilson 2004:7).[21]

Faisal Islamic Bank of Egypt had suffered major losses in 1991 because it had placed substantial funds with the Bank of Commerce and Credit International, a money-laundering institution that the Bank of England terminated that year. FIBE was hard pressed to pay competitive rates of return to its 'investors' who might otherwise prefer to deposit their savings in conventional banks. Like many other retail Islamic banks, FIBE had greater difficulty generating income from its investments than conventional banks because it was riskier to engage in sharia-compliant equity financing (*mudaraba* and *musharaka*) than in their functional equivalent for conventional banks of medium- and long-term lending. Arguably, new legislation originally proposed by the FJP for Islamic banks might increase their ability to engage in these more lucrative forms of financing.

---

21 Samer Soliman (2004:276) notes further decline by 1994, when Islamic banks held only 4.8 percent of the deposits.

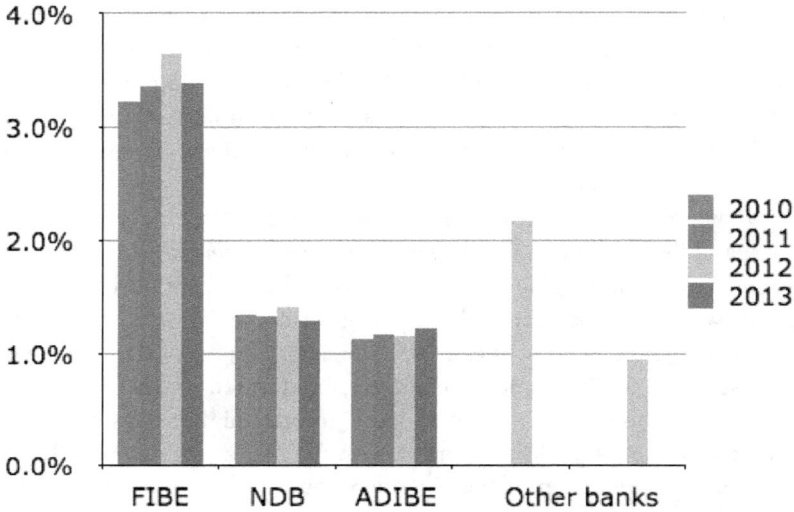

Figure 10.3. Market shares of Islamic bank deposits, 2010–2013 (total in 2013 of 8.9% of Egyptian deposits)

Today the official Islamic banking sector holds about 6 percent of the total deposits of the commercial banking system, and the Islamic windows of conventional banks such as Banque Misr hold an additional 3 percent. Faisal's share of deposits slightly increased after 2010, as figure 10.3 indicates, but stagnated in 2013. In the wake of the regime change that summer both Faisal and Al Baraka lost market share, but the Abu Dhabi Islamic Bank of Egypt was catching up with the latter.

Faisal regained its primary position and commands close to 40 percent of Egypt's sharia-compliant bank assets, while Banque Misr is second, holding 24 percent of them.[22] This large public-sector bank, originally opening Islamic bank branches to contain the private-sector banks, has sustained a steady 13 percent of its deposit base in sharia-compliant instruments despite opening only 33 branches, less than 7 percent of its total branch network, to sharia-compliant forms of financing.[23] Note,

---

22 As of September 30, 2012, according to the Egyptian Islamic Bank Association records kindly made available to me.
23 Soliman (2004:275, 279) and Galloux (1997) traced the earlier evolution of Bank Misr's Islamic branches.

however, that FIBE's 29 branches attracted substantially more deposits than Misr's Islamic ones.

The Abu Dhabi Islamic Bank Egypt (ADIBE) was the smallest of the three. Known until 2013 as the National Development Bank, it had earlier fallen on hard times but was steadily converting itself into an Islamic bank. Abu Dhabi Islamic Bank, which acquired a controlling share of the bank in 2006, is financing ADIBE's vision of becoming Egypt's premier Islamic bank and reconfiguring its consortium of regional banks. Increasing the share of Islamic banking from 10 to 35 percent of the total assets of the commercial banking system may be a bit ambitious, but this Brotherhood objective also implies continued peaceful coexistence and cooperation between conventional and Islamic finance.

Presently the Islamic banks are at a serious disadvantage. Except for Al Baraka Egypt, they have accumulated financing portfolios that are in even worse shape than those of Egypt's big public-sector banks. As figure 10.4 shows, ADIBE's "impaired" financing exceeded 40 percent of its entire financing portfolio in 2012 despite efforts under way since 2006, when Abu Dhabi Islamic Bank came to its rescue, to write off the NDB's bad debts. With branches in most of Egypt's governorates, NDB had probably served as a slush fund for provincial politicians. The Faisal Islamic Bank was in worse shape than ADIBE by the end of 2013, when most of the NDB's non-performing loans were finally written off. Faisal's percentage of non-performing assets was still double the national average.

Possibly some version of the legislation originally proposed in 2012 for these banks will accelerate improved financing and revenue flows. Their more lucrative equity-type financing with *mudaraba* and *musharaka* usually requires higher agency and monitoring costs than those needed by conventional banks for term lending. Pious Muslims, however, may be better able to monitor one another because they share common risks and aspirations.[24] Islamic institutions may hence become better able to compete with conventional banks by generating greater profits to distribute among their

---

24 See Moore (1990) for a further discussion of this point. It is also developed in Henry and Wilson (2004:288–289).

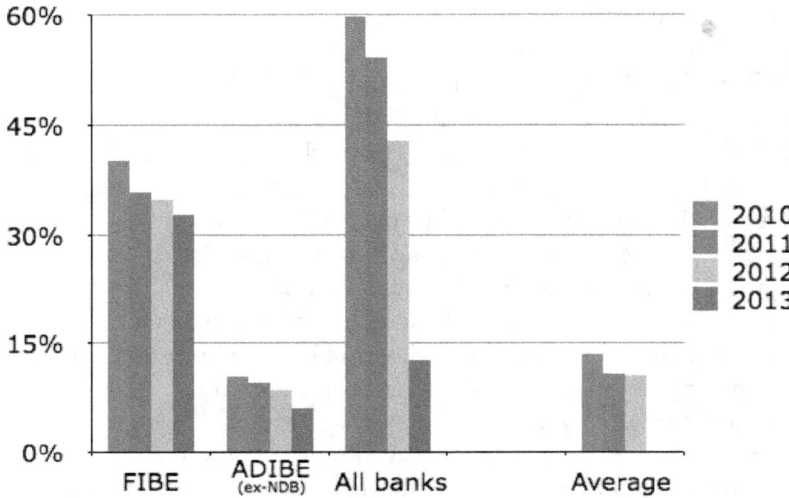

Figure 10.4. Non-performing as a percentage of total financing, 2010–2013

investor-depositors.[25] The draft of the legislation awaiting a new parliament also stipulates some Central Bank supervision of the sharia boards. Each Islamic bank will be required to have a board consisting of three sharia experts certified by the Central Bank, and no expert may serve on more than two banks' boards.[26] Such regulations, if implemented, may break up the virtual monopoly held by sharia experts in the world of Islamic finance. In 2008 11 sharia 'experts' sat on both the 18-man AAOIFI and the 19-man International Islamic Finance Rating Agency, the bodies that set the rules for the industry. Only three of them were not in turn members of at least 15 sharia boards of other

---

25 The Islamic banks actively compete with conventional banks for deposits and consequently must earn enough on their financing operations to pay profits on customers' savings accounts that measure up to prevailing interest rates. In his report on Al Baraka Egypt's financial performance for 2011, for instance, the CEO noted that "several banks . . . have raised the rates of return on their savings deposits in attempt to attract the biggest share of depositors, the matter that compelled our bank to raise its rates of return on the savings pools to keep pace" (ABE 2012:30).

26 "Islamists Draft Code to Boost Islamic Banks," Reuters, *Egypt Independent*, June 12, 2012, http://www.egyptindependent.com/news/islamists-draft-code-boost-islamic-banks

Islamic financial institutions. They legislated, adjudicated, and personally benefited from their multiple affiliations and complex conflicts of interest. Receiving an average yearly income of $10,000 to $50,000 per board membership, not to mention service per diems and first-class travel, they became "addicted to the new lifestyle." The majority of this self-anointed few served on 20 to 40 or 50 sharia boards, and one had accumulated a total of 61 such memberships by 2008.[27]

Ultimately, however, efforts to encourage Islamic finance depend on fostering a better business climate for conventional as well as sharia-compliant enterprises. In its flagship report on financial access, the World Bank outlined a series of reforms that would be needed to finance the small and medium enterprises needed for economic development (Rocha 2011). For instance, it calls for greater banking competition, less concentration of lending among leading banks to favored clienteles, and the extension of Egypt's private credit bureau to more "reporting entities (especially microfinance institutions, utilities, and retailers), and to widen the type of data collected" (Rocha 2011:120). Another suggestion, in addition to leasing that is fully compatible with Islamic as well as conventional finance, concerns reverse factoring, the use of an enterprise's accounts receivable to finance its operations (Rocha 2011:22). Islamic financiers could explore such means of servicing small and medium enterprises.

With Abu Dhabi's backing, ADIBE may also develop its microfinance capabilities. Since 1989, under its original identity as the National Development Bank, the bank has pioneered microfinance in Egypt. It has 44 microfinance units spread across 18 Egyptian governorates and claims to be the "only bank in the market to offer a full range of Shari'a compliant services to micro enterprises" (ADIB 2011:20). As a result of the deteriorating economic situation in the wake of the January 25 Revolution it gave 8,000 customers "a three-month repayment holiday,"

---

27 See Mahmoud El-Gamal, "Islam and Economic Solutions," part 2, June 17, 2005, for the quotation: http://elgamal.blogspot.com/2005/06/islam-and-economic-solutions-part-ii.html. When a data set of Islamic Financial Information Service (IFIS) briefly became available at the University of Texas in 2008, it was possible to analyze the composition of the sharia boards of 268 Islamic financial institutions worldwide. Subsequently Jamaldeen (2012:269) notes that 20 scholars occupied 621 sharia board seats, each holding from 14 up to 85 of them, whereas an additional 260 scholars accumulated only 520. Public access to the IFIS website (http://www.islamicfinanceservice.com/) no longer offers such information.

but its portfolio of these loans ranging from 1,000 up to 50,000 Egyptian pounds contracted from 215 million (ADIB 2011:15) down to 31 million by the end of 2012 (ADIB 2012:12). It then announced that it was preparing to book new business and seemed positioned, were Egypt to regain stability, to forge ahead. Other research indicates that a sharia-compliant form of financing micro-enterprises may enjoy greater success and acceptance in Egypt than the Grameen model (El-Gamal et al. 2014). In theory, too, some resources may become available from Egypt's quasi-autonomous Social Fund, which received a loan of $50 million in 2013 to study and promote Islamic microfinance.

Taken together, these initiatives spell a deepening of Egypt's financial system and possible extensions of Islamic finance to micro as well as small and medium enterprises. Even by MENA standards Egypt has among the lowest ratios of loans to SMEs to total loans as well the highest loan concentration ratio (Rocha 2011:104, 105). The appeal of Islamic finance may well extend financial intermediation beyond the 10 percent of the Egyptian adult population having bank accounts.[28] With proper regulation encouraging small and medium enterprise, the dynamo in Turkey and elsewhere of economic development in the current era, Islamic finance may bring Egypt's huge informal sector out into open, competitive financial markets, expanding the credit needed for these businesses to prosper. These neoliberal guidelines of economic development in a globalizing world are likely to inform any Egyptian government in the 'teens of the twenty-first century, whatever its partisan coloring.

Conclusion

Egypt seems likely to accentuate trends, already visible before Mubarak's fall, of catering to the tastes of local constituencies and potential GCC investors for Islamic forms of finance. With Malaysia as a possible model, Egypt may issue tens of billions of dollars' worth of corporate as well as sovereign *sukuk*, once a measure of stability and investor confidence returns. There is no reason to doubt peaceful coexistence between Islamic and conventional forms of high finance,

---

28 The World Bank (2004:10) recorded 12 million Egyptians holding postal service accounts amounting to LE23 billion ($4 billion) in 9,000 centers throughout the country, but these accounts were not part of the banking system.

however intense the conflicts on the ground between Islamists and more secularly minded political forces. Major international banks such as JPMorgan, Citibank, Deutschebank and Hongkong Shanghai are as comfortable with *sukuk* as with other forms of financial engineering. On the retail side, conventional banks in Egypt, as elsewhere, have opened Islamic windows. In Saudi Arabia they have converted virtually the entire retail sector, and others in Egypt are positioned to follow suit. The market share of Islamic banks noted in figure 10.3 already marks a slight increase since 1996, when the banks held 5.1 percent and the Islamic windows of Banque Misr an additional 3.0 percent (Henry and Wilson 2004:6).

Market forces will drive Islamic finance in Egypt. In addition to the lure of recycled 'Islamic' petrodollars, hundreds of thousands of Egyptians returning from the Gulf are likely 'investors' in Islamic banks or windows of some of Egypt's premier banks. Following Banque Misr, the National Bank of Egypt and the Commercial International Bank opened sharia-compliant services. In the countryside the huge Principal Bank for Development and Agricultural Credit (PBDAC) launched a major Islamic retailing initiative in February 2013 designed in time to triple its clientele of one million farmers (out of 5.8 million freeholders). The bank management hoped their expanded and revitalized Islamic branch network would attract many farmers who avoided the bank for religious reasons.[29]

A concluding irony is that these market forces have become a substitute for policy that may dampen or at least further confuse debates between the Islamists and their oppositions. Ibrahim Warde recently observed that "secularists will see supporting Islamic finance as a way of stealing the thunder of the Islamists by giving people an outlet to express their religiosity. . . . Even groups that were opposed to political Islam looked to Islamic finance as a way of preventing extremism."[30] It seems that its time has come, whatever government prevails in the new Egypt.

---

29 Reuters, "Egyptian Farm Bank Launching Retail Islamic Services," *Egypt Independent*, February 12, 2013, http://english.ahram.org.eg/NewsContent/3/12/64611/Business/Economy/Egypt-farm-bank-launching-retail-Islamic-services.aspx

30 Reuters, "A New Chance in Egypt for Islamic Finance," April 21, 2011, http://www.egyptindependent.com/news/new-chance-egypt-islamic-finance. Ibrahim Warde has written extensively on Islamic finance. See his chapter "Islamic Finance and Politics: Guilt by Association," in Warde (2010:214–233).

References

Abu Dhabi Islamic Bank—Egypt (ADIB). 2010–2013. Financial Reports. http://www.adib.eg/financial-results

Al Baraka Bank Egypt. 2012. *Annual Report of 2011.* Cairo.

Ali, S. Nazim, ed. 2005. *Islamic Finance: Current Legal and Regulatory Issues.* Cambridge, MA: Islamic Finance Project, Harvard Law School.

BP Statistical Review of World Energy. 2014. http://www.bp.com/en/global/corporate/about-bp/energy-economics/statistical-review-of-world-energy.html

Galloux, Michel. 1997. *Finance islamique et pouvoir politique: le cas de l'Égypte moderne.* Paris: Presses Universitaires de France.

El-Gamal, Mahmoud. 2005. "Limits and Dangers of *Shari'a* Arbitrage." In S. Nazim Ali, ed. *Islamic Finance: Current Legal and Regulatory Issues,* 117–132. Cambridge, MA: Islamic Finance Project, Harvard Law School.

———. 2006. *Islamic Finance: Law, Economics, and Practice.* Cambridge: Cambridge University Press.

El-Gamal, Mahmoud, Mohamed El-Komi, Dean Karlan, and Adam Osman. 2014. "Bank-insured RoSCA for Microfinance: Experimental Evidence in Poor Egyptian Villages," *Journal of Economic Behavior and Organization,* Supplement, July, 103:S56–S73. http://karlan.yale.edu/p/EMF-05-12.pdf

Haneef, Mohamed Rafe Md. 2005. "Recent Trends and Innovations in Islamic Debt Securities: Prospects for Islamic Profit and Loss Sharing Securities." In S. Nazim Ali, ed. *Islamic Finance: Current Legal and Regulatory Issues,* 29–60. Cambridge, MA: Islamic Finance Project, Harvard Law School.

Henry, C. M. 1996. *The Mediterranean Debt Crescent: A Comparative Study of Money and Power in Algeria, Egypt, Morocco, Tunisia, and Turkey.* Gainesville: University Press of Florida.

Henry, C. M., and R. Springborg. 2010. *Globalization and the Politics of Development in the Middle East.* 2nd ed. Cambridge: Cambridge University Press.

Henry, C. M., and R. Wilson, eds. 2004. *The Politics of Islamic Finance.* Edinburgh: Edinburgh University Press.

Jamaldeen, Faleel. 2012. *Islamic Finance for Dummies.* New York: Wiley.

Kahf, Monzer. 2004. "Islamic Banks: The Rise of a New Power Alliance of Wealth and Shari'a Scholarship." In C. M. Henry and R. Wilson, eds. *The Politics of Islamic Finance*, 17–36. Edinburgh: Edinburgh University Press.

Luciani, Giacomo. 2005. "From Private Sector to National Bourgeoisie: Saudi Arabian Business." In Paul Aarts and Gerd Nonneman, eds. *Saudi Arabia in the Balance: Political Economy, Society, Foreign Affairs*, 105–123. London: Hurst.

McMillen, Michael. 2005. "Structuring a Securitized *Shari'a*-Compliant Real Estate Acquisition Financing: A South Korean Case Study." In S. Nazim Ali, ed. *Islamic Finance: Current Legal and Regulatory Issues*, 77–104. Cambridge, MA: Islamic Finance Project, Harvard Law School.

Moore, Clement Henry. 1990. "Islamic Banks and Competitive Politics in the Arab World and Turkey," *Middle East Journal*, 44(2): 234–255.

Rocha, Roberto R. 2011. *Financial Access and Stability: A Road Map for the Middle East and North Africa*. Washington, DC: International Bank for Reconstruction and Development/World Bank.

Soliman, Samer. 2004. "The Rise and Decline of Islamic Banking Model in Egypt." In C. M. Henry and R. Wilson, eds. *The Politics of Islamic Finance*, 265–285. Edinburgh: Edinburgh University Press.

Warde, Ibrahim. 2010. *Islamic Finance in the Global Economy*. 2nd ed. Edinburgh: Edinburgh University Press.

World Bank. 2004. *The Role of Postal Networks in Expanding Access to Financial Services. Country Case: Egypt's Postal Finance Services*. http://siteresources.worldbank.org/EXTINFORMATIONAND COMMUNICATIONANDTECHNOLOGIES/Resources/PostalFinSvcesCountryStudies.pdf

Zahlan, A. B. 2012. *Science, Development, and Sovereignty in the Arab World*. New York: Palgrave Macmillan.

About the Contributors

Deena Abdelmonem has a BA in psychology from the American University in Cairo and currently works in elementary education.

Dr. Zeinab Abul-Magd is associate professor of modern Middle Eastern history, Oberlin College.

Yasmine Ahmed is a PhD candidate in social anthropology, University of Cambridge.

Dr. Sandrine Gamblin is director of the Middle East Studies Center, the American University in Cairo.

Dr. Ellis Goldberg is emeritus professor of political science, University of Washington.

Dr. Clement M. Henry is visiting research professor at the Middle East Institute, National University of Singapore.

Dr. Nicholas S. Hopkins is emeritus professor of anthropology, the American University in Cairo.

Dr. Dina Makram-Ebeid is research fellow at the Max Planck Institute for Social Anthropology.

Dr. Hans Christian Korsholm Nielsen is director of the Danish-Egyptian Dialogue Institute, Cairo.

David Sims is an independent economist and urban planner.

CAIRO PAPERS IN SOCIAL SCIENCE

Volume One, 1977–1978
1   *Women, Health and Development*, Cynthia Nelson, ed.
2   *Democracy in Egypt*, Ali E. Hillal Dessouki, ed.
3   *Mass Communications and the October War*, Olfat Hassan Agha
4   *Rural Resettlement in Egypt*, Helmy Tadros
5   *Saudi Arabian Bedouin*, Saad E. Ibrahim and Donald P. Cole

Volume Two, 1978–1979
1   *Coping With Poverty in a Cairo Community*, Andrea B. Rugh
2   *Modernization of Labor in the Arab Gulf*, Enid Hill
3   *Studies in Egyptian Political Economy*, Herbert M. Thompson
4   *Law and Social Change in Contemporary Egypt*, Cynthia Nelson and Klaus Friedrich Koch, eds.
5   *The Brain Drain in Egypt*, Saneya Saleh

Volume Three, 1979–1980
1   *Party and Peasant in Syria*, Raymond Hinnebusch
2   *Child Development in Egypt*, Nicholas V. Ciaccio
3   *Living Without Water*, Asaad Nadim et al.
4   *Export of Egyptian School Teachers*, Suzanne A. Messiha
5   *Population and Urbanization in Morocco*, Saad E. Ibrahim

Volume Four, 1980–1981
1   *Cairo's Nubian Families*, Peter Geiser
2, 3 *Symposium on Social Research for Development: Proceedings*, Social Research Center
4   *Women and Work in the Arab World*, Earl L. Sullivan and Karima Korayem

Volume Five, 1982
1   *Ghagar of Sett Guiranha: A Study of a Gypsy Community in Egypt*, Nabil Sobhi Hanna
2   *Distribution of Disposal Income and the Impact of Eliminating Food Subsidies in Egypt*, Karima Korayem
3   *Income Distribution and Basic Needs in Urban Egypt*, Amr Mohie el-Din

Volume Six, 1983
1 *The Political Economy of Revolutionary Iran*, Mihssen Kadhim
2 *Urban Research Strategies in Egypt*, Richard A. Lobban, ed.
3 *Non-alignment in a Changing World*, Mohammed el-Sayed Selim, ed.
4 *The Nationalization of Arabic and Islamic Education in Egypt: Dar al-Alum and al-Azhar*, Lois A. Arioan

Volume Seven, 1984
1 *Social Security and the Family in Egypt*, Helmi Tadros
2 *Basic Needs, Inflation and the Poor of Egypt*, Myrette el-Sokkary
3 *The Impact of Development Assistance On Egypt*, Earl L. Sullivan, ed.
4 *Irrigation and Society in Rural Egypt*, Sohair Mehanna, Richard Huntington, and Rachad Antonius

Volume Eight, 1985
1, 2 *Analytic Index of Survey Research in Egypt*, Madiha el-Safty, Monte Palmer, and Mark Kennedy

Volume Nine, 1986
1 *Philosophy, Ethics and Virtuous Rule*, Charles E. Butterworth
2 *The 'Jihad': An Islamic Alternative in Egypt*, Nemat Guenena
3 *The Institutionalization of Palestinian Identity in Egypt*, Maha A. Dajani
4 *Social Identity and Class in a Cairo Neighborhood*, Nadia A. Taher

Volume Ten, 1987
1 *Al-Sanhuri and Islamic Law*, Enid Hill
2 *Gone For Good*, Ralph Sell
3 *The Changing Image of Women in Rural Egypt*, Mona Abaza
4 *Informal Communities in Cairo: the Basis of a Typology*, Linda Oldham, Haguer el Hadidi, and Hussein Tamaa

Volume Eleven, 1988
1 *Participation and Community in Egyptian New Lands: The Case of South Tahrir*, Nicholas Hopkins et al.
2 *Palestinian Universities Under Occupation*, Antony T. Sullivan
3 *Legislating Infitah: Investment, Foreign Trade and Currency Laws*, Khaled M. Fahmy
4 *Social History of An Agrarian Reform Community in Egypt*, Reem Saad

Volume Twelve, 1989

1   *Cairo's Leap Forward: People, Households, and Dwelling Space*, Fredric Shorter
2   *Women, Water, and Sanitation: Household Water Use in Two Egyptian Villages*, Samiha el-Katsha et al.
3   *Palestinian Labor in a Dependent Economy: Women Workers in the West Bank Clothing Industry*, Randa Siniora
4   *The Oil Question in Egyptian-Israeli Relations, 1967–1979: A Study in International Law and Resource Politics*, Karim Wissa

Volume Thirteen, 1990

1   *Squatter Markets in Cairo*, Helmi R. Tadros, Mohamed Feteeha, and Allen Hibbard
2   *The Sub-culture of Hashish Users in Egypt: A Descriptive Analytic Study*, Nashaat Hassan Hussein
3   *Social Background and Bureaucratic Behavior in Egypt*, Earl L. Sullivan, el Sayed Yassin, Ali Leila, and Monte Palmer
4   *Privatization: the Egyptian Debate*, Mostafa Kamel el-Sayyid

Volume Fourteen, 1991

1   *Perspectives on the Gulf Crisis*, Dan Tschirgi and Bassam Tibi
2   *Experience and Expression: Life Among Bedouin Women in South Sinai*, Deborah Wickering
3   *Impact of Temporary International Migration on Rural Egypt*, Atef Hanna Nada
4   *Informal Sector in Egypt*, Nicholas S. Hopkins ed.

Volume Fifteen, 1992

1   *Scenes of Schooling: Inside a Girls' School in Cairo*, Linda Herrera
2   *Urban Refugees: Ethiopians and Eritreans in Cairo*, Dereck Cooper
3   *Investors and Workers in the Western Desert of Egypt: An Exploratory Survey*, Naeim Sherbiny, Donald Cole, and Nadia Makary
4   *Environmental Challenges in Egypt and the World*, Nicholas S. Hopkins, ed.

Volume Sixteen, 1993
1 *The Socialist Labor Party: A Case Study of a Contemporary Egyptian Opposition Party*, Hanaa Fikry Singer
2 *The Empowerment of Women: Water and Sanitation Initiatives in Rural Egypt*, Samiha el Katsha and Susan Watts
3 *The Economics and Politics of Structural Adjustment in Egypt: Third Annual Symposium*
4 *Experiments in Community Development in a Zabbaleen Settlement*, Marie Assaad and Nadra Garas

Volume Seventeen, 1994
1 *Democratization in Rural Egypt: A Study of the Village Local Popular Council*, Hanan Hamdy Radwan
2 *Farmers and Merchants: Background for Structural Adjustment in Egypt*, Sohair Mehanna, Nicholas S. Hopkins, and Bahgat Abdelmaksoud
3 *Human Rights: Egypt and the Arab World, Fourth Annual Symposium*
4 *Environmental Threats in Egypt: Perceptions and Actions*, Salwa S. Gomaa, ed.

Volume Eighteen, 1995
1 *Social Policy in the Arab World*, Jacqueline Ismael and Tareq Y. Ismael
2 *Workers, Trade Union and the State in Egypt: 1984–1989*, Omar el-Shafie
3 *The Development of Social Science in Egypt: Economics, History and Sociology; Fifth Annual Symposium*
4 *Structural Adjustment, Stabilization Policies and the Poor in Egypt*, Karima Korayem

Volume Nineteen, 1996
1 *Nilopolitics: A Hydrological Regime, 1870–1990*, Mohamed Hatem el-Atawy
2 *Images of the Other: Europe and the Muslim World Before 1700*, David R. Blanks et al.
3 *Grass Roots Participation in the Development of Egypt*, Saad Eddin Ibrahim et al.
4 *The Zabbalin Community of Muqattam*, Elena Volpi and Doaa Abdel Motaal

Volume Twenty, 1997
1 *Class, Family, and Power in an Egyptian Village*, Samer el-Karanshawy
2 *The Middle East and Development in a Changing World*, Donald Heisel, ed.
3 *Arab Regional Women's Studies Workshop*, Cynthia Nelson and Soraya Altorki, eds.
4 *"Just a Gaze": Female Clientele of Diet Clinics in Cairo: An Ethnomedical Study*, Iman Farid Bassyouny

Volume Twenty-one, 1998
1 *Turkish Foreign Policy During the Gulf War of 1990–1991*, Mostafa Aydin
2 *State and Industrial Capitalism in Egypt*, Samer Soliman
3 *Twenty Years of Development in Egypt (1977–1997): Part I*, Mark C. Kennedy
4 *Twenty Years of Development in Egypt (1977–1997): Part II*, Mark C. Kennedy

Volume Twenty-two, 1999
1 *Poverty and Poverty Alleviation Strategies in Egypt*, Ragui Assaad and Malak Rouchdy
2 *Between Field and Text: Emerging Voices in Egyptian Social Science*, Seteney Shami and Linda Hererra, eds.
3 *Masters of the Trade: Crafts and Craftspeople in Cairo, 1750–1850*, Pascale Ghazaleh
4 *Discourses in Contemporary Egypt: Politics and Social Issues*, Enid Hill, ed.

Volume Twenty-three, 2000
1 *Fiscal Policy Measures in Egypt: Public Debt and Food Subsidy*, Gouda Abdel-Khalek and Karima Korayem
2 *New Frontiers in the Social History of the Middle East*, Enid Hill, ed.
3 *Egyptian Encounters*, Jason Thompson, ed.
4 *Women's Perception of Environmental Change in Egypt*, Eman el Ramly

Volume Twenty-four, 2001
1, 2 *The New Arab Family*, Nicholas S. Hopkins, ed.
3 *An Investigation of the Phenomenon of Polygyny in Rural Egypt*, Laila S. Shahd
4 *The Terms of Empowerment: Islamic Women Activists in Egypt*, Sherine Hafez

Volume Twenty-five, 2002
1, 2 *Elections in the Middle East: What do they Mean?* Iman A. Hamdy, ed.
3 *Employment Crisis of Female Graduates in Egypt: An Ethnographic Account*, Ghada F. Barsoum
4 *Palestinian and Israeli Nationalism: Identity Politics and Education in Jerusalem*, Evan S. Weiss

Volume Twenty-six, 2003
1 *Culture and Natural Environment: Ancient and Modern Middle Eastern Texts*, Sharif S. Elmusa, ed.
2 *Street Children in Egypt: Group Dynamics and Subcultural Constituents*, Nashaat Hussein

3   *IMF–Egyptian Debt Negotiations*, Bessma Momani
4   *Forced Migrants and Host Societies in Egypt and Sudan*, Fabienne Le Houérou

Volume Twenty-seven, 2004
1, 2   *Cultural Dynamics in Contemporary Egypt*, Maha Abdelrahman, Iman A. Hamdy, Malak Rouchdy, and Reem Saad (eds.)
3   *The Role of Local Councils in Empowerment and Poverty Reduction*, Solava Ibrahim
4   *Beach Politics: Gender and Sexuality in Dahab*, Mutafa Abdalla

Volume Twenty-eight, 2005
1   *Creating Families Across Boundaries: A Case Study of Romanian/Egyptian Mixed Marriages*, Ana Vinea
2, 3   *Pioneering Feminist Anthropology in Egypt: Selected Writings from Cynthia Nelson*, Martina Rieker, ed.
4   *Roses in Salty Soil: Women and Depression in Egypt Today*. Dalia A. Mostafa

Volume Twenty-nine, 2006
1   *Crossing Borders, Shifting Boundaries: Palestinian Dilemmas*, Sari Hanafi, ed.
2, 3   *Political and Social Protest in Egypt*, Nicholas S. Hopkins, ed.
4   *The Experience of Protest: Masculinity and Agency among Sudanese Refugees in Cairo*, Martin T. Rowe

Volume Thirty, 2007
1   *Child Protection Policies in Egypt: A Rights-Based Approach*, Adel Azer, Sohair Mehanna, Mulki Al-Sharmani, and Essam Ali
2   *"The Farthest Place": Social Boundaries in an Egyptian Desert Community*, Joseph Viscomi
3   *The New York Egyptians: Voyages and Dreams*, Yasmine M. Ahmed
4   *The Burden of Resources: Oil and Water in the Gulf and the Nile Basin*, Sharif S. Elmusa, ed.

Volume Thirty-one, 2008
1   *Humanist Perspectives on Sacred Space*, David Blanks, Bradley S. Clough, eds.
2   *Law as a Tool for Empowering Women within Marital Relations: A Case Study of Paternity Lawsuits in Egypt*, Hind Ahmed Zaki
3, 4   *Visual Productions of Knowledge: Toward a Different Middle East*, Hanan Sabea, Mark R. Westmoreland, eds.

Volume Thirty-two, 2009
1 *Planning Egypt's New Settlements: The Politics of Spatial Inequities*, Dalia Wahdan
2 *Agrarian Transformation in the Arab World: Persistent and Emerging Challenges*, Habib Ayeb and Reem Saad
3 *Femininity and Dance in Egypt: Embodiment and Meaning in al-Raqs al-Baladi*, Noha Roushdy
4 *Negotiating Space: The Evolution of the Egyptian Street, 2000–2011*, Dimitris Soudias

Volume Thirty-three, 2010
1 *Masculinities in Egypt and the Arab World: Historical, Literary, and Social Science Perspectives*, Helen Rizzo, ed.
2 *Anthropology in Egypt 1900–1967: Culture, Function, and Reform*, Nicholas S. Hopkins
3 *The Church in the Square: Negotiations of Religion and Revolution at an Evangelical Church in Cairo*, Anna Jeannine Dowell

www.ingramcontent.com/pod-product-compliance
Lightning Source LLC
Chambersburg PA
CBHW071919070526
44583CB00016B/2051